SWEET FRUIT
FROM THE
BITTER TREE

61 Stories of Creative &

Compassionate Ways out of Conflict

— MARK ANDREAS —

SWEET FRUIT FROM THE BITTER TREE:
61 Stories of Creative & Compassionate
Ways out of Conflict

non-fiction

Published by:

Real People Press
1221 Left Hand Canyon Dr.
Boulder, CO 80302
RealPeoplePress.com

ISBN 978-0-911226-45-4 (paperback)

Cover illustration & design by Rene Eisenbart

Printed in the United States of America
10 9 8 7 6 5 4 3 2 1

Acknowledgements

My most sincere thanks to everyone who contributed a story to this project. Whether your story ended up as part of this collection or not, I have learned from and appreciated them all. Without you, this would have been a very short book.

Thanks to the friends and family members who read these stories and gave me feedback to help make this collection really shine. A special thanks to Tom Best for suggesting the title "Sweet Fruit from the Bitter Tree," and to Mark Gerzon for encouraging me to write the afterword.

Finally, thanks to my grandmother Lois Jean, for giving me the initial idea for this book.

Mark Andreas

Out beyond ideas of wrongdoing and rightdoing,
there is a field. I'll meet you there.

When the soul lies down in that grass,
the world is too full to talk about.
Ideas, language, even the phrase "each other,"
don't make any sense.

—Rumi

Contents

Introduction

In our media, entertainment, and culture today, we are continually bombarded with examples of winning through force, losing through lack of force, or losing *despite* using force. This can make it easy to believe that these are the only options available to us when we find ourselves in difficult situations of conflict. But in between domination and submission there is a whole world of possible action upon which people are drawing every day. This book is reassuring proof, inspiring example, and warm reminder of that fact.

The true stories in these pages include a wide range of conflicts, contexts, and solutions. There are stories of extraordinary situations, and everyday life. There are stories of navigating the physical dangers of war and crime, and stories of healing conflict in marriage, family, the community, the schoolyard, and even within one's self. There are stories of people who discovered deep wisdom, and others who didn't act so gracefully. Yet all found a way out of crisis: whether through a sense of humor, a loving presence, the ability to think quickly, or a willingness to act outside the norm. These stories show how ordinary people around the world have found ways to thread their way through the dangers and discover the opportunities that can exist even in times of crisis.

The idea for this book came when I was telling my family a story I had read that was both amazing and inspiring to me. In this story, a woman told of how she awoke one night to find that a man had broken into her house and kicked in the door to her room. He was verbally abusive as he walked up to her bed. She had a gun under her pillow, but couldn't imagine him waiting patiently while she reached under her pillow for the weapon. In that moment she had the thought that she believes saved her life, steering them both away from the violent ending that seemed so inevitable. The story is included in this book, so I won't tell you more here, except that I thrived on hearing this kind of example of someone using the full range of communication and connection that is available to human beings—rather than falling into the limited either/or choices of fight or flight.

As I finished telling my family this story and launched into another, my grandma, Lois Jean, said to me, "I just love these stories. You should write a whole book of them so that other people can read them and learn from them all around the country and even the world."

It was one of those things that grandmothers say—a nice idea, but of course it would never happen. Too much work...

As you can see, the seed was planted.

When I finished college and had no more papers to write, it seemed like a good time to begin collecting these stories of people's experiences of conflict resolution and transformation. Having the book project was a wonderful excuse to ask complete strangers to tell me some of the most meaningful events of their lives. And as I did, an interesting thing happened...

I had begun the project with my own specific idea of what constituted a "conflict resolution" story. My goal was to gather as many as I could and share them with a world largely dominated by paradigms of violence. But as I interviewed people, I encountered stories that didn't fit into my *own* paradigm of "conflict resolution." I remember thinking things like, *This is a fantastic story, but it isn't conflict resolution.* Then, after some time, I would return to it and realize I had been wrong. The more stories I collected, the

2

more I found my own limited idea of "conflict resolution" opening up wider with yet new possibilities. So in writing this book, I have already done for myself what I set out to do for others.

Most of the stories in this book were told to me through in-depth, recorded interviews that I later transcribed, edited, and had checked by the author for accuracy. The rest were either written by the author, or reprinted from previously published sources. In some of the stories, names and places have been omitted or changed to preserve privacy.

When putting these stories together into one manuscript I considered many possible ways I might organize them into a coherent whole, to give you, the reader, the most optimal journey from one story to the next. But every idea for organization that I came up with had some problem with it. I was seeing the truth to Mark Twain's statement that, *"Ideally a book would have no order to it, and the reader would have to discover his own."* Finally, I decided that the most fitting presentation was to not impose any categorization on these stories. They are simply arranged so as to give you the greatest possible variety from one story to the next. I think you will find this the most satisfying journey through this book—a journey true to life, which follows no simplistic design. These pages invite you into the real experience, just as it was for the person recounting their tale. Anything might happen on the next page.

I want to make it clear that this book doesn't overtly teach anything. (If you're interested in hearing some of the broader learning I've taken away from these stories, be sure to read the afterword). There are already many resources that teach theories and tactics for dealing with conflict without the use of force. This book does something different: it is simply a rich collection of effective things that real people actually did. Here are the stories. Stretch out in the sun or curl up on a rainy day, and simply enjoy what they offer you. In my experience, the deepest learning comes from the story itself.

Finally, I think it's important to mention that the most successful and elegant examples of conflict resolution and transformation never even reach the point of becoming a story. Einstein once said, *"Intellectuals solve problems. Geniuses prevent them."* The stories in this book are of solutions to imminent crisis or conflict, but when disaster is prevented from ever threatening in the first place, those stories remain invisible. Success is all around us; let's not forget that either.

I hope these stories teach you and inspire you, bring tears to your eyes, make you want to shout or laugh out loud, open your heart, or raise goose-bumps at the things you never thought possible. That is what they have done, and still do, for me.

Mark Andreas

1

Opening the Door

A twenty-year prison sentence is not a short amount of time to be locked up.

I was at a small reunion with my brother George and his wife Anne. Anne's cousin Jeremy was the reason for the gathering. When he was very young, for whatever reason, he had decided to participate in an armed robbery and had gotten himself arrested and sent to one of those chain-gang type prisons down south. He had been there for some 14-15 years of his full sentence. Now he was finally eligible for parole, but he needed a sponsor to live with, so my brother and his wife decided they'd vouch for him and provide him a place to live. George and Anne had gone down to meet Jeremy at the prison, and they'd flown him back to their home. Anne's sister and her husband had also flown in for the mini-reunion, wanting to be there to welcome Jeremy out of prison.

Jeremy was average height, a little on the thin side, but muscular, with salt-and-pepper hair. The second night after he arrived home with George and Anne, we were all deciding what to do, and Jeremy said he wanted to go see some hippies. It was the mid-seventies now, and I remember thinking, *Wow, he's been in prison a long time if he's never seen any hippies.* We went downtown to a popular bar and he was just amazed to see how people dressed—bell bottoms, beads, tie-die, leather vests, leather wrist bands and head bands. He commented on the strange music, but most of all he couldn't believe how many guys wore their hair long.

It was then that Jeremy said something to one of the hippie guys there. The guy said something back which all of us took to be innocuous—his response was a little sarcastic, but nothing mean-spirited. Well, Jeremy took it the wrong way, and he got this grim, mean look on his face. As we found a table Jeremy started muttering things like, "I should teach that mother fucker a lesson. I should kick his ass." We kept trying to calm him down, telling him the guy didn't mean what he had said, that it was just how people talked these days, but Jeremy's mood didn't improve. Soon we decided it was better we all just went home.

When we got back to George's house Jeremy was still in a dark mood. We all sat down in the living room, all except Jeremy, who kept pacing back and forth in a heightened state of anxiety. The others tried to calm him. Someone suggested that he sit. He did, but I could see that it only made him more agitated. Before long he jumped back up and stormed into my brother's bedroom. I don't know how he knew my brother had a gun in there, but he came back with my brother's gun. "I'm gonna go down there and teach that son-of-a-bitch a lesson!" he growled, sticking the gun in his belt.

At that, total pandemonium broke loose in the house. The women and the guys were pleading and arguing with him, trying to talk him out of this. They kept blocking his entrance to the door and he kept yelling, "Get out of my way, get out of my way! I'm gonna go back down there and show that asshole!" My brother managed to get the gun, but it just made Jeremy angrier and more intent on storming back to the bar for a fight. The women were starting to cry, "Oh, Jeremy, please don't do this, please!"

And it just kept going *on* and *on*. The pitch of hysteria was getting higher and higher, and Jeremy's rage was only building. Finally after five or six minutes I just got sick of the whole thing, so I walked over to the door and opened it. I looked at Jeremy and I said, "Go! Get out of here!" I didn't give it any conscious thought at the time, but nothing anyone else was doing was working, so I just tried something else. I was going to let him go and then I was going to call the police. "Go ahead," I continued, "You must *want* to go back to prison. You must be afraid of making it in the real world so go ahead back to your nice safe warm prison cell and spend the rest of your life there!"

He kind of froze, and everything changed. I could see something was going on in his brain. Then he grabbed me and hugged me and started crying and sobbing, and it was over.

We sat down as a family and talked about how there were a lot of things Jeremy was going to have to learn in order to live well in the outside world. One of those things was that people might say something he didn't like. "The way we handle it here on the outside," we explained, "is that we either ignore it, or say something back and then just let it go and be done with it."

We also talked about the false sense of security of being thrown back into prison. In prison you don't have to make any decisions about your life—you let someone else do it for you. "Out here in the world," we said, "You get the opportunity to make your own decisions and go forward." We talked about all the positive things that could happen in his life and we asked him what skills he had. It was then that he told us he had learned to be a welder while in prison.

"Well there you go," I said. "You already have a skill you can use out here; there are plenty of welding jobs around."

Years later I was over at my brother's on Christmas night when Jeremy called. He asked to talk to me so he could thank me. Over the phone Jeremy told me that when I opened the door those years ago, it changed his life. He said that in that moment, in a way, he really *had* wanted to go back to prison, because he *didn't* feel like he knew how to make it in the real world. That realization stopped him in his tracks, and allowed him to think about what he needed to learn in order to make a life for himself. He told me that after staying with my brother, he had met a gal who he eventually married, and together they moved down south where he started his own welding business. Now he had children and he was living happily together with his family.

Anonymous

7

2
You Have My Wallet?!

It was late in the evening in Glasgow, and I had decided to walk back to my Bed and Breakfast rather than take a taxi.

Now Glasgow, like just about any city of a reasonable size, tends to have its more and less "challenging" parts of town, and by challenging I mean the kind of place where you're likely to have interesting experiences with the city's more problematic residents...

In Glasgow, however, this is even more interesting because there is often very little separation between the nicer and, er, *less* nice parts of town. One wrong turn and you can quickly wind up having a *very* different experience.

While walking back to the B&B I went a few blocks too far and found myself at a construction site, walking through a passageway that obscured me from the street. Out of the shadows six young men approached me before I could get through.

The first young man came up to me, smirking in a way that was simultaneously friendly and menacing. It reminded me of the smile I saw on the delinquents in the movie *A Clockwork Orange*. With that same kind of attitude, he stated, "I'll have your wallet."

Now there are a number of ways that I could have responded. I'm a pretty big strong guy, so I could have grabbed the young man by the arm and twirled him about, threatening to knock all his friends down. I also could have been subtler and used some martial arts tomfoolery to disabuse them of this particular notion of how to have a good time earning pocket money. And yet, there was something about his phrasing and mock friendly tone that caught my attention, "I'll have your wallet..."

My face lit up with surprise and happiness. "You have my wallet?" I said. It was only a small misinterpretation of his words, and it came out of my mouth without thinking. "That's wonderful!"

Without giving him a chance to say anything else, I immediately went into a frantic stream of consciousness, explaining to him just how incredibly *relieved* I was, as I was supposed to be on a plane out tomorrow; I couldn't find my passport; I wasn't sure how I was going to get on the plane—there was no cash in my wallet but all my credit cards were there and I didn't know how I was going to pay for the hotel! Then I proceeded to ask him how exactly he knew that I had lost it around here. Did he see me drop it the last time I walked by, or did he recognize my face from my ID card?

As I barraged him with this information, I grabbed his hand and started shaking it while I patted him on the shoulder. This was not only a good way to startle him out of his previous pattern of intent, but it would also serve me in good stead if he didn't respond the way I thought he might.

"I... I don't have your wallet!" He stuttered, his face awash in confusion.

"You don't have my wallet?" I asked. "Then why did you tell me you had my wallet!" Still holding his hand, I launched into a diatribe about being completely screwed and not knowing what I was going to do. I really let that forlorn emotion register not only in my voice but all across my face.

"You lost it around here?" He asked, mirroring my concern.

For the next 15 minutes he and his friends helped me look, searching in the nooks and crannies around the fence of the construction site to see if we could locate my wallet. As we did, I don't think anyone was more amazed by what had happened than I was. I'm not sure I could have done what I did if I'd had to think about it in advance. It was just one of those times where I got into a flow state and magic happened.

Finally, after what I thought was an appropriate amount of time, I told them it was no use to continue. I shook all of their hands, in turn thanking each one of them in a heartfelt way for being kind enough to help me look. I told them that I was lucky to run into such great and kind people. I wished them all a wonderful night and sent them on their way still looking more than a bit confused.

I like to think that the next time those guys need to collect a little money to buy a few pints they might just find it more difficult to objectify someone and think of them simply as an easy way to grab a few quid.

Who knows?

Maybe one day they'll even step in to help somebody else having problems because they found out just how good it feels to help out a fellow human being.

Or maybe not…

I have no idea really, but I'd like to think that some good came of our interaction—not just for myself in keeping my wallet, but also for the young men.

Michael Perez

3
Soul Force

The phone call came just after dinner. It was my cousin
Philip, "We need you to come home. Daddy has been
killed."

A few months ago I conducted a workshop on active
nonviolence, what Gandhi called "Soul Force." My
audience was a wonderful group of Christian activists, fully
committed to working for social justice. When I asked them
how they had applied the principles of active nonviolence,
and what affect it has had on their lives, they spoke of sit-
ins, marches, leafleting, demonstrations, petitions, civil
disobedience, boycotts and arrests. They spoke of civil
rights, women's rights, human rights, peace and justice.

I asked, "What about your personal lives?"

They were puzzled by the question.

I tried to clarify. "What are the ways in which the
principles of active nonviolence have affected your
relationships at work, in church, in school, with family,
with personal friends and enemies?"

After a moment of silence, one of the participants said,
"I'm not sure I understand what you mean."

We spent the rest of the time we had together discussing the principles of active nonviolence, and the implications of Soul Force with regard to disarming our own hearts— opening up to the possibility of healing and being healed in our day-to-day lives. It didn't occur to me to share this story until after the workshop had ended...

My cousin Philip's words echoed through my mind, "... *Daddy has been killed.*" How could this be? I had just been to Kingston the previous summer for the fabulous celebration my hometown put on to honor my Uncle John on his 75th birthday. He had been Kingston's first black physician, and had served that town for 50 years. How could Uncle John have been killed?

When I was a little girl, I liked to ride with him on Saturday mornings as he made his rounds in his big red Edsel station wagon. We would start off with visits to his patients in town, and then head out on dusty tobacco roads to the shacks and trailers where the sharecroppers and mill workers lived. Folks would pay him whatever they could—money if they had it, a handful of eggs, firewood, a handshake, a prayer. Who would kill my Uncle John? He built a clinic on Reed Street. It was the very first, and for many years it had been the only clinic or hospital where Black folks could go without having to wait until last to be seen by a doctor. Why would anyone kill my Uncle John?

Philip told me that some punk kid, poor white trash, had broken into the clinic with a gun in his pocket, looking for something to steal. Uncle John caught him by surprise, and was shoved hard against the wall. He fell to the floor, gasping for breath. The kid dialed 911, and then he tried to run for it. But it was too late—Uncle John was dead of a heart attack and the cops were at the door.

My cousins were arguing with one another when I arrived in Kingston. *Shock, fatigue, heartbreak, anger and grief.* Visitors had been stopping by to let them know that the whole town was outraged by the crime. My cousins had been assured by one and all that the DA would do as he had promised—send that good-for-nothing poor white cracker punk kid straight to death row.

But the public defender had come by too. He confirmed that the DA was planning to charge the kid with a capital offense, and said that the kid had made up his mind to plead guilty. He said, "The charge doesn't fit the crime. That boy committed a crime for sure, and it is a terrible tragedy, but it would be a real stretch of the law to call it a capital offense." He had a question and a favor to ask. Did our family want justice or did we want vengeance? *Shock, fatigue, heartbreak, anger and grief.* Would the family be willing, he asked, to speak to the DA on the behalf of justice? Would we be willing to ask the DA to file charges that were truly commensurate with the crime?

My cousin Donny threw him out of the house.

"What a lot of nerve!" Donny shouted.

"What do you think Daddy would have wanted?" Rhonda asked.

"Would it hurt to talk to the DA?" Philip asked.

"Over my dead body!" Donny bellowed.

"It's not fair," Frank said. "It's not our job to tell the DA what to do."

"I think the public defender is right, and you know it too!" Ellen insisted.

"I don't care!" Donny cried. "A punk like that is going to end up on death row sooner or later anyway. Our father is dead because of him. Don't talk to me about justice. Where was the justice in Daddy dying like that?"

"I don't know," Rhonda said. "All I know is how awful all of this is. I don't know what the right thing to do is."

I asked, "Has anybody considered the possibility of talking to the kid?"

Donny stayed behind. The rest of us piled into the van and headed for the jailhouse. We bullied, badgered, threatened, and made a whole lot of noise before the attorneys would agree to set up the visit. It was awkward at first. The punk sat on one side of the table, staring down at his hands. We sat on the other side, taking in every detail: blue eyes, thin lips, pointed nose, dimpled chin, brown hair, crooked teeth, high forehead, ragged fingernails bitten down to the quick.

Rhonda broke the silence. "You know, the DA is calling for your life. And your lawyer said you're going to plead guilty."

He nodded.

"I need to know what happened. We need to know why. We need to understand this thing."

He was silent.

"Tell me!"

He raised his eyes, "I'm sorry about your father."

"It's too late for sorry," Rhonda said. "How old are you?"

He had just turned 19. His name was David. He'd grown up in the trailer park known as "The Bottoms," down by the river, just outside of town. Squalid. Ignorant. Dangerous. Crackerville. We asked questions, and he talked for more than an hour. He told us what happened. He said he owed a guy some money; money he didn't have; money he had no legitimate way of getting; money the guy was willing to kill him for.

"Look. I'm sorry about your daddy. I really am. He was a good man. I remember him coming down to the Bottoms a long time ago, knocking on doors, letting everybody know that us kids could come to the clinic and get shots and such. My mama took all of us. Said there wasn't too many people around like him that cared anything about Bottom folks."

David said he wasn't scared of prison. No, he hadn't been "inside" before; he'd never been caught. "I been in the wrong place, doing the wrong thing, for the wrong reason plenty times." He said prison didn't seem like it would be too bad; he'd lived a lot worse. He said his daddy was inside, and so was an uncle and one of his brothers; maybe they'd hook up.

Death row? "I ain't never expected to live to no ripe old age anyway." He had quit school in the 9th grade. He said that if he had it to do all over again he would join the military. He had tried to enlist, but had failed the test. "You got to have your reading up to be in the Army nowadays," he said.

Afterwards we sat in the van and talked.

"Jeez, what a loser."

"Uh huh."

"He's only 19."

"Face it, David doesn't have a snowball's chance in Hell of turning his life around."

"He's illiterate."

"Yep."

"Pathetic."

"Uh huh."

"I hate to say this, but prison just may be a step up for him."

"He could learn to read in there."

"Rhonda, what are you doing?"

"I'm making a list of books. What if we suggested that he had to learn to read, and finish a long list of books, and had to get his GED as conditions for parole? And what if, as a condition for probation, he had to learn a trade, and keep a job, and do some serious community service work for 5 or 10 years after he was released?"

"Well, he is only 19."

"Add the Autobiography of Malcolm X to your list."

"If David could make good somehow, then maybe Daddy's death would have some meaning."

"This is crazy."

"Yep."

"So do we talk to the DA?"

"Uh huh."

The DA was incredulous. But we stood our ground and made our case. He agreed to reduce the charges against David and to submit our recommendations to the court.

Donny was so angry at us that he threatened to boycott the memorial service. His wife had only been able to talk him into coming at the very last minute. To make matters even worse for Donny, the court had, with the family's consent, granted David's request to attend the service. It had been agreed that David and his mother would join us in the opening procession, and would sit with us during the service. There were hundreds of people in attendance. The aisles were filled. Every seat was taken. One after another, Uncle John's family and friends stood and came forward, to tell a story, to share a song, to recite a poem, to remember him, to speak of loss and to say goodbye.

When David stood, I was confused at first. I thought that perhaps he was preparing to leave. But no, he turned to the congregation and began to speak, "A good man is dead because of what I did. I'm sorry." He gestured towards my cousins. "They spared my life. I didn't deserve that. I'm going to be in prison for a very long time, but I'm not being sent there to die. What I want to ask all of you here is, is there any way you can forgive me?"

The pastor reached out to David and asked him to kneel. He called for a laying on of hands, placed his right hand on David's head, and began to pray. The pastor prayed for forgiveness. Ellen was the first to rise and place her hands upon David's back. The pastor prayed for mercy. Phillip and Rhonda rose and joined them. The pastor prayed for reconciliation. Even Donny stood and added his hands. He prayed for young people like David whose lives we've given up on. The rest of the family rose together, and we added our hands. Before long the entire gathering had come forward, laying hands on one another until we were all connected. The pastor prayed, and we prayed with him. We prayed for David to be healed and we prayed for ourselves to healed, and then we sang Amazing Grace.

Cynthia Stateman

Adapted from *Living with the Wolf: Walking the Way of Nonviolence*, Ed. by Peter Ediger, Pace e Bene Press, 2000. Used with permission.

4
Muslim Extremist Encampment

Blindfolded, his arms tightly gripped by his two armed captors, UN diplomat Giandomenico Picco was brought to a room where the leader of the kidnappers was waiting for him. It was 1991, and Picco had been sent by the Secretary-General of the United Nations to negotiate for the release of hostages being held at a secret location in Beirut. Though he had agreed in advance to be picked up in the middle of the night by masked Muslim terrorists, he was still terrified.

When they removed Picco's blindfold, he found himself facing a well-built, black-haired Arab man in his late thirties, wearing a ski mask. Behind the narrow slits in the ski mask, Picco could see nothing except the dark, suspicious eyes of his captor.

"You may know something about me," Giandomenico Picco said, after a period of silence. "But I know nothing about you."

"What do you want to know?" the masked leader asked Picco.

Picco paused before he spoke again. He knew the words he chose would determine their fate—and his own.

Imagine, just for a moment, that you are this official envoy. Completely at the mercy of your captors, you wonder if you will survive the night. You think of your loved ones, afraid that you may never see them again. What do you say when words are all you have?

"Do you have children?" Picco asked.

"Yes," the man replied.

"So do I," Picco replied. "And are you doing this because you want to give your children a better world?"

"Of course."

"Well, I am, too. So it turns out that we are both fathers who want to give our children a better world."

The man in the ski mask quietly shifted. He leaned toward Picco, peering directly into his face.

"Where the hell do you come from?" he asked with intense curiosity.

Reflecting on this life-and-death conversation years later, Picco told me that this initial conversation "blew the man in the ski mask out of his chair." Picco had chosen the right words, at the right time, to bring his adversary into relationship. They had, in a word, connected.

With consummate skill, this UN envoy began to create a shared context with his captor. Beyond all their deep differences and conflicting political views, Picco and his captor had discovered at least one common identity: they were fathers who loved their children. Even though it would have been easier for both the "terrorist" and the "diplomat" to remain walled off from each other inside those one-dimensional identities, they both stepped out of those narrow, separate cages and found a place to stand together. Their conversation required courage from both men, and eventually led to the release of the hostages.

"Why did you begin the conversation this way?" I asked Picco during one of our conversations.

"Each of us has multiple identities," he explained. "Each of us is more than one thing. I knew that was true for me, and also for the man in the ski mask. I knew that finding an identity that we had in common would build a bridge."

"Please say more about bridging," I probed. "What exactly is involved?"

"It was clear when I was brought into their hideout that they thought I was from a different planet. I knew that I had to overcome that notion, otherwise I would get nowhere. Discovering that we were both fathers who cared about our children was the first step. It changed the dynamic between us. I believe that this first exchange is what opened the door to a successful negotiation."

Mark Gerzon

From *American Citizen, Global Citizens*, by Mark Gerzon. Published by Spirit Scope (2010), Boulder, CO. International edition available under the title *GLOBAL CITIZENS* (Ebury Press: London). Used with permission.

5

The Third Hand

Walking around Westfield, New Jersey, I passed an art gallery owned by the father of a child I had taught in Kindergarten 13 years ago. Mike, Angelica's father, had always been complimentary about his daughter's Kindy experience. It had been a long time since we had a conversation. I thought that I would like to go into his gallery and have a short talk, "catch up" as it were. I went in.

"Hi, Mike," I said.

He embraced me and began to talk about how great a teacher I had been. I thanked him, and seeing that he had a customer, I tried to exit.

He said, "Don't go. I have to talk to you. I want you to know that you changed Angelica's life."

I thanked him, said something about how wonderful Angelica was…

He stopped me and looked directly into my eyes: "You changed her life. *Really* changed it. She was ashamed and embarrassed about having me for a father because of my accent. She didn't want me to come to school or meet her friends, and she refused to learn Spanish. It affected her personality in many ways. She felt less than others because she was the daughter of such a man.

"When Angelica told you her feelings, you had a talk with her and she suddenly saw things in a different way. Something changed inside her head. She was proud of me and proud that I was smart enough to know two languages when most people knew only one. She suddenly heard the way I speak English as like a beautiful song. Everything because of you, Daren. You changed her life."

I remember what happened:

I had asked all my parents to come as guest teachers to share a passion, a job, hobby, etc. I wanted Angelica to ask her Dad to come to class and share his passion for art and what he did in his work. Angelica refused to discuss it. Eventually she told me why she didn't want to invite her father. People had made fun of his accent.

We sat next to each other while I thought about this. There were two things: other people's reactions, and her feelings. And whenever you find yourself saying that there are two things, "on the one hand... on the other hand..." there is always a third somewhere. The third was how she was processing the reactions of others.

I told her she was right. Some people do make fun of other people. I asked her, "How smart are the people who make fun?"

Angelica didn't answer.

I said, "I know a secret a lot of kids and even grown-ups don't know. And even if I told them the secret, most of them wouldn't be able to understand it. You're very young, Angelica, but I think you are smart enough to understand." ("Smart" meant a lot to Angelica.)

Her eyes lit up. "Will you tell me the secret?" she asked.

"OK," I said. "The truth is that people who make fun of other people usually don't know what they're doing; they're not really using their brains. (We studied brains in Kindy). They're not thinking. So what could we do?"

Angelica ventured, "Punch them?"

21

"Or teach them," I said. "Most people learn how to speak one language, but your Daddy knows two. And his accent sounds beautiful, like music. I love to listen to him speak and I wish I could learn to speak another language as well as your Daddy does."

She thought for a while and then asked, "You mean Daddy is smarter than you?"

I paused, wondering how to answer this. It would be a problem if she began telling the other children that her Daddy was smarter than theirs because their Daddies spoke only one language. For my part, I do think that someone who speaks a second language fluently *is* smarter than I am, in a certain way. But with children, the "teachable moment" is very brief and won't withstand a discussion about the many facets of intelligence!

We were in this moment together and I took a risk.

"Yes," I said. "Think about it."

Her expression changed. The next day she said she wanted her father to come in and teach.

Our conversation lasted two minutes at most; add on another five for both of us thinking in silence. Later we shared our thoughts with the class and everyone talked about experiences of someone making fun of them or someone they knew. Solutions were explored. Differences between ignorant behavior and bullying were considered. Some children shared times when they made fun of someone else. It's really interesting to listen to five-year-olds; they give you so much to think about.

Angelica is now in her first year of college. She wants to be a teacher. She is fluent in Spanish.

Daren Driscoll

6
Seeing Each Other

A few years ago a woman called me up and asked me if I did couples counseling. I said yes. Then she asked if I did work over the phone. I said yes.

"Well," she said. "Will you do phone work with a couple if only one half of the couple is willing to do the work?"

"I am assuming you're the willing half?"

"Yes."

"Well that depends on how willing you are to actually do your part."

In our first session I found out that she and her husband still lived in the same house, but that was about as far as their relationship went. In fact they had divided up the house so that when her husband came home from work he went straight into his side of the house and locked it off! They hadn't spoken with each other for four years, except about who was going to pick up the kids, or go get the groceries. Any and all communication between them was strictly limited to the logistics of maintaining their children. She described him as "the biggest asshole in the world," and told me the only reason they were still together was for the sake of their kids. It made me wonder what the children thought of this arrangement!

I asked her if there was ever a time when they lived together and *did* get along.

She said, "Oh yeah, we used to be very much in love, but that was a long time ago."

"Well," I said. "What would it be like if you looked at him that way again, and treated him the way you used to when you were both very much in love?"

"Well I wouldn't do that, because he's not the same any more. He doesn't care about me anymore. He does all these awful things to me—he's rude, he criticizes me, he thinks he's always right, he doesn't listen to what I say, he doesn't hold to his responsibilities with the kids...." She had *lots* of evidence proving that this guy was now a real jerk—a long way from the man he used to be.

I asked her to step into his shoes a little bit. "Do you do anything to reinforce how *he* is being?" I asked. "Do you treat him in such a way that he would then view you differently and treat you differently from the woman he once loved?"

"Well, yeah, I suppose so."

That helped her begin to recognize that she played a part in the negative relationship. I pointed out that this was a good thing to notice, because now she could have some control over how she participated in the relationship. Now I wanted to find out what personal abilities she had already developed, that would support her seeing her husband in a generous and useful way.

First I found out that she was a fundraiser at a very high level. She raised a *lot* of money, millions and millions of dollars. I asked her, "When you're fundraising, do you ever come across people who are initially objectionable to you?"

She laughed immediately and said, "*All* the time."

"So I suppose you must treat them just like you treat your husband," I concluded.

"No!" she said. "I'd never get any money from them."

24

"How *do* you treat them?"

"I look at them as decent human beings. I think to myself, 'How would *I* want to be treated?' "

"Well, what if you did that with your husband?" I asked.

"Huh," she said. "I never thought of that."

I continued to draw upon abilities she already had in other areas of her life. I asked her, "What about your kids? When they do something you don't like, do you treat them like you treat your husband?"

"No. I mean, you know, they're precious."

"What if you viewed your husband in the same way even when he does things you don't like?"

With both her kids and the people from whom she raised funds, what kept her on track was that she had a very clear long-term vision of her outcome. If she went to ask somebody for $100,000, a good relationship with that person was vital to making that happen and to keeping open the possibility of continued support further down the road. And with her kids she had a strong vision of wanting to support them in growing and learning—coming fully into their lives. Both were very nurturing approaches.

"What has your goal been with your husband?" I asked.

"To punish him," she said, and I noticed her voice soften a bit at the realization.

"That's a little different approach, isn't it? What if you viewed him the same way you view your kids, or the people from whom you raise money? You may feel like punishing him in the moment, but what do you want to be happening a year down the road?"

That gave her a very different orientation.

Two weeks later, in our second session, she asked, "What happens if I'm seeing him in this new way and he still reacts like a horrible person? He said he was going to pick up the groceries on Wednesday and he didn't do it!"

I just brought the question right back to those abilities she already had. "If your kids said they were going to take out the trash that day and they didn't do it, would that make them horrible people?"

"No."

"Then why would it make your husband a horrible person? It's true he didn't keep an agreement, so that's something to notice, but should that really take him to this extreme of being a bad person?"

Most of the session was just basic coaching on other options she could take if he said this or did that, getting a more objective view and walking through future scenarios so she could practice using her new ways of interacting with him. At the same time I continued to bring up her awareness of how she had viewed him when they fell in love, reinforcing that memory.

"What would it be like to interact with him in that way again?" I asked. "How would you look? What would your voice tone be? When you were falling in love, how did you view his behaviors when he did something a bit goofy?"

"It was kind of endearing."

"What if you looked at his slip-ups as endearing again?"

The whole thing was pretty straightforward—how do you view him, and consequently how do you treat him?

After another two weeks she called up and said, "I don't need the third session. I don't need your help anymore."

"OK, that's fine. Can you tell me why?"

"Yeah, we're like teenagers in love. It is so good! It's better than teenagers in love because now we're adults and we bring so much more to the relationship. He's actually this really good guy and we just had a misunderstanding. I thought he didn't care about me, and he thought I didn't care about him! But that wasn't true at all!"

This taught me a lot about the dramatic change that one simple shift in viewpoint can manifest in any relationship. And almost a year later, when I checked in on her, she and her husband were still wonderfully in love.

Mark Hochwender

7
Defense Through Disarmament

I was awakened late one night by a man kicking open the door to my bedroom. The house was empty. The phone was downstairs. He was somewhat verbally abusive as he walked over to my bed. I could not find his eyes in the darkness but could see the outline of his form. As I lay there, feeling a fear and vulnerability I had never before experienced, several thoughts rushed through my head: First, the uselessness of screaming. Second, the fallacy of thinking safety depends on having a gun hidden under one's pillow. Somehow I could not imagine this man standing patiently while I reached under my pillow for my gun.

I believe the third thought saved my life. I realized with some clarity that either he and I made it through this situation safely—together—or we would both be damaged. Our safety was connected. If he raped me, I would be hurt both physically and emotionally, *and* he would be hurt as well. If he went to prison, the damage would be greater. That thought disarmed *me*. It also released me from paralysis and a desire to lash out. It freed me from fear's control over my ability to respond, even though I still had feelings of fear. I found myself acting out of concern for the safety of us both, reacting with firmness but with little hostility in my voice.

I asked him what time it was. He answered. That was a good sign. I commented that his watch and the clock on my night table had different times. His said 2:30, mine said 2:45. I had just set mine. I hoped his watch wasn't broken. When had he last set it? He answered. I answered. The time seemed endless. When the atmosphere began to calm a little, I asked him how he had gotten into the house. He'd broken through the glass in the back door. I told him that presented me with a problem: I did not have the money to buy new glass. He talked about some financial difficulties of his own.

We talked until we were no longer strangers and I felt safe to ask him to leave. He didn't want to; he said he had no place to go. Knowing I did not have the physical power to force him out, I told him firmly but respectfully, as equal to equal, that I would give him a clean set of sheets, but he would have to make his own bed downstairs. He went downstairs, and I sat up in bed, wide awake and shaking for the rest of the night. The next morning we ate breakfast together and he left.

Several things happened that night. I allowed someone of whom I was afraid to become human to me, and as a result I reacted in a surprisingly human way to him. That caught him off guard. Apparently his scenario had not included a social visit, and it took him a few minutes to regain his sense of balance. By that time the vibes were all wrong for violence. Whatever had been motivating him was sidetracked, and he changed his mind.

Angie O'Gorman

This is a portion of a 1983 essay adapted from *The Universe Bends Toward Justice: a reader on Christian nonviolence in the US* edited by Angie O'Gorman, New Society Publications, 1990. Used with permission.

8

Navajo Handshake

I was spending the 4th of July in Telluride, Colorado with my wife and two kids as we have every summer. This year we were camping next to a family that was taking off on the morning of the 4th for Durango. As they were waking up I saw an extensive Navajo family of about 16 parked near the campground entrance. A young Navajo man in a white T-shirt left one of the cars and strolled over to our neighbor's camp. He must have been in his twenties, and the multiple scars on his hands and head, a black eye, and his scabbed knuckles made an immediate impression.

When I first saw him I felt the Holy Spirit within me say in a quiet voice, "Him, that guy," a gentle prompting to connect. I ignored it. I was on vacation. As if you can vacation from the Holy Spirit.

I watched this man slink right into our neighbor's camp and start talking to the father of the family there. I couldn't hear what they were talking about, but I could see the father was really uncomfortable being confronted by the young man. It was the 4th of July and most of the campsites were taken, so I guessed the Navajo was intentionally trying to intimidate our neighbors into leaving quickly so his family could move into the site. I could tell the father was trying to avoid him, and the whole family was rushing to get out of there.

As soon as our neighbors left, the cars at the campground entrance rolled in and the Navajo man's family piled out, setting up a crowded camp beside ours.

I returned to my camp and walked around trying to "look busy," but the longer I avoided that internal calling, the more the prompting intensified, until finally I felt an overwhelming need to be back in alignment with the rhythm of the Spirit.

I observed the young man for a while around his family. He yelled a lot. I could see how agitated he was as he paced back and forth. His whole family walked on eggshells around him. He had two young boys, about three and four, and a small child just over a year. One of the boys was getting into something he shouldn't have and the man yelled "Dóoda! Dóoda!" The boy scurried away behind a camp chair.

Once they were set up he came up to me. I had the sense that he might try to intimidate our family into leaving too, to give his large family more space. At that moment I let myself crawl into the back seat in my head, and simply opened myself for the Spirit to speak through me. It was afternoon now, and the sun was low.

The young man was saying something incoherent as he reached out his hand, and at that moment I remembered something my friend Steve had told me in passing many years ago, about his time on the Navajo reservation in the 1950's. Steve told me that when two Navajos meet, instead of shaking hands vigorously as we do, they place their hands together gently and hold them there while looking into each other's eyes, silently sensing each other.

I reached out my hand and as he began to shake it I just kept my hand still, staring into his eyes and sensing his presence.

He murmured something, and I could see that he was dumbfounded that this white man was greeting him culturally correctly. I just stood there and he kept grunting, as if in disbelief.

"Huh…!

"Huh…!

"Huh…!

We stood like that for over two minutes. Finally he asked.

"Who are you? What's your name?"

"I'm Scott."

He said, "Hey, man. You know… You're cool man, you're cool."

I said, "Thanks, what's your name?"

"Jim."

Then he walked off. I could tell he was utterly bewildered by what had just happened. He paced around his camp. After a little while he came back and asked where we were from.

"California."

"You came all the way from California?"

"Yes."

"Why?"

"We're here for the 4th of July in Telluride. Are you here with your family?"

"Yes, those are my boys over there."

His sons were little ruffians. They were throwing sticks and rocks and leaves at my three-year-old daughter, who retreated to a safer place in our camp. When I saw she was fine I turned back to Jim. I could tell that the Navajo greeting I had given him had instantly developed a deep connection between us. I asked him more questions and we talked for hours about the struggles in his life—why he gets into lots of fights, his drinking, his anger at the world, America, and whites.

When I asked him why he was so angry he said,

"People are bad, white people are bad, but you're cool though, you're cool. But white people are bad. I fight a lot." He gestured to his black eye. His knuckles were more than scabbed. They were black and blue and torn up. He had been fighting *hard*.

"I see you fight a lot," I said. "What is it that you are fighting against?"

"Anything that tries to hurt me. I think I'm going to die soon."

"What is important to you in your life?"

"My family."

"Why would you want to allow yourself to die and rob your children of their father and the future that you can give them?" I asked. We talked more about his family. "What are the things you want your sons to have in their lives?"

"I want them to be happy," he said.

"Do you have that happiness?"

"No."

"How do you expect to give them the gift if you don't have that yourself? Is happiness important enough to give to your sons that you can find it for yourself?"

"I'm just not worth it," he said. "I'm not worth anything." He welled up with tears and left.

While he was gone I remembered him using the sharp directive "Dóoda!" with his sons, which clearly meant "no." So I went to my three-year-old daughter, who's quite verbal and outgoing for her age. I said to her, "If those kids throw stuff at you again, you tell them 'Dóoda!' really loudly."

After pacing through his camp Jim returned and we talked more about the things that he wanted his sons to have in their lives. What most impacted Jim was the idea that he was modeling what his children would learn, and that he could create a different path for his children. He began to see that they represented a specific mission in this world that he was here to carry out—and that mission transcended his environment, and all he had been through. He was greatly moved by the realization that he was of value to his sons in spite of his own beliefs about himself. The whole time his family just stood in jaw-dropped amazement that he was talking so long to this strange white man.

During our conversations Jim went back to his campsite many times because he got so emotional. He didn't want me to see him welling up with tears, so he'd walk off and sort of murmur to himself for a little while, but each time he would come back. I knew we were connecting at a very deep level. I was touching something that he couldn't close the door on; it was so compelling that he had to get some kind of closure on it. What I was doing and saying didn't fit any of his initial presumptions about who I was.

When he returned again I said, "You are the pathfinder for your sons. You are going to lay out the path that they will follow. Are you going to lay out a path where you teach them that they're going to have to beat up people and fight?" He was already shaking his head. "Or will you lay out a path where they're seeking what's peaceful and loving and beautiful in life?"

He nodded, "That's what I want, that's what I want."

"Then that's your mission and that's your purpose that you need to be here for."

He got very emotional again and we hugged, and I saw his family with that deer-in-the-headlights sort of look. They couldn't believe that Jim, whose only physical contact with others was with his fists, was actually hugging and crying with this white man.

Jim left again, walking through his camp, clearly turned inward. When he came back I said, "You've walked around this field of your life and you haven't realized that there is real treasure inside of *you*. You need to be digging for that treasure, not only for yourself, but to share that with your children. What looks like a desert to you, underneath the soil, and in your heart, are beautiful things that can grow. That's what you need to dig for, that treasure is worth fighting and digging for." That made an impression on him, and he began to realize even his own beliefs about himself could be changed easily and did not have to be formed by his environment.

I said to him, "Look Jim, there is a specific reason God had us meet, and he cares for you so much that he made sure I drove 997 miles from Thousand Oaks California, so that we could talk. This is the most important conversation that I've had all week in Telluride. Now you tell me that you don't have a special purpose on this planet?"

That just landed right in his heart. He put his hands over his face and wept and walked away. He came back several times, but couldn't speak without breaking up.

When he was finally able to speak, he said, "I'm not deserving."

I said, "Jim, there are reasons for people meeting." The more we talked the more he understood that the reason I was there was to have that conversation with him. "If you weren't worth it, why would God send me?" I asked.

That created another shift for him. He got choked up again and I could tell that he was beginning to see that maybe he *was* worth something. We hugged again, and the tears kept flowing despite his efforts to control himself. We continued talking at length about how his own identity will shape his mission in the world, and how his mission and identity will shape those of his sons, and grandsons and great-grandsons, seven generations down.

I told him, "You appear to be someone who is wasting your energy on fighting people on the outside, when you should be fighting for yourself on the inside—someone so worthy deserves someone to fight for their survival.

"If anyone came up to your child and tried to hurt him, what would you do?"

"I would kill him! I would kill anyone who tried to hurt my family."

I put my hand on his shoulder, "So you really have a strong sense of protecting your children, don't you?"

He nodded.

Then I touched him over his heart and said, "This wounded heart in here needs the same protection and the same care. You wouldn't let some outsider come up and harm your son, then why would you let thoughts, patterns, and your own behavior harm that little boy's father? Your little boys are going to use you as their model for the rest of their lives, to know that they were of value to you and to themselves. They will forever either say, 'I want to be like my daddy' or 'I don't want to be like my daddy.' You need to choose today, who you will be to your sons and who you will be to yourself. Jim, we were supposed to have this talk, and you have a blank map to draw the journey of your life. Decide today that you will fight just as hard for the survival of yourself as you would for your sons." Again he left weeping...

That night I had been cooking a hamburger for myself on the campfire while his family was getting ready to have hotdogs for dinner. I asked him if he would be interested in some steak that I had that I wasn't going to be able to cook since we were leaving the next day. He said he had no way to cook it. I told him that I would be happy to cook it for him and I pulled out a huge 2-inch-thick rib eye steak and started to cook it for him. He stood amazed, and kept staring at it, because again what I was doing didn't fit into his old beliefs about white people. When it was finished and I gave it to him he asked, "Why are you doing this?"

"Doing what, Jim?"

"Why are you eating a hamburger while you cooked me this steak?"

"Why?" I said. "Because of my faith, I do what I would want someone to do for me, and I want you to have my best." Tears in his eyes, he left with the food. I watched him standing in his camp holding the steak and just staring at it for about twenty minutes before sharing it with his family. He was staring a *lot* that whole evening, clearly thinking things through inside. I imagine he was digging up the treasure in his heart that he never realized was there before.

After dinner, sure enough Jim's boys started throwing stuff at my daughter again. She pointed her finger at the Navajo boys and yelled. "Dóoda! Dóoda!" Their eyes got as big as saucers. Just like their dad, they had no idea how this little white girl could be addressing them in their own language. It was really cute to watch.

The next day I noticed that Jim's shoulders had relaxed and his chin was up. He had stopped yelling with his family, and the anxious and intimidating presence of the day before was gone. He seemed to be at a centered peace with himself.

We had to leave that morning, but before we left he came over and said that our conversations had a deep impact on his life and that I was a blessing from God. He actually asked me to take him with us. I said I couldn't do that, but I promised I would pray for him. I said, "Somebody will come next, to take you to the next place or help you with the next thing you need to learn."

Scott Leese

9
The Ranch

I had met up with three other moms to ride our horses together at the Ranch as we often do. I was happy to be there with them and the horses; riding my horse Chinook is one of the greatest things I do in my life. We walked our horses out into the pasture together and I relaxed into the friendly atmosphere and the beauty of the Ranch.

I was particularly enjoying the company of my friend Mary, who I ride with more often than the others. She's fun to go out on the trail with and just "shoot the breeze," so to speak. She's always willing to share what she has, whether it's useful information on this or that, or a helpful hand with the horses.

When we got back from our ride we brushed the horses down and I gave Chinook a treat while I picked her feet and put a treatment on her hooves that keeps them clean and well oiled. Then we turned the horses back out to pasture.

As we were walking back to the cars I noticed Karli's truck in the parking lot, and there was Karli by my car. She was a slender woman, moody and irritable most of the time, despite the beautiful setting of the Ranch.

As we approached my car I could see she was at the end of her rope already. She started in on me at once.

"What are you doing parking your car like this?!" she demanded to know. "It's too close to the horses! I'm not responsible if my horse kicks your fucking car. If that happens it'll just be too bad and I'm not going to pay for it!"

When I saw how angry she was, my first thought was, *Why is she being such an asshole about this? If she has something to say, why can't she just say it to me in a way I can hear? Like, "Do you mind parking your car differently?"*

Instead she was being incredibly rude. But that wasn't all. She just kept going on and on: "What's your problem? I don't know what's wrong with you!" she shouted. "Can't you see this is too fucking close?!"

It was then that something shifted for me and I thought to myself, *You know what? This is just somebody who is in a lot of pain right now.*

When she took a break for a minute I said, "Karli, this seems a little inappropriate for you to yell at me like this over my car." I was doing my best to stay centered, but looking back I can see that what I said was still judgmental.

Not surprisingly, she started in again with the same dialogue.

But now I realized I could—not help her—but *love* her. I could just stand there and let her do whatever she needed to do while staying in my own space in my heart. It didn't matter if it turned out in any particular way, but I didn't have to join her pain.

When she paused a second time I said, "Karli, what's going on? This can't be about me. It seems like there's something else going on with you."

At this point my friends were just gaping, watching this entire thing in total disbelief because Karli was so off the wall, and I was so off the wall to them in terms of how I was reacting to her—I simply wasn't jumping back at her with anger.

Karli went off on another rant, blaming me for how I had parked the car. I just stayed with her, saying, "Karli, it really seems like there's something happening for you that you're blowing this out of proportion. I don't feel like

I deserve the way you're talking to me, and it feels like you have something else that's going on inside of you."

At that point Karli stopped and just *looked* at me, and I *looked* back at her.

"It seems like you're really upset about something," I said. "Do you want to talk about it? What's going on for you?"

At that point her whole mood shifted. We continued looking at each other and I just held out my arms and she walked right into them and started crying.

"Thank you so much for not buying into my shit," she sobbed, "and for really staying with me. I'm really having a hard time in menopause right now, and sometimes I can't control my anger. Thank you so much."

When she left, Mary looked at me with amazement.

"What are you, enlightened?" she said, only half joking. "That was unbelievable what you just did. I can't believe I just got to witness that. I would have done just the opposite in that situation, and it would have ended very differently."

"Boy we just had an incredible lesson in life," said my other friend Susan.

"The next time I have a confrontation like that I hope I can do it in a similar way," Mary said. "Until now I always thought that responding like you did would just get me walked all over."

Even though my first reaction was not a great thought about Karli, it turned out very lovely in the end. Nobody got hurt, and I avoided the pain and confusion I would have felt if I had let myself feel attacked personally, and had come back at her with anger. I learned later that Karli told several other people what had happened that day. She told them how grateful she was that I didn't yell back at her like she expected, but instead kept inviting her to a different place.

Anonymous

10

Why Did You Look Up?

Jill had been a victim of almost unbelievable abuse. She struggled mightily—having been in and out of the psychiatric hospital several times where she'd accumulated quite a list of diagnoses. Though she was 36, she was still utterly afraid of her mother, who somehow still ruled the roost of her seven grown kids. I say *somehow* because none of them was dumb; each was highly intelligent. I'd estimate Jill's IQ at roughly 130—around the 95th percentile. Yet despite their smarts, Jill and her six siblings were still dominated by their mother.

Jill came in one day in the middle of a panic attack.

"What's going on?" I asked.

"Mother's back in town... she's called... she wants to meet and she wants to have everybody together, and everybody's upset!" Jill's parents moved around a lot. They often upset people by the strange things they did, and so they would just pick up their stuff and move on. Now they were back.

"What would happen if your mother walked in right now?" I indicated toward the door. She followed my gesture, but then her eyes darted up and she literally flinched.

"Wait a minute," I said, "We're pretending here, she's not actually here." Jill took a breath. "Why did you look up?" I asked her.

"I don't know," Jill replied.

"How tall is your mother?"

"I don't know, she's... she's four eleven."

"How tall are you?"

"Five one."

"When you imagined your mother you looked up as if she were about five nine or ten. Why did you look up?" She couldn't tell me. "Let me guess. You looked up because suddenly you felt like you were a small girl, a small child, didn't you?"

She paused and said, "That's exactly how I felt. Something bad was going to happen when mother showed up." The minute she even *imagined* her mother walking into the room, she suddenly became a little girl again, with this huge powerful mother towering over her.

"OK," I said. "Let's take control of this. I want you to imagine in a moment that your mother is over there. She walks in and now you remember you're an adult. You are five one; she is four eleven. I want you to see her as four eleven, just her regular size. Can you do that?"

She braced herself but she could do it without panic.

"OK, now if you can do that. Why don't you make her smaller? After all, this is *your* image."

"OK" She shrank her willingly. We did this a couple of times, and each time mom got smaller, Jill's posture got a bit straighter.

"Is that better?" I asked.

"Oh, you bet!"

"Can you remember now how tall she really is and who you are?"

"Yes."

Then we imagined a future situation where Jill would probably see her mother. It was a family gathering of some sort. I helped her visualize that scenario in the same way, seeing her mother at her real height, while remembering that she was an adult and even slightly taller. That was all. What we did was really very simple.

When Jill went to the family gathering, her mother was again doing her thing, dominating the environment and making some outrageous statements.

Jill stood up and faced her mother. She said, "Mother, that's a bunch of crap and you know it. Why don't you just sit down and shut up!"

Jill's mother got a wide-eyed look on her face and just sat down. Everybody there wheeled around to look at Jill, who had been the scapegoat of the family for many years. They were shocked.

From that point on Jill actually became the spokesperson for her siblings. Now when mother is bugging them, they turn to Jill for help.

Steve Watson

11

Size Matters

A woman at a noisy summer party in the older part of a large city went out to the fire escape to sit down, cool off and have a smoke. With the loud sounds of the party behind her, and her attention on the city lights before her, she was in her "own little world." When she felt something on her shoulder, she looked over and saw a man's penis there. She said casually, as if musing to herself, "Hmmm, that looks like a penis, only smaller." We'll probably never know what kind of response he expected, but evidently that wasn't it. The penis—and it's owner—vanished back into the party crowd.*

A "flasher" had been reported in the neighborhood of a Catholic girls' school, and the staff had expected that sooner or later he would "show up" at the school. So the staff rehearsed all the students in what to do if he did. Sure enough, a week later the flasher arrived in his car, and called to some of the girls. Several of them went over near his car,

---

* From *Transforming Yourself* by Steve Andreas, pp. 250-251. Copyright © 2002 Real People Press, Boulder, CO.

43

and when he "did his thing," they all looked sorrowful, as they said, "Oh, we feel so sorry for you. It's *so* small!" He scowled and left immediately, and was never seen at the school again.[*]

Steve Andreas

---

[*]From *Six Blind Elephants, Volume I* by Steve Andreas, pp 276. Copyright © 2006 Real People Press, Boulder, CO.

12

One Question

In 1999 the Chief of the White House Commission on Complimentary and Alternative Healthcare, Dr. Jim Gordon, set up a team to do international post-war trauma work. He knew I had been doing this work in my own practice for twenty years, so I was invited to be on his team of ten health care professionals. Our intention was to teach various methods to other healthcare professionals in post war zones, giving physicians, nurses, psychiatrists, and school psychologists more methods to deal with the trauma surrounding them. Jim received a grant from USAID, and along with other private funding we set off on our first trip in the fall of 1999.

We had to cross the border into Kosovo on foot from Macedonia; then we continued into Prishtina where the Kosovar refugees were just returning. KFOR, the fifty-thousand member multi-national peacekeeping force, had finally arrived in a delayed response to the sweeping genocide. The help came so late it seemed to me we hadn't learned anything, as a country or as a world, from the genocide five years previously in Bosnia. We gathered 144 of the refugees who were healthcare professionals, and we paid to put them up for a week of training in the Prishtina hotel. There we taught them the straight medical model behind our work, and of course we worked with their own personal trauma—they were all in shock.

The Serbs had taken out two power plants in the province, and KFOR had only gotten half of one back up and running, so electricity would go out most of the time, leaving us in a horrible dark hotel that one of Milosevic's head criminals had used as his headquarters. Rape and torture and all kinds of terrible things had gone on there, but it was the only place we had. Despite the aura of despair, every day we taught 4 hours of lecture and 2-3 hours in small groups. I led a group of twelve, and their stories were all horrifying.

Each day I set up a circle of chairs around an altar, opening the group with a blessing for all of us and an intention to work together for healing. I expressed compassion for the loved ones they had seen die, and for their eleven-year ordeal of being shut out from any kind of education or life as they had previously known it.

I started out with art therapy to assist in opening up to their repressed trauma. During this process I noticed that one Albanian man was unique. He seemed to have come to a different place within himself than the others had. He was more tranquil—both steady and focused in our group.

He told me an incredible story about how conflict can be taken care of, and it will stay in my mind forever. I learned that he had grown up in the town of Prishtina next to a Serbian family that had a boy the same age as him. The two families had become best friends, and the two kids had grown up together side by side, from small children to middle-aged men. Their two families had been like blood relatives, but in the spring of 1999 the Serbian family turned the Albanian family in to the Serbian police. He had to watch as his mother was beaten, and his father was brutally killed in his own home.

He fled to the mountains where he hid for four months before returning to Prishtina. While in hiding he had some time to think about what had happened. He told me he came to the conclusion that the betrayal of his family was part of the human condition, *period*. The depth of that broad acceptance, not just saying it intellectually, but actually *getting* it, allowed him to move to a place of strength that none of the others could get to yet. He was in a state of fluidity, dialogue, and negotiation—I could just see it. The other people in the group could see this as well, and it was in stark contrast to where they found themselves.

I asked him how he arrived at such an emotionally healthy place with all the horrible tragedy around him.

He said, "I asked myself one question over and over again, and one question only: *How can I prevent this from happening to my own children?*"

That's what did it. He realized that if he held onto the anger and bitterness and hate, it would only help repeat the same kind of trauma that he had experienced. He knew he had to let that go and start a new path.

By asking that question he was laying the foundation to build bridges between two ethnic cultures. When I visited later I got to witness his work in transforming ethnic conflict using many of the methods for processing trauma that we had taught him. Eventually he took the healing process all the way to organizing his old neighborhood to once again incorporate both Albanians and Serbs.

Christine Hibbard

13
Guests in the Night

I t was a family adventure trip. My wife, Judith, our two-year-old daughter, Leila, and I had rented a small camper and were traveling through Baja California. The day before our return to San Diego, we parked the camper near a beach for one last night in nature.

In the middle of the night I was awakened by Judith poking me with her elbow and yelling at me to get up. My first impressions were of noise and banging. Fairly disoriented, I jumped down out of our little loft-bed, and standing stark naked, faced the windshield.

What I saw woke me quickly out of my half-dazed state. The van was surrounded by masked men banging on the windows.

Having watched a lot of adventure movies, I always wondered what I would feel and do when confronted with danger. Well, I leapt right into the hero's role. I felt no fear—time to "save the family."

I dove for the driver's seat and turned the ignition. The camper had started perfectly at least 50 times that trip. Now it tried to turn over, sputtered a few times, and died. There was the sound of breaking glass, and a hand reached in through the driver's side window. I smashed the hand. (Non-violently of course! Actually, my lifelong inquiries about pacifism didn't stand a chance in the energy of the moment. I've often thought that I'm glad I didn't have a gun because I probably would have used it.)

My hand was bleeding from the broken glass. I figured I had one more chance to start the car. Having played hero successfully a thousand times in fantasy, I never doubted I would do it. I turned the key. The engine sputtered to life ... and died. Then someone jammed a rifle into my throat. I remember this thought, *You mean I don't save the family?* I was really quite surprised.

One of the bandits, who spoke a little English, was yelling, "Money! Money!" The rifle still at my throat, I reached under the driver's seat and handed one of them my wallet through the broken window. I was hoping this was the end of it.

It wasn't.

Releasing the latch through the broken window, they opened the door. The man with the rifle pushed me hard and sent me sprawling onto the floor. They entered the camper.

They looked remarkably like Mexican bandits from a grade-B movie. They had standard-issue bandannas over their faces. There were four: the one with the rifle, one with a rusty carving knife, one with a huge machete and one unarmed. I was half surprised they weren't wearing bullet-filled bandoleers slung over their shoulders. Maybe their weapons were really props from Central Casting.

While one man held me to the floor with the rifle against my neck, the bandits started tearing the camper apart, yelling in Spanish.

It's interesting. While I could do something (or at least had the illusion of being able to do something) like start the car or save the family, I felt no fear, although there was adrenaline to spare. But as I lay naked on the floor, cold steel against my neck, I started feeling quite helpless. Then I felt afraid. I began to shake.

Now this was an interesting situation. I was just about to get pretty in tune with my fear; in fact, I was only a moment or two from losing it. In a fleeting shred of self-consciousness, I reminded myself that this might be an excellent time to meditate and seek guidance. I remember breathing into my heart and asking God for help.

I heard quite clearly this passage from the 23rd Psalm:

"Thou shalt preparest a table before me in the presence of mine enemies."

These words were met inside with a resounding, *Huh? ... I don't get it!*

Then I saw an image of myself, serving the bandits a feast. I thought to myself, *I'm living in a reality where bandits have attacked me, I'm resisting, and it's a generally bad scene.*

Well, what if this wasn't so? What if they weren't bandits? What if they were old friends of ours, come to visit us out of the cold desert night? What if I were glad to see them, and welcomed them as I would honored guests? What if I prepared a table for them?

While one aspect of me was busy fantasizing horrendous scenes of rape and murder, a clear, quiet space opened inside that was intrigued by this new possibility. *These, too, are children of God. How many times have I declared that my purpose is to serve others? Well, here they are!*

I looked at the bandits from this more heartfelt awareness. *Wait a minute! These aren't bandits! They're kids!*

It was suddenly apparent that these "bandits" were quite young, obviously inexperienced and rather inept. They also seemed nervous. Their violence and yelling seemed more a product of their fear than their power. Also, in their thrashing about, they were making a terrific mess of things and losing a lot of the good loot. In a rather bizarre flash of insight, I saw that "serving a table" in this moment meant to help them do a better job of robbing us.

I turned to the young man who spoke English and said, "Hey, you're missing some of the best stuff! Under that pile over there is a very nice camera."

He gave me a peculiar look.

He yelled something in Spanish to one of the other young men, who found the camera buried where I had pointed. "Thirty-five millimeter ... takes great pictures!" I offered helpfully.

I spoke to the English-speaking man again. "Your friends are making such a mess, you're going to miss things. I'd be happy to show you where all the good stuff is."

He looked at me strangely again. My responses were clearly not matching his script for bandits and victims. As I pointed out other items and their hiding places, his suspicion gave way. I offered to get things for him and his friends.

The next thing we knew, it was show and tell. "Nice guitar!" I demonstrated a few chords. "Who plays? Here, do you want it? ... Sony Walkman, headsets, batteries, some tapes! Who wants it?" I thought about the Native American giveaway. I realized that given our respective access to money, it seemed right somehow that they should receive our goods, a kind of balancing of wealth. I began to enjoy the feeling of gifting them. I tried to think which of our possessions they would most enjoy.

Although my out-of-role behavior was clearly having some impact on the scene, it was not yet a total transformation. The young man with the carving knife seemed particularly erratic, perhaps drug-intoxicated. Every few minutes he pushed me or yelled at me. His English vocabulary seemed to consist of: "Drugs! Booze! More money!" He found a bottle of Lomotil (for diarrhea) in a kitchen drawer. I tried to convince him that he didn't want the pills, though when he became violent about it, I must confess the thought, *It serves you right* crossed my mind.

My English-speaking "friend" increasingly began to play a calming role with the others.

Well, I'd given away everything I could think of. I looked toward the back of the van where Judith and Leila were huddled, wrapped in a blanket. Judith, of course, was having her own inner adventure, managing her fears of rape for herself and kidnapping of our child. Leila, who in her whole two years of life had never encountered someone who wasn't "good," kept interjecting things like, "Daddy, who dese nice men?"

I thought to myself, *What's next?* Then I found myself spontaneously asking, "Would you like something to eat?" The English-speaking young man translated. Four pairs of incredulous eyes looked at me as I proceeded to open the refrigerator. Now we had a cultural problem. As I surveyed the shelves of tofu, sprouts, yogurt and nut butters, I had that sinking feeling like when you're hosting a dinner party and someone shows up on a special diet. It was obvious that we had nothing recognizable as food. Then I saw a nice Red Delicious apple. *Okay, that's normal food.* I took out the apple and held it out toward the man with the machete. This felt like an important moment. In most cultures, the sharing of food is a kind of communion, an acknowledgment of friendship, or declaration of peace. As I continued to hold out the apple toward him, I sensed him struggling for a moment, in his own way letting go of the roles in which we had met. For an instant he smiled, then took hold of the apple. I flashed on the image of E.T. extending his light-tipped finger. As our hands met on the apple, I felt a subtle exchange of energy.

Well, we had given presents and shared food. Now the English-speaking man said we were going for a ride. Fear came back. I didn't know where they were taking us. If they were going to kill us, this was as good a place as any. They didn't seem competent enough to pull off a kidnapping and ransom. I suggested that they take the car and leave us here. We were in the middle of nowhere, but anything seemed better than going driving with them. We exchanged views on this several times, then all of a sudden they were back to threatening me with weapons. I got it. As soon as I switched back into fear mode, they became bandits again. "Okay Let's go!"

I climbed in the back next to Judith and Leila, and away we went. I had my pants on now, which further improved my state of mind. I flipped in and out of realities, at some moments, just driving through the desert. Then, seeing lights, I planned how I might open the door and push Judith and Leila out if we slowed down near people.

As we drove along, I asked myself, *What would I do if I were driving along with my honored guests?* Sing, of course!

Judith, Leila and I started singing:

Listen, listen, listen to my heart's song.
Listen, listen, listen to my heart's song.
I will never forget you, I will never forsake you.
I will never forget you, I will never forsake you.

Leila kept smiling her outrageously cute smile. She'd catch the eye of one or another of the young men. Several times I saw them trying to keep it straight. ("Come on kid, cut it out. I'm trying to be a bandit.") Then they'd smile despite themselves.

They seemed to like the singing. We did. Then I realized I was failing to be a good host. They didn't know any of the songs. I thought for a moment. Inspiration!

Guantanamera, guajira, guantanamera.
Guantanamera ....

That did it. They began singing along. The energy came together. No more bandits and victims. Feet were tapping and spirits lifted as we sailed through the desert night.

We passed through a village without a chance for my great rescue attempt. Then the lights faded away as we entered some remote, hilly country. We pulled down a dark, dirt road, and the RV came to a halt. Judith and I looked at each other as we both had the thought that they were going to kill us. We rested deeply in each others' eyes.

Then they opened the door and began to get out.

Evidently, they lived far from the scene of the robbery. They had driven themselves home!

Several of them said "Adios" as they exited. Finally, there was just my English-speaking friend. In halting English he struggled to communicate. "Please forgive us. My hombres and me, we are poor people. Our fathers are poor. This is what we do for making the money. I'm sorry. We didn't know it was you. You are such a good man. And your wife and child, so nice."

He apologized again and again. "You are good people. Please do not think bad of us. I hope this won't ruin your vacation."

Then he reached into his pocket and took out my wallet. "Here." He handed me back my MasterCard. "We can't really use this. Better you take it." He also gave me my driver's license. As one of his hombres stared in amazement, he peeled off a few Mexican bills. "Here, for the gasoline."

I was at least as amazed as his fellow bandits. He's giving my money back to me! He wants to make things right between us.

Then he took my hand. He looked into my eyes, and the veils were gone between us. Just for a moment, we rested in that place. Then he said, "Adios": "With God."

Our bandit guests disappeared into the night. Then my family held each other and cried.

Robert Gass

14
The Farm Culture

In the 1980s a large multinational pharmaceutical company was having difficulties between its British and American research and development groups. Instead of cooperating by sharing their research, the two groups had gotten increasingly competitive until they were actually withholding scientific data from one another. This meant the company was not getting the comprehensive research it needed to support the delivery of its new drug. If the company couldn't show government agencies that its drug merited approval, it would never go on the market and the company wouldn't make any money, so this was a serious issue.

I was hired as a mediator from the US, along with a British mediator named David Gaster. We met on the East Coast with the American and British R&D groups in order to facilitate a solution to the problem. As background, I knew that the British and American groups had been separate companies that had recently merged, so they weren't used to working with each other. What's more, after the merger the company headquarters had been moved from the US to the UK, and the British R&D group had received a lot of fancy new equipment. The Americans were jealous. As David and I found out more, it became clear that the top British guy and the top American guy had gotten into it with each other. They were competing instead of collaborating, and that competition was cascading down into their teams.

One of the main issues was that the American guy was under a lot of pressure from the American marketing department, which wanted information so it could create marketing materials in anticipation of the release of the new drug. The British guy wouldn't give the American the information needed to do that. Instead he would insult the American by saying, "Oh, for goodness sakes! Get a spine and just tell the marketing people to fuck off!"

As we asked more questions we learned that in British companies during that time, departments were very divided from each other. If you were in charge of a department, what you said went, and you didn't talk a lot to the departments around you. You ran your own show, and they ran theirs. There wasn't a lot of interdepartmental collaboration. Well, things didn't work that way in the US, and the British guy didn't understand the situation he put the American guy in when the American couldn't provide the information his marketing people needed.

Ultimately, what we had to do was figure out a way for these two guys to save face so they could move on from what had become a very personal battle of wills. This was especially true of the British guy, who was very military in his management style—very hierarchical, top down, command-and-control. We had to come up with a way he could do an "about-face" in the way he was engaging with the American guy, while still maintaining his undisputed leadership of his R&D group.

We pulled them aside to do this, and I don't know where this came from, but as we were sitting there talking I said, "You know, until about 50 or 75 years ago, well over 90 percent of the people in the United States lived on farms. In farming communities no family ever stood alone. If you were not there to help your neighbor bring in his crop before it rained, and the crop spoiled, that family starved. Because of this history, corporations in this country are run in an atmosphere in which cooperation is assumed and unspoken. It's just a legacy of US culture that you can't be a renegade or run your company with a castle mentality. That wouldn't work on a farm, therefore that's not how people here think. So in order to work within the culture in this country, one of the things companies have to do is collaborate and cooperate with each other."

I didn't know if what I said had had any impact. We went back into the main plenary session, which included each man's team, and I swear that within a minute and a half the British guy said to his team, "You know, you have to understand, that until 50 or 75 years ago, over 90 percent of people in the US lived in farms…" And he continued to repeat the very story I had just told.

It did nothing more than give him a face-saving way to remain in charge and still tell people what to do, but to do it in a way that led in a direction of cooperation rather than competition.

The intervention was a success and the R&D groups started to cooperate with each other. They even started several joint research projects, and the new drug hit the market on schedule.

Lara Ewing

15
The Living God Inside You[*]

Lu Yung-cheng and Gladys were standing in the courtyard when a messenger rushed in waving a piece of scarlet paper. He gabbled at such a rate that Gladys found it difficult to understand him.

"What's the paper for, anyway?" she asked Lu Yung-cheng.

"It's an official summons from the *yamen*," said Lu Yung-cheng nervously. "A riot has broken out in the men's prison."

Gladys was really not very interested. "Oh, has it?" she said.

"You must come at once," said the messenger urgently. "It is most important!"

Gladys stared at him. "But what's the riot in the prison got to do with us? It can't have anything to do with my foot inspection." [Gladys had been authorized by the provincial governor of Yangcheng in northern China to implement a new law forbidding the binding of the feet of young girls.

Gladys Aylward was an independent British missionary in Yangcheng, south of Peking, China, from 1930 to 1941.]

"You must come at once!" reiterated the messenger loudly. "It is an official order." He hopped from one foot to the other in impatience.

Lu Yung-cheng looked at her doubtfully. "When that piece of red paper arrives from the *yamen*, you must go." There was a nervous tremor in his voice.

"All right, you go and see what it's all about," said Gladys. "It's obviously a man's job. I know nothing about prisons. I've never been in one in my life. Though I really don't see what you're supposed to do."

She could see from Lu Yung-cheng's face that the prospect did not appeal to him.

"Hurry, please hurry!" cried the messenger.

Reluctantly, Lu Yung-cheng trailed after him to the door. Gladys watched him reach the opening, take a quick look behind at her, then dodge swiftly to the left as the messenger turned to the right. She could hear the sound of his feet running as he tore down the road.

Within two seconds the messenger discovered his loss. He stormed back through the doorway crying "Ai-ee-ee!" and shaking his fist in rage. He raced across the courtyard toward Gladys, a little fat man without dignity.

"Now you must come," he shouted. "This is an official paper. You are ordered to come. You must come. Now! With me! If you refuse you will get into trouble!"

"All right," she said mildly. "I'll come. I really don't know what's the matter with Lu Yung-cheng. He must feel ill or something. But I certainly don't see what a riot in the prison has to do with me."

They hurried up the road and in through the east gate. A few yards inside the gate the blank outside wall of the prison flanked the main street. From the other side came an unholy cacophony: screams, shouts, yells, the most horrible noises.

"My goodness!" said Gladys, "it certainly is a riot, isn't it?"

The governor of the prison, small, pale-faced, his mouth set into a worried line, met her at the entrance. Behind were grouped half a dozen of his staff.

"We are glad you have come," he said quickly. "There is a riot in the prison; the convicts are killing each other."

"So I can hear," she said. "But what am I here for? I'm only the missionary woman. Why don't you send the soldiers in to stop it?"

"The convicts are murderers, bandits, thieves," said the governor, his voice trembling. "The soldiers are frightened. There are not enough of them."

"I'm sorry to hear that," said Gladys. "But what do you expect me to do about it? I don't even know why you asked me to come."

The governor took a step forward. "You must go in and stop the fighting!"

"I must go in…!" Gladys's mouth dropped open; her eyes rounded in utter amazement. "Me! Me go in there! Are you mad! If I went in, they'd kill me!"

The governor's eyes were fixed on her with hypnotic intensity. "But how can they kill you? You tell everybody that you have come here because you have the living God inside you."

The words bubbled out of the governor's mouth, his lips twisted in the acuteness of distress. Gladys felt a small, cold shiver down her back. When she swallowed, her throat seemed to have a gritty texture.

"The—living God?" she stammered.

"You preach it everywhere—in the streets and villages. If you preach the truth, if your God protects you from harm, then you can stop this riot."

Gladys stared at him. Her mind raced round in bewilderment, searching for some fact that would explain her beliefs to this simple, deluded man. A little cell in her mind kept blinking on and off with an urgent semaphore message: "It's true! You have been preaching that your Christian God protects you from harm. Fail now, and you are finished in Yangcheng. Discard your faith now, and you discard it for ever!"

It was a desperate challenge. Somehow she had to maintain face. Oh, these stupidly simple people! But how could she go into the prison? Those men—murderers, thieves, bandits, rioting and killing each other inside those walls! By the sounds, louder now, a small human hell had broken loose. How could she...? "I must try," she said to herself. "I must try. O God, give me strength."

She looked up at the governor's pale face, knowing that now hers was the same color. "All right," she said. "Open the door. I'll go in to them." She did not trust her voice to say any more.

"The key!" snapped the governor. "The key, quickly." One of his orderlies came forward with a huge iron key. It looked designed to unlock the deepest, darkest dungeon in the world. In the keyhole it grated loudly; the immense iron-barred door swung open. Literally she was pushed inside. It was dark. The door closed behind her. She heard the great key turn.

She was locked in the prison with a horde of raving criminals who by their din sounded as if they had all gone completely insane. A dark tunnel, twenty yards long, stretched before her. At the far end it appeared to open out into a courtyard. She could see figures racing across the entrance. With faltering footsteps, she walked through it and came to an abrupt standstill, rooted in horror.

The courtyard was about sixty feet square with queer cage-like structures round all four sides. Within its confines a writhing, fiendish battle was going on. Several bodies were stretched out on the flagstones. One man, obviously dead, lay only a few feet away from her, blood still pouring from a great wound in his scalp. There was blood everywhere. Inside the cage-like structures small private battles were being fought.

The main group of men, however, were watching one convict who brandished a large, blood-stained chopper. As she stared, he suddenly rushed at them, and they scattered wildly to every part of the square. Gladys stood there, aghast at this macabre form of "tag." The man on the ground with the gash in his skull had obviously been well and truly "tagged."

No one took any notice whatsoever of Gladys. For fully half a minute she stood motionless with not one single cell of her mind operating to solve her dilemma. The man rushed again; the group parted; he singled one man out and chased him. The man ran toward Gladys, then ducked away. The madman with the ax halted only a few feet from her. Without any instinctive plan, hardly realizing what she was doing, she took two angry steps toward him.

"Give me that chopper," she said furiously. "Give it to me at once!" The man turned to look at her. For three long seconds the wild dark pupils staring from bloodshot eyes glared at her. He took two paces forward. Suddenly, meekly, he held out the ax.

Gladys snatched the weapon from his hand and held it rigidly down by her side. She was conscious that there was blood on the blade and that it would stain her trousers. The other convicts—there must have been fifty or sixty men cowering there—stared from every corner of the courtyard. All action was frozen in that one moment of intense drama. Gladys knew that she must clinch her psychological advantage.

"All of you!" she shouted. "Come over here. Come on, form into a line!" She knew vaguely that the voice belonged to her, but she had never heard it so shrill. She screamed at them, gabbled at them like an undersized infuriated sergeant-major, like a schoolmarm with a class of naughty children. "Get into line at once. You, over there! Come on, form up in front of me!"

Obediently the convicts shambled across, forming into a ragged group before her. She regarded them stormily. There was silence. Then suddenly her fear had gone. In its place was an immense, soul-searing pity that pricked the tears into her eyes. They were so wretched. They were so hopeless. A mass of thin faces: angular cheekbones, puckered lips; faces contorted with misery, pain, and hunger; eyes, dark with fear and despair, that looked into hers.

They were remnants of humanity, half-men dressed in rags, caked in dust, running with lice; animals more than men, and the cages in which they were penned around the arena were those of brutes. She could have wept openly that human creatures could be so wretched. With an effort she tightened her lips and took command again. The fear had gone, yes; but she knew she must still cow them with her authority.

"You should be ashamed of yourselves," she said, berating them like an irate mother scolding a crowd of naughty children. "All this noise and all this mess!" Mess! She waved her arms to indicate the bodies and blood the battle had left behind. "The governor sent me in here to find out what it was all about. Now, if you clean up this courtyard and promise to behave in the future, I'll ask him to deal leniently with you this time."

She tried to keep her eyes away from the still figures of the dead. She knew she must focus their attention until all the desperate violence had seeped away. "Now, what is your grievance?" she snapped. "Why did you start fighting like this?"

There was no answer. Several hung their heads in shame. "I want you to appoint a spokesman, then," she went on. "He can tell me what the trouble is. And then you can start cleaning up this courtyard at once. Now go over in that corner and appoint your spokesman. I'll wait here."

The convicts trooped over into the corner she indicated and talked among themselves. A few moments later, one of the taller men of slightly better physique approached. Like the others, he was dressed in rags.

"My name is Feng," he said. "I am their spokesman."

While they swabbed up the blood with rags, and moved the dead bodies into less spectacular positions, Gladys listened to his story. Later she learned that he had once been a Buddhist priest; he had been convicted of theft from the other priests of the temple and sentenced to eight years in jail. He explained that no one really knew why, or how, the riot had started. They were allowed the chopper—he indicated the ax which Gladys still carried—for an hour every day to cut up their food. Someone had quarreled over its possession, someone else had joined in, and suddenly, without anyone knowing exactly why, the volcano of passion had erupted and a lava of blood flowed everywhere.

He could not explain this strange occurrence. Perhaps it was that many of the men had been there for many years, he said. As she knew, unless their friends or relatives sent in food, they starved. It was hard to sit up against a wall and starve to death while other men ate. Sometimes they took one of their number out into the square and executed him. That terror hung over many heads. He could not explain the outbreak, but the walls were high and the doors were strong; they never saw the outside world, women or the mountains, a tree in blossom or a friendly face; sometimes the spirit grew so oppressed that it burst out of a man in a wild tumult of violence. That, he thought, is what had occurred. They were all very sorry.

"What do you do all day in here?" asked Gladys seriously.

"Do? There is nothing to do."

"No occupation of any sort?"

"None!"

"But a man must have work, something to do. I shall see the governor about it."

It was at that moment she became conscious that the governor and his retinue were behind her. She did not find out until later that there was a small opening toward the end of the tunnel through which they had heard everything. The noise of the riot had died, and they had now thought it safe to enter and take an official part in the peace treaty.

The governor bowed to Gladys.

"You have done well," he said gratefully. "We must thank you."

"It's disgraceful," she said bitterly. "These men are locked up here week after' week, year after year, with nothing to do. Nothing to do at all!"

"I do not understand." His bewilderment was rather ludicrous.

Gladys could, however, sense his gratitude and decided to press her point. "Of course you have riots if they've nothing to occupy their time year after year. You must find them occupations."

The governor was still completely puzzled. "Occupations?" he repeated.

"They must have work to do. We must get looms so they can weave cloth; we must find them all sorts of jobs so that they can earn a little money and buy food and get back a little self-respect."

The governor nodded. Whether he agreed or not she could not tell. "We will discuss it later," he said amiably.

"I have promised them there will be no reprisals," she said.

The governor nodded again. A few corpses were rarely the subject of an official inquiry or even an embarrassment to the Chinese penal system. "As long as there is no recurrence," he said, "we shall forget all about it."

"That is good," said Gladys. She turned to Feng. "I'm going now, but I shall come back. I promise I will do all I can to help you."

She saw upon her the dark eyes of the priest who was a thief. "Thank you," he said. "Thank you, Ai-weh-deh."

She did not know at the time what the word "Ai-weh-deh" meant. That evening she asked Lu Yung-cheng when he returned from the long walk he had so suddenly decided to take.

"Ai-weh-deh?" he said curiously. "It means the virtuous one."

She was known as Ai-weh-deh for all her remaining years in China.

Gladys Aylward

16

The Imam and the Pastor

Nigeria's Muslims and Christians lived in peace until the last quarter of the 20th century, when economic decline, religious extremism, and political turmoil combined to strain communal relations to the breaking point. In recent decades, the country has been repeatedly rocked by violence between Christians and Muslims. Tens of thousands of people have been killed in the clashes, and whole communities devastated.

It was against this background in the late 1980s that Pastor James Wuye, a Pentecostal minister and a passionate evangelist, decided to join a Christian militia group.

James Wuye:
I became a part of this militia group because I wanted to protect our people. Christians were being killed, pastors were being killed, and I needed to do something about it. If the Muslims had their lives, then we could go take them. Even just one Muslim life—I wanted to put it on the line. My hate for the Muslims had no limits. That was how I became militia.

In 1992, the Zangon Kataf religious crisis began over the relocation of a market place. For a long time the economy of the place had been dominated by Muslims. In the conflict that ensued, most of the people killed were Muslims. The corpses of those people were transported to Kaduna state, to a place called Tudun Wada. The Muslims of Tudun Wada, seeing the corpses of their kin, decided to pounce on the Christians who were there in the city.

As a person trained to protect the Church, my militia group swung into action. Some of the boys who were with me were killed in that battle, and I lost my right hand in trying to defend the Church.

Muhammad Ashafa:
I came from a very strong religious family, a family of custodians of the Islamic heritage. My father was a spiritual leader, and I found myself growing up and learning about the Quran and teaching it to younger ones than myself. I wasn't able to go to western education because my family had a serious struggle with western colonial authority. My family were learned people; they knew how to read and write in Arabic and how to communicate in the Arabic language. But when the colonialists came with their own system they changed the language of communication to English, and that led families like my own into serious withdrawal from anything to do with the west. We had a reformatory zeal of protecting and reviving the glory of Islam. Such was the family I came from.

I was a member of the Muslim militia in Tudun Wada, and took part in the 48 hours of fighting there. I was full of passion, maiming and killing others, believing I had to defend my faith. But at the end of the day, my spiritual teacher, about 75 years old, had been murdered by the Christian community, and two of my cousins had also been killed.

I learned that it was James' militia group that organized themselves against my group. I was full of anger and wanted to take revenge, so for three years my group was planning to eliminate the leaders of James' group.

James:

In May 1995 I met Ashafa unexpectedly at a gathering of community leaders convened at the residence of the Governor of Kaduna state. A mutual acquaintance introduced us to one another and challenged us to make peace.

Our meeting was full of suspicion. Ashafa's posture and the way he dressed was the embodiment of an Islamic fundamentalist. We Christians saw such a man as an obvious fanatic who believed in Islam only, to the exclusion of all other religions. My fear was that because of my training, Ashafa might be planning to identify me and my friends for possible attack whenever a convenient occasion presented itself.

Ashafa:

Before I met James in person, I had spent three years seeking revenge against him. Then one day I found myself in the Mosque, and the Imam was talking about the power of forgiveness. He said, "Yes, it is written in the law that you can seek revenge equal to the evil done to you. You have a right to take redress. However, the Quran teaches further: It is better to turn away evil with that which is good."

Suddenly I had to wonder, *if I am a Muslim today, and I refuse to forgive those who persecute and hurt me, how can I be a true embodiment of Muhammad?*

The Imam continued, reminding us of how Muhammad was persecuted and humiliated and turned out of Mecca. Muhammad went to the city of Taif, a city very close by, and there he preached. But people gathered to stone him, people sent by those who didn't want Muhammad's message to be heard. The stones flew and blood poured down Muhammad's body. Then the angel that moves mountains came to Muhammad and said, "Oh you prophet of Allah, do I destroy these people? What do you want me to do? Give me a verdict. I will do whatever you want me to do with them. You, Muhammad, are Allah's messenger." Muhammad opened his mouth and said, "No, I don't want them destroyed. Oh, Allah, forgive my own people."

When I heard the Imam recounting this I wept into tears. I was crying, tears flowing down my face. *How can I forgive this enemy of mine? This man James, who maimed and killed my spiritual teacher and two of my brothers?* Then the Imam looked in my direction and it was as if he knew exactly what I was thinking. He said, "Muhammad has forgiven you. You have to forgive." I was in an ocean of confusion, or an ocean of war—between my conscience and desire for revenge, and the reality of this new standard. And in that moment the Imam finished and said, "Let's pray."

We prayed, and after that I started thinking, and I really forgave James and decided I needed to meet with him.

James:

After my first tense meeting with Ashafa, my mother took ill. To my surprise, Ashafa came with a group of young Muslim men to see her and visit her in the hospital. That was when I started changing. I said, "Wow, how is it that this Muslim comes to greet me as a Christian? Eventually my mother passed on, and again Ashafa came with a group to pay her their respect. That was what broke my resistance to interacting with Ashafa.

I decided to visit his Mosque. Well this was like, "I will swallow my heart," because I wasn't sure I would come out of the place alive. But I did come out alive, and I kept visiting, and eventually I developed confidence. My relationship with Ashafa began to grow, and we started to discuss what we could do to stop all the horrible violence from continuing.

Our reconciliation caused controversy. Religious groups in the area asked us to explain our change of heart. But our relationship was still fragile. When we shared rooms, sometimes I was tempted to take my pillow and suffocate him while he was sleeping to retaliate for the loss of my hand. But then this force would pull me, "Thou shalt not kill." For three years this feeling would arise, telling me to kill him. What finally removed that from me was when the pastor of the Family Worship Center in Abuja said, "You cannot preach Christ with hate. Christ is love and the message he is carrying is love."

The pastor said to me, "James, I know you, and I know what you are doing with Ashafa. If you will truly do this work, you must learn to forgive them for every hurt against you or against anyone you have ever loved." That broke me finally. After that I was eager to meet Ashafa, like a lover looking for his loved one. I wanted to demonstrate this new insight. This was my real turning point—the moment when I really got into the work of reconciliation.

*   *   *

Imam Ashafa and Pastor James began working together in earnest in Kaduna, long known as being one of the flashpoints for conflict. In Kaduna the relationship between the Christian and Muslim communities, roughly equal in size, continued to be tense. In the midst of this situation, Pastor and Imam set up the "Christian-Muslim Interfaith Mediation Centre" to advocate for peaceful coexistence and re-integration in divided communities. Responsibilities at the interfaith centre are shouldered equally by Muslims and Christians, who travel throughout the region teaching peace-building workshops, promoting good governance, and fostering community empowerment through various projects directed toward the needs of those affected by conflicts. The centre also deprograms militia groups, transforming them into interfaith ambassadors of peace by teaching the need for harmonious coexistence. Educating the general public on the need to sustain the environment is another important mission of the centre, as pollution of natural resources and the over-cutting of trees for cooking fuel are significant problems that give rise to conflict.

In 2001 James and Ashafa brought together prominent religious leaders in Kaduna to work on a joint peace agreement. After months of discussion, the governor of Kaduna signed a historic peace declaration along with eleven Muslim leaders and eleven Christian leaders, and the president of Nigeria unveiled a plaque of the agreement. The 22 people who signed the declaration went to monitor elections, and there was no rigging or violence at any of the places that were monitored. Now when there is a problem in Kaduna, the Christian ecumenical center leadership is able to communicate with the Muslim ecumenical center. They can talk and sort out the truth amongst themselves.

Many conflicts that would have led to bloodshed have been resolved by the communication between these two centers.

Over the years, as the work of the interfaith mediation centre continued to expand, teams of pastors and Imams began journeying to trouble spots to lead workshops and seminars. The rapport between Pastor James and Imam Ashafa became the foundation of their trust-building work with religious and community leaders. But traveling long distances together as an interfaith team presented its own challenges.

Ashafa:

As a team on the road the Christian members will wait in the bus and car while the Muslims go to say their prayers. And on Sunday, the Muslims will wait while the Christians go to prayer. You see, there is mutual respect for one another, absolute trust, absolute unselfishness in action.

At the Mosque of Samaru Kataf was where we first began our work as mediators between Muslim and Christian communities. During the Samaru Kataf crisis, the Mosque was almost demolished from an attack by the Christian community. We brought the youth here, both the Christian and the Muslim youth, and we talked about reconciliation. We facilitated negotiation between various stakeholders—both the government and other civil-society organizations—and our initiatives were able to broker peace within the community.

James:

We disagree on certain things. And that disagreement can put us apart for two or three days during which we won't talk to one another. Once we were asked to write papers on the death penalty, for example. I say, "Jesus came to forgive, so the death penalty should be eradicated." Ashafa felt the death penalty should remain in Nigeria. We came from the same organization, but we had different opinions.

One time we had one of these disagreements that kept us from talking to each other. If Ashafa had a message for me he would write it on a piece of paper and stick it under the door to my office. And if I had one for him, I would drop it in his office. Then we would take the same taxi to go to meetings and appointments together, and at the meetings we would laugh together with everybody, but when we came back we still refused to talk to each other and there were no "Good nights."

We are like a husband and a wife that must not divorce. If we divorce, our children will suffer. And because of our children—the Nigerian youth, the Christians and Muslims, the global community—we cannot separate. Ashafa and I have developed a system of helping ourselves. When I am hurt, and he is hurting me, I will say, "Ashafa, I need your help." Then he will quickly know he has hurt me. And he will say the same to me if I am hurting him. When one of us asks for help from the other in this way, we go and talk with one another, and we call this "Let's go for some clinic" (a heart to heart talk, so as to foster dialogue). This is how we have been able to resolve our differences over the last 15 years. We are stuck together in this; no separation whatsoever is possible.

*   *   *

In 2004, clashes between Christians and Muslims from different ethnic groups erupted in the town of Yelwan Shendam. The spate of killings was furious and terrible. Hundreds of corpses had to be buried without proper ceremony in mass graves. James and Ashafa decided to focus their energy on a bid to bring healing to Yelwan Shendam. They made 17 separate visits to the area, sharing their own experience, mediating, and preaching peace. Little by little, apologies were shared and trust was rebuilt.

Ashafa and James worked for five months with Muslim and Christian leaders to hammer out a peace affirmation. During this process the idea formed to put on a festival where former enemies could come together in a celebration of peace, culminating in the reading of the peace affirmation. At the festival the various communities arrived to celebrate with their respective dance troupes. The crowds were exuberant, but the situation was still volatile, so the security forces remained vigilant.

One citizen at the festival said, "I witness this day as the happiest day of my life, because it's come to an end of the bloodshed in the town." Another said, "I lost my father, my brother, and my sister. I am staying with my relatives. I really appreciate the way that I saw people all gathering here. Both Muslim and Christian, to share ideas together, and even dance together. We are all one."

Political and religious leaders joined the crowds, including the governor of Plateau State, and letters of apology were read for everyone to hear. Then representatives of the different communities addressed the gathered people:

"I want to make it very clear that as far as I am concerned, the issue of religion was far, far secondary to what happened here. We have come back here to embrace ourselves in that old spirit, and to live here together once more as brothers and sisters."

"It is time for Muslims and Christians to go back to the original teachings of their religions. Because we, the preachers—we misled you. I'm sorry. In most cases, we preach violence instead of preaching peace. That's the problem. We must go back to the real teachings of our religions."

"We are confident that with all that has been put in, today will mark the beginning of a lasting and sustainable peace among the Christians and the Muslims, and the peoples of different ethnic groups within this area."

A plaque was unveiled in the town, representing a commitment to peace and an enduring settlement. Then Ashafa and James gave the crowds two minutes of silence to pray to their almighty, in the best way they could pray to Him, in their own mother language. After this everyone came back to each other to celebrate peace and the end of violence.

James:

A lot of the people in Yelwan Shendam lost loved ones in the violence, so it can be a difficult task to show them that the life ahead is much more than what happened in the past. But Ashafa and I can show ourselves as examples. We used to be in militias. We lost loved ones. I lost my hand. So it is very clear to these people that we can empathize with their situation. Ashafa and I tell them that we have learned a bitter lesson. We say it is better to *dialogue* with people than to *deal* with people. When you *deal* with people, you live in fear and unforgiveness, and every day you are not sure what will happen the next day. But when you *dialogue*, when you talk and when you forgive, you have peace. We feel that in forgiveness there is strength. You are stronger when you forgive someone who has been against you or hurt you.

We are grateful to God that we have learned the ability to hear one another and create a safe space to dialogue. Without this we would be assuming things from afar and you can kill somebody based on assumption.

Ashafa:
I want all communities of the Islamic faith to be safe havens for other people from around the world who come from other faiths and traditions.

James:
Preaching Christ does not really mean verbalizing it. You have to live it. By living a Christian life, I can influence people positively without saying it out loud. I practice my faith vehemently. And Ashafa does too, and we are still coexisting and living together. Yes Christianity and Islam can coexist side by side, and the believers of each will still go to the heaven they dream of according to their scriptures' text. This is true.

Ashafa:
Even though we differ in some theological issues, we will make the world a safer place. Having thousands of people behind me—I lead a congregation in the thousands in prayers—I never compromise the principles of Islam. Islam says, "Create a space for others." We are a living example of this. Even though James is not a Muslim I like him; I would give my life to protect his honor and dignity. This is what Islam taught me to do, and I will live for these principles and I will die for these principles."

James:
I love Ashafa. I am told to love my neighbor as myself according to the bible, and I live by that principle now.

*   *   *

Pastor James Wuye and Imam Muhammad Ashafa have traveled to other countries to spread their work, and they have spoken at international gatherings on conflict resolution and development. Their story of forgiveness and the strength of their partnership has stirred debate and fostered hope, but creating peace between Christians and Muslims remains an ongoing challenge. For James and Ashafa and many others in Nigeria and around the world, the work continues.

Imam Ashafa and Pastor James

Adapted from "The Imam and the Pastor" (2006), A documentary by FLTfilms, London, UK. Director - Alan Channer; Co-Producer - Imad Karam; Executive Producer – David Channer. With additions from Pastor Dr. James Movel Wuye & Imam Dr. Muhammad Nurayn Ashafa.

17

Flex Cop

My buddy and I were on night shift when the police dispatcher asked us to respond to a domestic call. We came in and here was this guy who had just torn up the apartment. He was standing there in a fighting stance as we came in. Of course it's absurd that an unarmed guy would really want to take on two armed cops with sticks and mace and guns, but it looked like he might do it anyway. I looked at my partner and he nodded, so we immediately started rearranging the furniture and stretching our muscles like we were preparing for an athletic contest. The man just looked at us and said, "What the fuck are you doing?!"

"Hey, look," I answered, "You just tore this apartment up. You've been fighting for the last ten minutes while we've been sitting in our car."

"We're not loosened up," my partner added. "Give us a few minutes to get ready like you are so this can be fair."

The man looked at us like we were insane, but really our actions only brought to light the ridiculousness of the original situation. His rage was gone; there was no way he was going to try fighting us anymore.

This is the kind of incredible magic that I eventually came to experience fairly often during my time as a policeman. But first, I should tell you how it all began, and the low to which I sank before finding a better way.

In 1973 I got a job as a policeman. My dad was also a cop. He grew up in an orphanage, and in order to get out of the orphanage early he lied and joined the marines, where he got his high school GED. Then he left to join the Cincinnati police department where he had a great police career.

I looked up to my dad a lot. While I was in high school I remember thinking, *Wow, here's a guy who grew up in an orphanage and had no family to model after. He had to lie to join the marines and then became a cop, but not any old cop, he was a* homicide *cop. Yet even with all that he never brought his job home with him.* As a senior in high school I remember giving an impromptu speech where I said if I could be one-tenth the person my dad was, I thought that would be awesome.

My police training was a three-year program with the university of Cincinnati for an associate degree. Most police academies are six months, so this was a much more rigorous training. In 1976 Cincinnati had a big budget crunch, so they laid off about 150 police officers, and I was one of them. I couldn't even find other police jobs because they were worried that I'd go back to Cincinnati when they were ready to re-hire. In '79, two Cincinnati police officers were murdered on duty, so the city manager recalled all 150 of us to strengthen the force. I actually replaced one of the murdered officers. I went into work my first day and opened the time book, and scrawled next to this police officer's name was, "killed in the line of duty, march 6, 1979." Right under his name, my name was inserted. That was how my police-patrolling career began. A couple months later another police officer was murdered in the line of duty. We had three murders in two months, which was very unusual for a city our size. It wasn't a good way to start.

The traditional police training of the time was all fear-driven. The idea was to make criminals more afraid of us than we were of them. The focus was always on tactical use of weaponry. The traditional thinking was, *if we get a bigger gun, a bigger stick, maybe we can save more people.* I was caught up in that fear thinking because that was all that was taught.

About a year and a half later I was transferred to another part of town. We were working patrol one night and an undercover cop had arrested a 23-year-old kid for stealing a truck. The uniformed police have to do the transport, so we picked him up and brought him to the police station. While we were doing the paperwork to transport the car thief to jail, someone yells. "Get the key, he's hung himself!"

The stations at those times had little holding cells with bars in them. It was common procedure to take the person's belt, socks, and shoelaces, but this young man had on a windbreaker jacket. The arresting officers hadn't taken his jacket from him because he didn't have a shirt on underneath and they just didn't think of it. He had tied the windbreaker up into the ceiling bars and hung himself.

I ran and got the key and rushed in there, lifting him up to take the pressure off his neck. Then my partner cut his jacket and I cradled his head as we laid him on the floor to start CPR. When we took him down he was lifeless, and even though I had been taught CPR, I'd never had to do it before. I started doing the 15 chest compressions and he was doing the two breaths and finally I said, "I feel a heartbeat, I feel a heartbeat."

A third officer standing around said, "No, that's only your own palm beat." I was sweating. The incredible physical exertion it took to continue CPR was just unbelievable.

"You're not going to save him," I heard, but after a couple attempts the young man started breathing on his own and the paramedics arrived. The Lieutenant was saying, "Man, he owes you one. You guys saved his life!"

I'm not religious but I am a spiritual person. I remember going into the bathroom to wash my hands and I looked upward and I said, "Thanks, whoever you are up there, *thanks*." What an incredible feeling it was to bring a heart back under my own hands. I felt so high to know that I'd brought somebody back to life. It didn't matter that he was a so-called criminal. He was a human being.

I got out of the bathroom and I saw the paramedics still had him on a stretcher. I thought, *What's going on, why haven't they left yet?* Then he vomited brown bile and it didn't look good. Finally they transferred him to the university hospital.

About three hours later we got a call from the hospital letting us know he'd died anyway. The doctor had made a comment that maybe we'd let his neck break when we cut him down, implying that we just sawed the jacket and let him drop, when I had been carefully cradling his head the whole time. That accusation hurt. We had been so careful and we worked so hard to save him and now they were saying we might have caused his death.

The hanging happened at one in the morning. At five in the morning we got a call about unknown trouble. We showed up at the place and couldn't get in, so because of the nature of the call we forced our way in. (As a cop you have a right to break in under emergency circumstances if you think something dangerous could be going on). An intoxicated man was lying passed-out on the couch with a loaded shotgun. He turned out to be a friend of the man who'd hung himself. We learned later that he was planning on shooting a cop for killing his buddy. Fortunately he'd passed out or that cop might have been me.

Four months later I got a subpoena to the anti-police civilian review board. I was the target subject witness of the hanging death of Gary Downing for using improper procedure. I was so crushed. I had only been trying to save this guy's life. What's more, the civilian review board was headed by a convicted bank-robber who did 25 years in an Ohio prison. Now, I believe that when people pay their dues, they pay their dues, but you don't hire a pedophile as a teacher, you don't get a bank-robber working a bank, and you don't have a 25-year guy investigate cops.

To make a long story short, the man heading the civilian review board ended up being very sympathetic once he heard the whole story. Finally he said, "Wow, you deserved commendation for what you tried." Well at that point simply understanding the truth wasn't going to make up for being hounded and accused for four months. In fact it almost made me more upset. They had just ruined four months of my life only to say, "Oh, you did the right thing; you deserved commendation."

I was still hurt and angry. We had tried to save this kid's life, and instead the doctor suggested we killed him, his friend tried to kill one of us, and the civilian review board had been at our throats for four months. We even met with the young man's mother at the Catholic Church to tell her we tried our best to save her son, but nothing changed. Just because the review board finally saw the truth didn't take away the feeling that everyone was out to get us for doing the right thing.

My wife says I had turned into a zombie during those four months. I still went to work each day, but I didn't want to go out with people any more, or attend family events. By July 1983 I had been in the police over four years since my second hiring, and I was still stuck in this negative loop. I was starting to think there were only two kinds of people in this world: cops and bad guys. I was loosing my sense of right and wrong, and I was losing hope. A job I started out feeling very, very proud of, I was now dreading to go to every day. I knew I was stuck, but I didn't know how to change. It seemed that most of the other people I spoke to on the job were stuck too.

The traditional police training got a person comfortable around negativity. The unspoken rationale was that you wanted people to talk bad to you at a traffic stop because then you didn't feel guilty giving them a ticket. A common joke was we wanted the guy to wave at us with one finger as we pulled him over. I sought out negativity and was "rewarded" by looking for the wrong in people. I found myself feeling comfortable when things were negative because it was my justification for being miserable.

Then I went to a convention in San Francisco, and had the tremendous fortune to attend Donald E. Dossey's seminar *Keying in Success*. In the seminar he gave me an introduction to a form of communication and personal growth called Neuro-Linguistic Programming (NLP). As a result I went back to my police job with a new flexibility that would change my life.

What I wanted on the job was the chameleon-like ability to adapt to what needed to be done without losing myself in the process. The traditional police teaching was very simplistic and reactionary, based on what the marines had developed in World War II by associating a color with a state of readiness. There were three states: yellow meant cautious, orange meant alert, and red meant alarmed. I realized I wanted a color chart that was *gold*, orange and red. I wanted to play off the golden rule rather than yellow which is associated with cowardice. I even developed a half-moon chart, making the first color gold instead of yellow. Starting with gold I would be the nicest guy in the world while still being realistic that there are some violent people out there. I wanted to deal with everyone in the most peaceful way possible. I wanted this for my *own* protection, both physically and also emotionally, so that doing police work would no longer change *me*. Any benefits the other person gained would be an extra bonus.

My new chart was like a thermostat rather than the thermometer of the marines. I wanted to use my language and demeanor to *guide* my interactions with people, rather than resort to the traditional *reactionary* escalation of force that would negatively affect me as well as the other person. If I could achieve this, then at the end of the day it would be easy to come home and toss ball with my kids, take my wife out to dinner, and not get into my previous belief that the world was going to hell.

I continued to study with Dr. Dossey and I bought every book I could find on NLP. Finally I told my wife, "When I go in to work, I'm going to go as a researcher."

"What do you mean?" She asked.

"Well, I'm going to try this stuff out."

I even had a meeting with the police chief and he was convinced before I'd even tried anything out. "Wow," he said, "We need to have you go to the police academy to teach this."

"No," I said. "I need to prove this works on the street. I don't have the credibility to claim to teach this without applying it first."

So I went into the inner city area of town on permanent night shift, and I put a little recorder on myself, because I wanted to see if my new skills would really work. I was very blessed to have a guy named Mike Broering as my partner. I called him Barney, because he looked like Barney from the Flintstones. I said, "Barn, I need your help. I'm not going to be one-tenth the person my dad was if I continue this negativity. I want to try some things out with you, will you trust me to go along with it?" He was terrific. He knew nothing of this communication stuff I'd learned, but nonetheless he was up for trying it out.

The typical approach to traffic stops during night shift was to use floodlights—which are actually aircraft landing lights—to light up the car. It's good for safety, but it's intimidating to the person being stopped. We were also never taught to greet people, just a cold, "license and registration." Well that wasn't a conversation; it was a confrontation, especially after barraging a driver with intense floodlights.

My goals with every encounter were to get into communication rather than confrontation. I thought, *We truly are only enforcing traffic laws because we want to save people's lives, so why can't that come across?* I went into every situation with a gold state of readiness, not a yellow, orange, or red one.

During our night shift we'd still put the floodlights on for safety; then one of us would approach the driver. I began by saying, "Good evening sir, I appreciate you pulling over so quickly." It might have taken him three miles to pull over, but I wanted to embed the idea that he was appreciated. Most people don't attack those who appreciate them.

That was how we started out.

The idea was to thank people up front for being courteous, and bring that side of them out. I remember going back to the car and saying, "Barn, this is unbelievable. I'm not feeling the old distrust and I'm not walking up tense anymore." Even if someone *was* up to no good I felt better able to deal with them. I didn't shut down into tunnel vision the way I often had before, when expecting the worst.

Next I thought, *I'm going to add the idea that it's a safe spot.* At the next traffic stop whoever's turn it was would say, "Good evening ma'am, I appreciate you pulling over in a safe spot." Now if they're up to no good, we've just suggested that this is a safe spot, so maybe it's not worth trying anything.

Then it evolved and we always used the word "we" instead of "I" to imply that there were at least two of us there. I did this even when I was by myself, because at night with the floodlights on no one could see into the cop car.

Sometimes we would ease the tension by saying. "I'm not going to use that line everybody else does of 'I'm just doing my job.' " The admission lowered our defensiveness and invited the driver to do so as well. Yet at the same time the message remained that in fact we *were* doing our job. We didn't say it, but we still said it.

Communication rather than confrontation created an amazing shift. We stopped more people but issued fewer tickets, since most people were polite and the stop was all they needed to remind them to be safe. When we did give a citation at least six out of ten times the first words out of the driver's mouth as they signed the ticket was, "I know you guys are just doing your job, and I appreciate that." They were feeding back what we had said to them. Over and over again I was hearing words come out of the violator's mouth that I had *never* heard at traffic stops before. People said they appreciated us, they shook our hands, and they told us to "be careful."

We were two white cops in the inner city of a predominantly black neighborhood, and it always upsets me when people think conflict will naturally arise in such situations. Because of our new ways of communicating we were showing people that there were a lot more similarities between us than differences. I was so grateful for what I had learned, and what I was still learning. Finally I was becoming the peace officer I knew my dad would be proud of. And this was just the beginning...

(To be continued in the next story, *The Dork Police, Further Adventures of Flex Cop.*)

Michael Gardner

18

The Dork Police
Further Adventures of Flex Cop
(A continuation of the previous story)

Everyone in the field knows that the most dangerous part of police work is handling domestic disputes. Roughly one third of the police officer assaults and killings in this country occur during domestic disputes. A cop may go in to arrest the attacker and suddenly the spouse turns on him with the frying pan when she sees he's making an arrest. There's no telling who may be a problem, and people are much more likely to fight to defend their homes against intruders.

A lot of the calls we got on night shift were domestic violence runs. Cops hate making domestic runs because they're so dangerous, but for research purposes my partner and I asked other cops, "Do you mind if we start taking over your domestic runs so we can experiment with defusing hostile situations?" Of course we got no objections.

Traditionally, police officers are limited to only four choices for controlling situations—visual and verbal persuasion, chemical irritant, impact weapon, and deadly force. In training, most emphasis was on weaponry defense, without nearly enough on visual and verbal defense. My partner and I saw the need to stretch our flexibility to hundreds of choices in this uncharted territory.

The traditional approach in police work for a domestic run was to show up at an apartment and bang on the door using a raid-type knock with the police night stick, BAM BAM BAM BAM! I even hate it when the UPS or mail carrier bangs on my door to give me something I *want*, so I tried to imagine how someone already in emotional distress would be angered even more with a raid-type bang on their door. To be less intrusive and confrontational we started showing up and doing the "shave and haircut" knock, a very light "Rap ta-ta tap tap, tap tap." Even if the people inside didn't catch on to the jingle, it was a less invasive knock, and its association with a harmless advertisement was more to relax *us* than the people inside. It kept us at a condition orange—alert, but not the red of alarmed. We would even joke sometimes going into an apartment, "Hey let's be condition purple." What we were really saying was, "Hey let's not get red, because if we go in there red, we're going to have a fight."

The usual question police were trained to ask when entering a home was, "What's the problem here?" Well, if you enter after a loud raid-type knock and ask them, "What's the problem here?" They'll give you a problem, usually several. They may tell you their problems from twenty years ago.

Instead we'd ask something like, "What have you decided to do between the time you called us and the time we got here?" That put them in solution mode. Other times we'd ask people to step out into the hallway so they wouldn't feel the need to defend their turf. We also purposely wore our hats when we approached, so when we did enter their house or apartment we could take them off as a sign of respect.

My partner and I became known to our fellow officers as the Dork Police, because no one knew what crazy thing we were going to do next. They were equally amazed at our success in non-violent control of tense situations. We experimented daily with ways of startling subjects into confusion in order to interrupt their dangerous mental patterns and provide a space for something more positive.

For example, we would sometimes approach potentially dangerous domestic disputes with our jackets purposely buttoned improperly, or with our caps pulled down so our ears stuck out. Other times we'd say "no" while nodding our heads up and down. Unless the combatants were too intoxicated or high to observe this odd behavior, they stopped, at least temporarily. They couldn't help responding to what they saw. Then it was hard for them to pick up their fight where they had left off.

Sometimes we'd walk into a shouting match between a couple, and we'd just run over and switch the channel on the TV set. If one of them said, "Hey, what the hell are you doing?" We'd say cheerfully, "Hey, you're not going to listen to us anyway, so we're going to watch some TV."

All we were trying to do was get them to refocus out of their anger and onto something else. We would do anything to create a change. Once that was accomplished, we'd offer suggestions for where couples could go for longer-term help.

Using humor was particularly useful when performing routine, uncomfortable tasks like patting down or frisking a suspect. While maintaining physical control, we would like to say, "You don't have any hand grenades, swords, or bazookas hidden on you, do you?" Subjects generally laughed it off. Now and then, one would disclose that he had a knife or razor.

When couples were screaming at each other we'd start sniffing and shouting out. "Oh, do you smell gas? Where's your stove? There must be a burner on!" While the fight was temporarily stopped, my partner and I would go to the kitchen and pretend to check the stove for gas leaks. After a few minutes of sniffing the stove and kitchen area, we would advise the people that everything was OK, then ask "What else can we help you with?" The response was amazing. Often they said, "Nothing, officer..." If the argument did begin again, all my partner and I had to do was to sniff with a concerned look on our faces. With this pattern interruption, the subjects' personal fighting became secondary to the threat of a gas explosion in their home. They may even start getting an unconscious connection of, *Every time I start getting nasty there's danger, maybe I should try something else.*

Other times, we would enter a residence and be greeted by someone standing in a fighting position and shouting, "You two think you can take me? Come on!" We would mirror his stance, but hold our palms up instead of making fists, saying, "No way. We heard how tough you are. We can't beat you, we'd have to call ten more guys in here." If that statement had any effect, we would follow up with, "Why don't we talk first, then you can kick our butts." On several occasions the potentially violent subject changed his mind. And if he didn't respond to our initial statement, that signaled us to try something else. Initially it was hard for us to give this kind of "pull" statement when a violent subject "pushed" us verbally. We instinctively wanted to "push" back with an "attack" statement. Yet the patience of our "pull" statement always minimized the force of our arrest.

One time we had a husband and wife close to killing each other. They were shouting countless obscenities at each other, and their hand gestures were disjointed and out of sync with the tone and tempo of their verbal language. I remembered the metaphor of an orchestra conductor—when people talk in rhythm with their gestures it tends to be good venting; letting their anger come out verbally rather than physically. But when their gestures are short, choppy, stab-like motions, disconnected from their language, it is likely that they're about to explode physically. This couple was actually making verbal threats like, "I'm going to kill you, you son of a bitch!" "You're dead, mother-fucker!"

In a flash I said, "In all my years of police work, I've never seen somebody able to express their anger like you can! I appreciate that, because sometimes things really piss me off and I wish I could express my anger like you are!" I was empathizing with them to bring their attention to me and to the importance of what they were feeling, and away from a fight.

Another time we came into an argument with the woman yelling and screaming at her husband. I said to her, "I bet you don't talk to the mailman this way, do you?"

"What? Of course not!"

"And I bet you don't talk to your car mechanic that way, do you?"

"No, of course not!"

"Well the reason you talk to your husband like that is obviously because you care a whole lot more about what he says than what the mailman or the mechanic says."

"Yeah, well I guess so."

My questions first took her attention away from her emotions and what she was mad about. Then I offered her a new meaning for her outburst—it was because she *cared* about her husband. After about 15-20 minutes of me telling them how frustrated I was at not being able to express my feelings the way they could, they started counseling me. Soon it was apparent by the way they were sitting next to each other and looking at each other that they were eager to be left alone. I think we reframed their anger toward each other to such an extent that they wanted us gone so they could make up!

Once we came into a heated dispute and I said to the man, "Hey, you don't work for the city, do you?"

"NO!"

"That car out there with the lights on, that's not your car, is it?"

"NO!"

"You don't want us here, do you?"

"NO!"

"You'll be happy when we leave here, won't you?"

"Fuck yeah!"

This way I matched him and let him express himself. He was in the mood to disagree, so I started with questions all of which let him say "No." Then I shifted to a "Yes" question, leading him to a more positive place and getting his explicit agreement that when we left he'd be happy. It might sound like a small thing, but it made a huge difference. Now we were on the same page and he was more relaxed—no longer disagreeing with everything we said.

We'd also do a thing I called "word salad." I never did it in a disrespectful way, but when people get violent they're behaving worse than childish. Sometimes I'd say, "What you're saying here sounds like a phonological ambiguity to me, so rather than jeopardize any other litigation circumstances why don't you just take a walk and let things cool off?"

They got so confused by the first part of my sentence, they would jump on the first thing that made sense, usually responding. "I'll just take a walk and cool off a bit."

I'd say, "Great, I appreciate that."

Often we would use many of these different tactics one after the other, until we found what worked. By systematically attempting to stop violence by using our appearance or words, we put ourselves in a position where we would be much more justified—both emotionally and legally—if we ended up having to resort to a higher degree of force. Yet in all these experiments on permanent night shift, and during my thirty-year police career, I never fired my gun. I had to use mace on a person only once, simply because the man was so intoxicated I couldn't communicate with him. We had tried many things, but he just wasn't there because of the alcohol. He had a little paring knife that he wouldn't drop. Technically I could have shot him, but I had been relaxed and aware enough to keep a table between us, so I was able to subdue him with the mace. As amazing as these techniques were for defusing violence in the moment, our biggest success was that we stopped getting return calls from the places we visited. Before we started using these techniques, it was common to get calls from the same location two or three times a night. Sometimes my partner and I would spend 15 or 30 minutes out on a call, and we'd get in trouble from our supervisor because he wanted us in and out. If they didn't straighten up right away he wanted us to simply arrest them. But we knew we could save time in the long run by coming to a peaceful resolution.

Probably our most interesting encounter came in June of 1984. My partner and I were patrolling our beat on a Saturday afternoon, when the dispatcher's voice crackled over our radio:

"Car 405, Car 405, respond to 755 East McMillan Street, reference a man with a gun. The only description we have is he's male, black, and his last name is Large. He threatened to kill a person and stated he would kill the police. Car 405."

We replied, "Car 405, OK."

Our sergeant came on the air with, "Car 422, advise Car 405 to wait for my arrival before they approach the address. I'll respond with a taser gun."

Unfortunately for us, my partner and I happened to be on the one-way McMillan Street heading for that very address when the dispatch came out. Other police units were coming over the air advising that they would also respond. Since we were so close already, we parked near the location and advised our dispatcher that we were on the scene. Needless to say, our adrenaline was pumping. We often got calls where the details sounded frightening, but this one was different. We were afraid. As we approached an alley between two buildings, we observed a man in an army coat arguing with a woman. Without thinking, I blurted out, "Anyone here order a *large* pizza?"

The male subject turned and looked at me with a puzzled expression. Even my partner was looking at me funny. I could see the man's hands were empty. He said, "My name is Large…"

With that we knew who he was. We quickly handcuffed him and put him in the back seat of our car. Fortunately, he did not have a gun—something we did not know until after we had him under control. It turned out that he was a walk-away mental patient from the Veteran's Hospital Psychiatric Unit. He had been walking around threatening to kill people, hoping to force the police to kill him. Who knows what might have happened if Mr. Large hadn't been caught off guard. I sincerely believe that on this particular day the flexibility that I'd learned saved the life of a mentally disturbed veteran—and perhaps my life as well.

My partner, himself a Vietnam veteran, was able to chat with Mr. Large on the way to the Veteran's Hospital. Upon our arrival, the hospital staff was shocked that we didn't have to struggle with Mr. Large. I can't thank the people enough who taught me how to use these skills. Even though we may have been justified legally with some tactical force, we could never have lived with ourselves if we had hurt Mr. Large.

Unfortunately, it's very difficult to measure what *doesn't* happen, but I can say confidently that I was involved in hundreds of peaceful resolutions that would have ended up in arrests or fights had we used traditional police procedure. Ever since my eyes were opened to what is possible, I've been studying and researching how police officers everywhere can increase their choices by using visual and verbal persuasion to prevent, or at least minimize, their use of force in violent situations. Believe me, police officers all over this country need new tools for accomplishing their duties. They are hungry for positive education that will enhance their control over themselves and others. No group of professionals needs flexibility more than police officers.

Michael Gardner

19
Third Grade Bully

I was a third grade teacher in a small school in Oregon. One day the first grade teacher, Mrs. Nolan, came to me and told me that two of my third grade boys had bothered two of her first grade girls after school the previous day. The girls' parents were concerned and had contacted Mrs. Nolan, who talked to each of the girls individually the next morning. In her talk with them, the girls were both clearly still upset, and one of them had started crying as she retold what happened. The girls' stories matched pretty well: the boys had come up to them after school and Preston had thrown yogurt at their hair while Henry egged him on.

When Mrs. Nolan and I met with the third graders, they first tried to minimize what they had done, pretending like they hadn't really planned on throwing the yogurt, and that it had just happened as a joke. Henry even tried to say he had nothing to do with it, but finally the truth came out that actually he had been the instigator who'd convinced his friend Preston to throw the yogurt, and then encouraged him in the process. Henry had been particularly devious.

Next we called a meeting with all the children involved, and we asked the first graders to describe what happened so the third graders could hear their perspective. The girls had trouble verbalizing what they went through except that they were very upset. I asked them, "Were you angry? Or hurt? Or scared?" This helped draw out their feelings so the third graders could understand what it had been like for the girls.

I turned to the third graders, "Did you know this is how they felt?"

"We just thought it would be funny," one of them responded.

"Well from your perspective I can see how you might think that was funny," I replied. "But now imagine having yogurt in your hair, would you like that?"

Right away they both said, "Oh no, yuck!"

"What would it be like if the fifth graders were playing pranks on you and you felt very uncomfortable and afraid?" I asked.

They clearly didn't think that would be very much fun. I went on to remind them of the sheet of paper we have at the front of our classroom with all the rules we've created together, as a class. "One of the rules that you and the rest of your class created, is that the older students have a responsibility to set a good example for the younger ones."

Mrs. Nolan added, "This is a very serious situation because these girls are much younger than you, so they felt very much afraid."

The boys seemed to get it, so we asked them, "Now that you know what the first graders felt, what do you want to tell them?"

They both apologized in a very sincere way, meeting eyes with the first graders and expressing that they wouldn't do things like that anymore. They clearly weren't just trying to get the meeting over with, but came from a very genuine place. Then, in addition to their apologies, we had them balance out their bullying with something helpful to the first grade by washing their class' desks and blackboards.

The situation with the first graders was dealt with, but it had further revealed a dynamic I'd been noticing between the two third graders. This incident with the girls wasn't the first time Henry had pressured Preston into doing something not nice. I'd also seen two other boys participate in bullying Preston. There were many cases where Preston would totally lose it and get into a mode of very aggressive behavior. He was a boy who showed a lot of stress among his peers, and I had seen these three boys take advantage of it and prod him until he went over the edge. I decided to have another meeting with the four of them, and again Mrs. Nolan came with me to add emphasis to the importance of our talk.

The four boys were very nervous when I took them out of class for the meeting. Since we weren't holding it during recess, they wouldn't be itching to get out as soon as possible, and this was a sign that we were giving this meeting extra attention. I didn't tell them what the topic of the meeting was, because twice before Henry had manipulated other children to lie in order to cover him, and only later did I learn what really happened. This time no one could be pressured to make up stories to cover the one with the strongest social power in the group, because no one knew what was going to happen.

We took them to a free room with several exercise balls lying around. At first they were joking around, pretending like it was really cool that they got out of class to sit on these balls. I could see they were trying to act like cool dudes as they bounced up and down, but underneath it I sensed their worry.

Once they settled down we sat together and talked about how the behavior of the three boys had often contributed to Preston acting up in extreme ways that often hurt other children, usually in the younger grades. I said, "One thing I remember is during a game of kickball when Preston was getting upset, and several of you said things like, 'Oh you're just a crybaby!' or 'God, you cry as if you broke your leg!' Later when Preston tripped over someone's feet, he was still so worked up that he turned around and slammed the other kid really hard, thinking he'd been tripped on purpose. When someone feels like the others are after him all the time, even if it's not true, he'll get mad and lash out." I paused. "So what are the things that each of you can do to help change that and support Preston?"

Mrs. Nolan added, "Why don't you each say in your own words what you think you would like to change for yourself. Just talk about yourself, and if you need some help we'll give you some help."

I was amazed at what happened next. During that round the kids truly came out with the major points we had seen that we wanted them to change.

Henry said, "I need to make sure Preston is included in our games, and that we don't make fun of him."

The second boy said, "I have to work on not saying mean things."

The third boy, who was often on the periphery, but who we still felt was very much a part of the dynamic, said, "I need to say the truth. I should make sure that I don't just stick up for my friends and side with them when they're saying something that isn't true."

Each one of them said something different, and specific to himself, and totally true! It was wonderful.

Preston was the only boy who had difficulty thinking of what he could change. I think he was still too much in stress mode to see what he needed to do differently, so his friends actually volunteered what he could work on, and they did it in a very gentle way. Henry, the one who had bullied him the most, was actually the first to help him out, pointing out sweetly that he should watch his temper.

"When you get mad," he said, "You should just walk off or something like that, to cool down."

It was really dear. When our meeting was over they walked out with a sincerity that I never expected they would come to.

Afterwards I was watching one of their kickball games and each time Preston's team was up they were getting struck out very quickly. Preston was getting more and more angry. As his team struck out yet again, I braced myself for the regular comments that would either send Preston into a rage or cause him to fall apart crying.

Then I heard one of the boys say, "Hey Preston, it's just a game. Let's enjoy it."

Henry chimed in, "C'mon, it's not so bad, take a break if you have to cool off a bit."

The third boy said, "It's ok, we'll be up again."

I smiled in amazement at the change. Several times now I've seen the three boys gently remind Preston to take it easy, rather than pushing him further with negative comments or encouraging him to bully younger students.

Anonymous

20
The Decision Has Been Made

During my teenage years Vietnam was really heating up, and in 1965, at the age of seventeen, I became involved in serious demonstrations against the war. As I fully expected, this alienated me from the vast majority of people in my town and country. But then I started to notice something else that made me very uncomfortable. As Buffalo Springfield's rock and roll song later would say, "There's battle lines being drawn, Nobody's right if everybody's wrong ... Singing songs and carrying signs, Mostly saying, 'hooray for our side.' "

It seemed to me that there was a lot of mob mentality, a lot of herd consciousness, in the peace movement. I saw a lot of people who were more caught up in being part of their "gang" than in moving the country forward. And I saw that some of these people were self-aggrandizing into positions of leadership and cutting down other people just because they wanted to be the boss at the moment. It had nothing to do with the issue we were supposed to be defending. I became convinced that some of the peace movement leaders would have instantly switched to become generals in the war, if offered a couple stars on their shoulders and a bunch of people to command.

I became interested in Sufism and began reading G.I. Gurdjieff, who said that most of the worst of human misery is a result of the herd mentality. I came to believe that there wasn't going to be a political solution to the problems society was facing; a solution would have to be spiritual—something more subtle and deeper than simply defining one's political policies perfectly and getting the biggest following. When I reached this conclusion I started attending peace rallies with a quite different consciousness. I'd think to myself, *Here I am and here's this herd. I'll participate, but keep my wits about me.* This helped prepare me for the day where keeping a mind of my own would really matter to an innocent person trapped by a mob...

Of course I don't believe that mob consciousness is always a bad thing. I love being immersed, though not dissolved, in a complete frenzy of meaningless victory. That's just fine in its place. I had an incredible personal experience of this when my girlfriend and I happened to be at the NY "Miracle Mets" finale game in 1969. The Mets had come from being completely off the map, never finishing higher than next-to-last during their first seven years, and now in their eighth year they won the entire pennant and World Series! When that final out was made, crowning the Mets world champions, the stands erupted with a roar, hordes of fans rushed onto the field, and within seconds the outfield looked like the most mangy cat you've every seen – mostly brown and just a little remaining green, and pretty soon that was gone too. I asked my girlfriend, "What's going on in the outfield?"

She said, "People are grabbing pieces of the sod to take it home for good luck."

After half a minute our initial frantic cheering and screaming quieted down a tiny bit in the stadium, and above this we heard a new sound – the most overwhelming, enveloping sound I've ever heard in my life. I looked around and around, and it wasn't our crowd making that sound. "WHAT IS THAT?" I exclaimed.

We looked at each other and suddenly realized: it was Manhattan!

Manhattan Island is about 12 miles away, where everyone had been tuned into the game. As that final out was made, every train whistle, every fire engine's klaxon, every civil defense siren, every human throat, every steamboat whistle – it all went off at once. Sixty seconds later it hit us way out there in Queens.

I said, "Let's go to Manhattan!" So we ran out of the stadium ahead of the crowd and got into our car. We only got as far as Lexington Avenue because the entire island was a traffic jam. Manhattan was paralyzed. Buses were stuck in confetti two feet deep and the skies were dark with falling IBM punch cards and office files emptied from skyscraper windows. There were abandoned police cars with their sirens going, the police jumping up and down in the crowd or on top of their cars.

Now, New York has always had a lot of problems socially and economically, and 1969 was worse than usual—a lot of hurting people—but in those moments every human being on Manhattan Island absolutely loved every other human being. One match could have burned down the block and no fire engine could have gotten near it, but nobody lit a match. It was an astonishing outpouring of good will. So I like that. I really like that.

Meanwhile the Vietnam War had become more and more unpopular. Richard Nixon had actually been elected in 1968 as a peace candidate, claiming he was going to stop the War. One day in April 1970, when it became known that Nixon had in fact, been secretly bombing Cambodia for some time, in addition to Vietnam, the USA really went crazy. This was the opposite of ending the war. This was outrageous.

In Boulder Colorado, 10,000 people were gathering in the dark hours to protest this escalation of the war. Two of my friends, both brilliant human beings, met up with me and we caught up with the demonstrators as they passed along 9th Street at University. Half a mile uphill, we halted at the intersection with Baseline. Several people with megaphones addressed the crowd. They led a few songs, and began chanting anti-war slogans.

Soon I was astonished at the behavior of my two friends. All of a sudden they were yelling and shaking their fists. I didn't recognize them anymore. These were no longer people that I knew, even though I'd known them for years. I'd never seen such behavior from them. These guys were basically apolitical. Sure, if you'd asked them, "Are you against the war?" they would have said, "Yes," but they weren't going to make a point out of it. Now all of a sudden here they were with angry faces, echoing what was said over the megaphone and trying to be louder than the next guy. It weirded me out.

An announcement was made that we were going to go down to Highway 36 and shut it down. So all these thousands of people marched twenty blocks down to the turnpike, somebody built some fires on the road and they shut down the main corridor between Boulder and Denver. However it was not the only corridor. The police created a detour so that people could get through on back-roads, bypassing the demonstrators on the highway. Only two cars remained trapped, unable to make it into Boulder past the barricade of fires, and unable to retreat past the angry, shouting, torch-bearing mob. Just two cars trapped.

I was 100 yards or so from the fires and the cars and I was already thinking this was a little silly. I had mixed feelings. Yes, lighting fires on the freeway made me a little uncomfortable, but it also didn't strike me as necessarily a bad way to get ourselves noticed and into the news. We wanted to make a statement showing that a lot of people were really angry about this Cambodia bombing.

That was when a rumor came through the crowd. The person who reported it to me had absolutely no trace of concern as he conversationally mentioned, "One of the people in the cars has a broken leg, and he can't get to the hospital."

I was aghast when I heard that, staring back at him in astonishment. *Did he really just say that?* It was becoming a very ironic situation. Here there were all these people who were supposed to be for peace and love and compassion and good sense, yet they had fires built across US 36 and they wouldn't let two cars through so this guy could get to the hospital! He'd just have to sit there in the car with a broken leg and wait who knows how long.

I thought, *No, we can't do that. What am I going to do about that?* I looked around and saw this guy with a megaphone. I just walked up to him and in an authoritarian voice I said, "Give me the megaphone." He instantly obeyed me.

I turned it on and addressed the crowd, using my language carefully. My voice boomed: "THE DECISION HAS BEEN MADE TO ALLOW THESE CARS TO PASS. REMOVE THE FIRES IMMEDIATELY."

I didn't begin by commanding the crowd myself. Neither did I preach, nor exhort, nor reason, nor ask, all of which would have acknowledged possible resistance. Instead I simply said, "The decision has been made..." I was merely the messenger, obeying authority's order that the fires were to be removed.

Instantly, the people near the fires began obeying the order, in the same spirit that I was apparently obeying the order.

I'm guessing that most of the people in the crowd, in some part of their consciousness, felt the same concern for the man with the broken leg that I felt. But they had been caught up in the adrenaline and fire and yelling of the mob—the momentum of what the group was already doing. Nobody thought they could change this or do anything about it as just one person. So, for those who knew there was a man with a broken leg, I think they were probably relieved to cooperate when they heard: "the decision has been made…"

I held onto the megaphone until the fires had been completely moved. Soon they were gone, and the cars went on down the road.

Larry Frey

21

Only If My Mother Tells Me

Northern Uganda was locked in a horrific political and social struggle for over twenty years. Joseph Kony, founder and leader of a notorious rebel group called the Lords Resistance Army (LRA) believed he was doing God's work by fighting the Ugandan government and others in the area. But in the course of this long struggle the LRA has murdered, mutilated and raped tens of thousands of unarmed civilians; burned down homes, churches and whole villages; and abducted an estimated 30,000 children to be used as child soldiers or "wives." Over the years, the violence brought about a predictable reality of thousands upon thousands of victims, many of whom became perpetrators and then victims once again. The Acholi people and others in the region of Northern Uganda suffered beyond description.

Approximately 1.8 million people abandoned their homes and farms to live in Internally Displaced People (IDP) camps set up by the government in other parts of the North. In fact the Ugandan army *forced* most of these people into the IDP camps, on the grounds that the displacement was militarily necessary to help distinguish between civilians and fighters while combating the LRA. The government called these camps "Protected Villages," but in actuality little to no security was provided. Many of the IDP camps continued to be raided by the LRA, and the uprooted people found themselves even worse off than before—without reliable access to basic food and sanitation. Camp conditions led to acute malnutrition in children and the near-total destruction of social networks and cultural norms. More than 300,000 children under the age of five suffered from malaria, pneumonia, diarrhea and preventable diseases, and thousands of people were dying every month.

I first heard of all this on a winter morning at a small gathering of about 80 people who met in a UN building in New York City. Presenting at this meeting were Christian and Muslim and Indigenous leaders from the Acholi community in Northern Uganda, who had organized themselves into a group called the Acholi Religious and Cultural Leaders Peace Initiative. They told us, "We have lost everything, even our children. But we still have our political will. Please help us. Do you have the political will to help us?" Together these leaders spoke with absolute conviction that, "More killing is not the answer." It was an incredible place to come from after so much atrocity. Yes, there had been horrible killing and abductions and rapes in the past decades, but instead of getting lost in that, they asked, "What can be done to save our children from this violence and protect the vulnerable people alive today?"

Sadly, despite the phenomenal attention the UN has always given to Aftrica, there was no focus on this particular situation in Uganda. It was one of the most child-focused crises in the world, and it was not getting attention. (In 2005 it would be named one of the 10 most under-reported crises in the world). As a permanent delegate to the United Nations for a non-governmental organization (NGO), my responsibility was to advocate with the Security Council to provide a voice from the ground and from the churches, for the peace, security and development of all human beings in any given situation, *especially* the people in forgotten places like what I was hearing about now. Together with other NGO colleagues, we asked ourselves, "How can we help?" Without knowing it, this moment was the conception of the Northern Uganda Working Group—a collaboration of individuals and NGOs all working in and around Gulu, the capital of Northern Uganda, to support peace-building efforts for the Acholi people and the rest of civil society in the region and the country.

As a part of this Northern Uganda Working Group, I helped support the Acholi Religious and Cultural Leaders in their work towards peace. They continued to reach out, saying, "Joseph Kony, we need to talk to you. Come out of the bush so we can talk." They were advocating for a cessation of hostilities that would at least allow innocent people to be safe while continuing to deal with the LRA. It became a precarious movement of people saying, "Joseph Kony is a human being. We have to talk to him. We have to talk to our enemy." The idea is fairly astonishing to the western mind and others not yet reconciled to this alternative to fighting. You want to do what? You want to sit down with the LRA in the bush and talk to these killers? Really? This is crazy—*dangerous*! On the radio there had *never* been so much conversation about the LRA that wasn't just saying to shoot them, so the LRA were tuning in, you can be sure of that.

At the time, John Baptist Odama, a native Ugandan from the south of the country, was serving as Archbishop in the northern capital of Gulu. This gave Odama a unique position of neutrality with regards to the Ugandan Government and the LRA in hiding throughout Northern Uganda and the region. From this position, Odama became central to the new movement of forgiveness as a path to peace and justice. He preached how forgiveness was not only in alignment with God, but also practical and true to a long tradition of Ugandan local justice and culture. Odama said, "In Acholi society when someone forgives an aggressor, it doesn't diminish in any way the severity of the violence that was done. Instead it reminds the aggressor that he is from the same community. It reminds him of the fundamental dignity and humanity of every person in the community. It is not a matter of forgive and forget. For the rest of his life the forgiven person has to live publicly with that forgiveness."

Even when the International Criminal Court indicted Kony and other rebel commanders on multiple counts of crimes against humanity, Archbishop Odama said, "If you want to put somebody in jail take me, put me in jail. Putting Joseph Kony in jail is not going to end the war here." Regarding the ICC, to his own church leaders and cardinal, he said, "Take me. Take me if you want a body. I'm no one, take me." The depth of his authenticity rang as very courageous; he clearly held a deep belief that there was a way to peace through reconciliation and forgiveness. "I need to talk to the man," he said. "I need to see him and treat him like a human being whom I believe God loves." It was a radical disposition aimed at finding a humane solution.

By 2006, momentum was growing within the Ugandan government and the international community to create space for negotiation with the LRA. With dedicated effort and collaboration, many Ugandans and other interested parties supported Archbishop Odama to find a way to meet with Joseph Kony in the bush. All understood the tremendous risk of attempting this, but the Archbishop believed this was the right thing to do, at the right time. Finally, discretely and without fanfare, it was all arranged.

In his meeting with Kony, Odama said, "Joseph, this is not good, what you're doing is not good, it is not the way. If you believe you are doing God's will, I can tell you, this is not God's will. It would never be God's will to kill people. Your mother is not proud of you for doing this."

Joseph Kony said, "Let my mother come here and tell me that. If my mother tells me this is not God's will, then I will stop." Having lived in hiding in the bush with his rebels,

Kony had not seen his mother for many, many years. Was this just a clever way to get Odama to bring him his mother? Or was there some sincerity to Kony's statement?

When Odama returned from the meeting he told President Museveni that he had talked with Kony, and he relayed what Kony had said. The Archbishop decided to take Kony at his word. In no more than a few days, under much care and attention and with the help of the Ugandan government, Odama arranged for Kony's mother to be flown in to the bush to meet her son.

On the African continent, the mother is unquestionably the very source of life and all that's revered, so her words usually carry great weight. When she arrived at the meeting place, she looked into her son's eyes and said, "I am your mother and I love you, and I absolutely tell you, you must stop. This is not what God wants. Come out of the bush, let's find a way to negotiate and find peace."

Shortly after this Kony had a conversation with one of his primary enemies, the Ugandan President Yoweri Museveni. Out of that meeting came an intense and methodical process leading to the cessation of hostilities— an agreement to gather the LRA rebels into *assembly areas* in the region, where they were guaranteed their safety. Once in the assembly areas, the LRA would be provided with basic food and medical supplies in exchange for no longer raiding the villages of innocent civilians while the peace talks unfolded.

A call came in one day from a local colleague of mine. He was in the area where LRA fighters were marching toward one of the agreed-upon assembly areas. He told me, "If I didn't just see this with my own eyes, I wouldn't believe it. I've just watched as thoroughly-displaced Ugandan citizens, living a totally miserable survival existence, brought little brown paper bags of their limited food to give to these LRA soldiers for their journey. The same people who two weeks ago might have killed each other!"

I could hardly believe it either. Here was the most astonishing example that peace is personal, and that's what makes it possible. Archbishop Odama's prophetic voice rang through my mind, "Our hate for the LRA has killed our souls. We have to say that we're bigger than this, that we are capable of forgiving, so that we and our children might reclaim our lives and live again the life God gave us." Now, before the eyes of my friend, those words had become real; it was actually happening.

When Archbishop Odama returned to NY to address the Security Council at the United Nations, he came not as a representative of a government or political party. He came as a priest and a pastor and a member of the community. He brought the wisdom and cultural sensibilities of the Acholi people, whose basic message was, "Forgiveness, with all its implications, is greater and more powerful than killing."

This message transformed the international leaders' debate, confronting them with the reality that local and cultural mechanisms for reconciliation and healing from war are both practical and possible. A UN special envoy, former Mozambican president Joaquim Chissano, was appointed to help in finding a solution as negotiations continued. Chissano also went to the bush to meet with Kony, returning to say, "I have met Joseph Kony. I have seen the whites of his eyes, and I can confirm that he too is a human being made in the image and likeness of God. Even as we pursue justice, I can't just let you kill him, because that won't bring the end of this."

Again, as with the Acholi Religious and Cultural Leaders and Archbishop Odama before him, Chissano held the same firm conviction that killing was not the answer. Many were fascinated, others infuriated, with this alternative cultural approach. But for Chissano and Odama and many others, the question was and continued to be, *How do we achieve justice?* These were the responses of faith-filled individuals to horrendous violence. It could sound terribly naive, but in their presence it became clear that these were voices of reason and wisdom.

Along with the UN and many other groups, Archbishop Odama and the Acholi Leaders helped serve as brokers of the ensuing Juba Peace talks from 2006-2008. By the end of the talks, 13 agreements were signed, and roughly a million of the 1.8 million Internally Displaced People had returned home—back to their villages and farms. People in Gulu began to speak about being secure. "We have hope," they said. "We know there are still vulnerabilities in the region, but we have life today and we have peace." Today approximately 90 per cent of the Internally Displaced People have returned to their areas of origin or have resettled in new locations.

All this was made possible because of the utmost sincerity in not only recognizing the humanity of Joseph Kony, but of really listening to him, and being willing to bring his mother to him as he'd asked. Odama let Kony come to a change of heart in the way that he had requested, and a level of fragile trust was built. To be minimally associated with this absolute moment to say, *forgive*—it's the most humbling thing I've ever been a part of.*

A Peace Advocate

---

*In early 2009, while Joseph Kony never signed the final peace accord for reasons too complex to explore in this story, a significant measure of peace, security and hope was restored to Northern Uganda. Due to the Juba Peace Talks and the cessation of hostilities, many lives were saved. Families are farming again, and children are going to school. Unfortunately the LRA continues to bring violence and insecurity to neighboring countries, where Archbishop Odama, the Acholi and others are doing their best to address this regional problem. As of this writing, again there is a renewed UN and international effort to find a resolution to this horrendous situation. The search for peace clearly goes beyond borders, which is why we continue to work for peace by going wherever we are needed.

22

The Ganges River

In the city of Benares, India, the Ganges river is used for all practical needs and all spiritual rituals. Every Hindu bathes spiritually every morning, but they also go there to really wash themselves because most don't have running water. Because of this there are great wide stairs, called Ghats, leading all the way down into the water like the steps of middle-European cathedrals. The life of the city is out on these Ghats, and there are many who make their money ferrying people from one to another in little boats; it's one of the main ways to get around the city.

It was almost evening as I stepped out on one of these Ghats, looking out over the wide expanse of the Ganges. The sun was ready to set on a wonderful day. I had just finished buying lungis and sarongs, the traditional Indian clothing, as well as other items to send home to Switzerland. I had been particularly successful in negotiating good prices, and the storekeeper had even agreed to pack it all for me and take it to the post office.

I was happy that all had gone so well with my purchases. As I watched the water shimmer with the last rays of sunlight, I decided that this beautiful evening I would take a taxi boat

111

back home, about three Ghats upriver. I descended the stairs and waved one in, and soon a small rowboat pulled up with three men inside. One of them gave me a toothless grin as I jumped in and pointed up-river. All three were in their forties or fifties, clearly quite poor from the grime on their ragged clothing. It didn't surprise me at all. If you owned a boat for your personal livelihood it was very common that in off-hours you would ferry people around to make some extra money.

As usual the oarsmen rowed the boat a little distance away from the shore where the main traffic went, but soon I noticed that he didn't stop there. Instead he kept rowing the boat farther and farther out into the deserted middle of the river. The Ganges is a *huge* river, almost like a lake, so I started to get nervous. At one point the three men all talked in Hindi amongst themselves. They didn't say a word to me in English, so I didn't know what was going on.

Finally I asked, "Why are we going this far in the middle of the river?"

The only reaction I got was nervous laughter and uncomfortable expressions. At that point I knew something was absolutely *wrong*. Suddenly my high from the day was gone. I became very present, trying to figure out what was going on. It was clear that the men were into something together.

"What is going on?" I demanded.

Only one of them could speak English. He pointed at me and said, "*YOU*. Wester woman. Wester woman have sex many men. We have no sex, no woman. We have sex with you."

I said, "What? All three?"

"Yes," he said. In his halting English he told me none of them had ever had sex in their lives. If they ever did and others found out, it would take away any chance for them to ever get married. "We go in middle of river where nobody sees," he said.

"I don't want this," I said.

They chatted amongst themselves and then the translator said simply, "We know you have sex with many men."

No matter what I said they always came back with that. I couldn't exactly deny it, so I said, "But I always chose."

They spoke amongst themselves again, and the translator said, "We also choose now, we choose you." He told me they would just go a little bit farther and then they would begin.

At that point my thoughts raced. *What can I do?* I asked myself. When they weren't watching me closely I checked the water with my foot to feel how cold the water was. It was possible that I could get away by swimming, but the distance was far. Then I realized I was wearing a sarong. I knew the long cloth garment wouldn't be an easy item to swim in, so I dismissed that option. I was very clear that I would rather submit to them than put myself in a position where I might die. My first commitment to myself was not to die.

As I watched them they were clearly very decided on their course of action. It looked like they had made a genius move in getting me on that boat and abducting me into the middle of the river—not for me of course, but for them.

Then as I watched the men I picked up something new. There was some sort of hesitation around them. They started to speak back and forth, and from the little Hindi I knew, I understood that they were saying, "Not me, you." "No, not me, you."

What are they discussing? I wondered.

"We talk about order," the translator informed me before I even asked.

I realized they were arguing about who *had* to go first, not who *got* to go first. None of them wanted to be the first one. That realization gave me a sense of empowerment and soon a second commitment grew in me. Something in me said, "No. This is *not* going to happen." I felt very clear that I would decide my future *and* I wouldn't need to swim. But I didn't know yet how I was going to save myself.

113

That's when I looked down and noticed my mala, the 108 Hindu prayer beads hanging around my neck, each for one of the 108 names of Shiva. I was feeling desperate and very alert. I took the beads in my hand and began to pray to myself very intensely, "Om Namah Shivaya, Om Namah Shivaya…"

It was the mantra of every Hindu ashram, including the one where I had been studying. I wasn't very intimately connected to Hinduism, but I participated in the Indian culture as best I could while I was there. I was much more interested in my education with my particular teacher Babaji, and the wisdom he had to share with me. In the past week at his ashram I had said the prayer so many times that it was what first jumped to my lips. Directly translated it means "I bow to Shiva," the highest deity in Hinduism. However Leonard Orr, an American spiritual leader, translated it as "I bow to the higher self in me." I always held it that way. That's how it made sense to me, allowing me to say it and really mean it.

Soon I was praying to myself like I had never done before. I felt this was my safety; this could be my saving grace until the answer came. I prayed one or two minutes, and then I closed my eyes and didn't even look to see what the men were doing. I was just concentrating on, "Om Namah Shivaya, Om Namah Shivaya!" Soon I began to say it out loud—louder and louder. Not long into it I felt like I was in the middle of a balloon, and every "Om Namah Shivaya" made it grow a little bigger. Soon I felt like the balloon around me protected me to the extent that I was untouchable. I had no doubts any more that these guys absolutely could not get through. I just kept my eyes closed and continued praying as if my life depended on it. It was one of my very few experiences of single focus. I knew what I was going for and it was not a joke. I was determined I would not have three men over me.

I can't even say how long it was, but I just kept reciting the prayer with great conviction, growing my strength. Then

I felt the boat move. I heard an oar splash in the water and soon the movement became steadier, with a rhythmic pull to it. At one point I opened my eyes very quickly and I saw that we were going back to the shore, so I closed them again and continued praying with even more passion. I had first started praying in order to bow to the wisdom of my higher self, and be open to its guidance. I never guessed that the praying itself might be the answer. Somehow the mantra really did make me untouchable.

Soon I felt a jerk in the boat and the man who spoke English said, "You, go!"

I opened my eyes to see we were back at the Ghat, and oh my gosh how did I go! In moments I was out on the steps racing for a little wall not far away, still with the huge balloon glowing around me. I just made it there and sat down, watching the three men depart just as quickly in their boat. It only took them several minutes before they were completely out of sight.

At that point I don't know what happened to that balloon around me, but I looked down and my legs were shaking and wobbling. There was no balloon left. I just felt myself crying away without being sad, just releasing my nerves. For the next twenty minutes I cried. When I finally finished I found my way home, feeling very grateful and humbled by the whole experience.

Claudia Samson

23

Gratitude

When I worked as a women's counselor for the Boulder County Safehouse, part of my job was to lead groups for the women in the Boulder Jail. The whole intention behind this was to do outreach to this population of jailed women who might really need our services. But rather than focusing on domestic violence, the groups were a place of support to develop life skills. When I first started I was really nervous about facilitating these women who *certainly* didn't want to be in jail, and probably weren't very excited about being in the group either.

At least they had a choice whether or not to come to the groups, which were held in a room across the hall from the main locked cell area. The groups were always small, ranging from about three to seven.

At first I started with psycho-educational presentations on issues like communication. The groups were really dry, and people didn't participate that much. Something was missing.

Someone else covered the job for me while I was away for several months, and during that time I began to realize, "What I really want to do is just be present with these women, and see what they want, and what might be useful to them." I decided that when I returned, I would shift my focus.

On my first day back I was surprised to find that the group's location had been changed. Now it was taking place *inside* the women's locked unit. We were meeting in what was basically their living room or common area. And to add another dynamic, the group was now *mandatory*. Suddenly I'm not only leading this group right in their living space, but everyone *had* to attend regardless of interest, unless someone was in solitary confinement or locked in their room. Now there were about 18-22 women in the group—four times what I was used to!

I took a deep breath and started. This time, instead of giving a psycho-educational presentation, I just opened up to these women, sharing my own desire to hear what was up for them in the moment.

They were hesitant to genuinely express how they were feeling, so I said, "Imagine that in this moment, you were a box of cereal. What kind would you be?" We went around the circle and heard from each woman—it made it easy and fun for everyone to share. As they answered, I noticed the themes—shredded wheat, bran, grape nuts, soggy oatmeal.... I started sharing what I noticed, creating the rest of the group around naming those themes, and guiding people to talk more about them. I just trusted the process, and the entire group shifted, becoming quite lively. People started really connecting. The whole process was much more organic and satisfying than the dry presentations I had done before.

One day I walked in and there were about 22 women in the group. There was a lot of "I don't want to be here in jail" energy. We did a check-in, and there was a lot of, "This sucks." "I hate this." "I don't want to be here." "I don't trust these people in the room." "The people here are annoying." "I can't trust them." "I don't even want to talk in this group." "I don't want to share about myself." "The food sucks."

First I acknowledged how they were feeling. I said, "OK, I really get that this is not where you want to be. This is really a stressful place to be for you. And you don't have a lot of choice right now, either in your lives, or about who's here."

"Got that right!" One woman said, and others nodded.

"What I'm curious about is what helps you get through?" I asked. "What are the small things? Is it a person here? Is it a value you have? Is it someone at home supporting you? I want to just start the group today by giving everyone an opportunity to express any appreciations that they have in their life."

So people started sharing what they appreciated. One said, "I appreciate my roommate, she listens to me when I'm frustrated." Someone else said, "I really appreciate my kids. They're what get me through, and I can't wait to see them again." A few women said they appreciated their spirituality, and having that as part of what keeps them going, trusting that it was all for a reason, and that God was there for them. Someone else talked about her own inner resources, she had courage in knowing that she'd been through hard times before, so she could get through this. Another talked about the little moments of kindness from other people in the jail—sharing their food, or something else that they'd gotten.

Then one of the residents said, "I really appreciate Valerie." (One of the police officers who worked on the unit.) "Valerie totally treats us with respect and a lot of other police officers don't; I just really appreciate her and that she treats us like humans."

This went on for a really long time. It was just amazing because this simple offer of appreciation shifted the whole energy of the group. What I thought would be a ten-minute check-in just kept going. People kept talking about all the things they appreciated! We didn't do any specific problem-solving, but much of what had been problems when we started, simply dissolved in the atmosphere of appreciation.

At one point Officer Valerie actually walked through the unit, and one of the group members called out, "Hey Valerie, come over and join our group."

She stopped and asked, "What are you doing?"

I said, "We've been expressing appreciations, and one of the women here said that she appreciates *you*, and appreciates how you treat her."

The women asked, "What do you appreciate, Valerie? Do you appreciate anything?"

Valerie got really honest and said, "You know, I really love working on this unit. Honestly, when they first moved me here I didn't want to work here. I didn't want to work with women. I thought it was going to be harder, and I was really resistant. But after coming here I really enjoy working on this unit, and I really do care about you all."

Before anyone knew it, our two hours were up. By just expressing their appreciation, the attitude among these women had shifted dramatically, from focus on all the little conflicts to an awareness of the good and cooperative things in their lives.

Katie Asmus

24

Neither Violent Nor Victim

Maggie Harris, jogging through a city park at dusk, suddenly came face-to-face with a large man who had stepped out, blocking her path. She was terrified when he grabbed her arm. Just then she saw an old man walking his dog on a path across the park. She held back an impulse to call for help when she realized that the old man would likely get hurt if he tried to assist her. But this momentary change of focus toward the safety of the old man broke the paralysis of her fear.

With new courage Maggie jerked loose from the man's hold, grasped his arm, and said, "Let's go over here and talk." She led him to a less-secluded spot. After she expressed concern that he might be having some kind of trouble, he began to share about his plight and despair. Later he walked her home without harming her, thanking her for being his friend.

Peggy Faw Gish

From *If a violent person threatened to harm a loved one… What Would You Do?* By John Howard Yoder, p 130. Copywrite © 1983 by Herald Press, Scottdale PA.

25
Doggedly Determined

A couple came seeking couples counseling at the therapy group practice in which I worked. They were very embittered with one another, but couldn't get a divorce because they had a dog that was the center of their lives. Neither of them was willing to give up even partial custody of the dog.

When we worked with them, we discovered that the wife resented her husband's habit of not even acknowledging her when he came home from work. When he walked through the front door he would simply head straight upstairs to shower. By the time he arrived back downstairs, she would be livid, and they would get into a terrible argument.

The husband complained that the wife was not physically affectionate. He longed for her to sit next to him on the couch while they were watching TV, or to cuddle up and kiss him. He would complain sarcastically that he must have body odor when she sat some distance from him.

We asked what the dog did when the husband arrived home that was different from what the wife did. It turned out that the dog would run to the door, greet the husband and get a nice rubbing in return. The wife would wait in the other room for the husband to seek her out, which he didn't do.

We discovered that the dog was very assertive when he wanted affection. He would come over and sit next to the person from whom he wanted affection. If they were distracted or unresponsive, the dog would put his paw over their arm or nuzzle them with his cold nose until they petted him or snuggled.

So we gave the couple this task: they were to study the dog, and make him their teacher and guru. When they each saw how the dog got what he wanted from the other, they were to copy that behavior and try it out for themselves.

They had great fun with this, and began to turn their relationship around. Soon they no longer wanted a divorce.

Bill O'Hanlon

26
It Was Like a Spring Thaw

Japanese troops approached the abandoned American university a couple of miles outside a little Chinese village. Morgan, a lone American missionary,[*] could hear the menacing rattle of machine guns in the distance, but he decided to stand his ground at the gate of the institution where he had taught until the Japanese invasion drove the students and other teachers westward.

The troops came along the road—dirty, disheveled, tense, and utterly weary. *As tired looking a bunch of men as I've ever seen*, Morgan thought. It was a small contingent, a sort of advance guard. They would trot along the road a hundred yards and then squat down, set up a machine gun, and spray the road ahead. They paid little attention to the man standing by the gate as they went by.

By the next day the nearby village had become a field headquarters for the Japanese, and Morgan's tribulations began. As he had anticipated, the Japanese officers cast

---

[*]The American Protestant missionary recounting this experience was a member of the Fellowship of Reconciliation, in whose journal, *Fellowship*, it first appeared in the January 1945 issue.

covetous glances at the university buildings. Soon a group of them called on Morgan and demanded the keys.

The missionary declined, politely but firmly. He explained that the property belonged to American mission boards, that it had been entrusted to his care, and that he was not at liberty to hand it over to anyone else. An hour and a half of discussion, with the missionary remaining always courteous and friendly but firm, convinced the Japanese, and they left.

Unfortunately, that was not the end. Periodically, on an average of every two weeks, the village garrison changed, and each new contingent had to be persuaded all over again. Through it all Morgan did his best to remain calm and friendly.

But then came a major crisis. This time something had happened to make the Japanese less patient, less willing to listen to the missionary's arguments. Morgan sensed the tension in the air immediately. He could not help reflecting that, isolated as he was, the Japanese could do with him as they would. No "neutral" witnesses could be summoned to testify against them. A dead missionary could easily be explained by a "stray bullet—so sorry!"

Nevertheless, he greeted them cordially, as always, and refused their request for the keys of the building with his usual regretful firmness. This time, though, the most eloquent arguments appeared only to inflame the soldiers more. Finally the officer in command of the detachment delivered an ultimatum.

"Surrender the keys," he demanded flatly, "or we shoot you!"

The missionary stood a little straighter. "I have told you how it is," he replied quietly. "I wish you no harm, but I cannot do what you ask. I cannot."

Grimly the officer counted off three men and lined them up facing the missionary.

"Ready!" he commanded, and rifles were raised to shoulders. He turned to the missionary. "Surrender the keys!"

"I cannot. I have told you I cannot. I have no hatred against you. I have only the friendliest feelings for you. But I cannot give you the keys."

Morgan thought he could see admiration in the soldiers' eyes—admiration and baffled wonderment, as though they could not understand what held him erect and smiling in the very face of death.

Later he said, "I felt no fear. I was perfectly calm. My only prayer was for enough love to disarm my attackers. I tried to show them—the men as well as their officers—that I had in fact the friendliest feelings for them, that I recognized them as brothers and would refuse to cooperate with them only when they wished me to do something wrong. I tried to put that into my eyes as well as into my words."

"Aim!" The officer's voice was gruff as he turned once more to the missionary. "Your last chance," he said. "Surrender the keys!"

There was a pause. Morgan looked directly at the men who stood with leveled rifles facing him He spoke to them, as one man to other men, as brother to brother.

"I cannot," he said. "You know that I cannot."

The stillness was absolute. The missionary looked steadily at the men. The officer seemed uncertain, the men uneasy. Then, one at a time, they relaxed. Rifles lowered; sheepish grins replaced their looks of grim determination.

But the danger had not passed. One man of the firing squad apparently was disgusted and embarrassed at the outcome of this situation. He gripped his rifle and glared at Morgan.

"Father," the missionary prayed, "a little more love. Let me show a little more love."

The soldier had decided. Abruptly, with fixed bayonet on the end of his rifle, he launched himself full tilt at the missionary.

"He came fast," Morgan recalls, "and he came hard. At the last instant, when the point of his bayonet was not a foot from me, I dodged. He missed, and the force of his charge carried him up to me. I reached around him and with my right hand grabbed the butt of his rifle. (I thought that under the circumstances even a pacifist might be forgiven for holding a rifle!) With my left hand I grasped him around the shoulders (and that was a pretty hefty grip, too, for a pacifist) and pulled him tight up against me. I was taller than he, and he had to look up at me. When our eyes met, his face was contorted with fury.

"Our glances locked and held for seconds that seemed ages long. Then I smiled down at him, and it was like a spring thaw melting the ice on a frozen river. The hatred vanished and, after a sheepish moment, he smiled back!"

That was the end. A few minutes later the soldiers, like a group of bewildered children, were trailing the missionary into his living quarters—to have tea before their tiring journey back to the village.

Anonymous

Used with permission of *Fellowship* magazine: www.forusa.org/fellowship

27
Jail Break

Many years ago when I first started in the field of human services, I hired on as a Detention Home Group Supervisor—long title, short wages. I worked for the Juvenile Court officially, and I was in charge of the boys (usually ages 12 to 17) who were detained. It was a kind of junior jail in a corner of the County Corrections facility on the top floor of the County Hall.

On Sundays the main entrance was locked, so to get to the boys I had to first go to the basement and enter the Sheriff's office. From there I took the jail elevator to the top floor where I walked through the administrative part of the jail into the Juvenile Detention area. There was no other access to the top floor on Sundays.

The kids I dealt with were often runaways or shoplifters; a few were charged with violent crimes, even all the way up to homicide. Detention Hall Sundays were visiting days for parents of the detained youth. This particular Sunday during the early afternoon, three kids' parents were visiting, meeting with their sons in extra rooms or out in the hall. I oversaw the visits while keeping an eye on the other boys through a plexiglass window in the main office.

Suddenly I heard, "BAM! Crash!" and indistinct voices were yelling from over in the jail area. What the hell was going on? I ran down the hall leading to the jail in order to find out. Immediately I found myself confronted by a 23-year-old man in jail coveralls. In one hand he held a knife, and in the other was a sap (a head slammer) made of a sock with something heavy inside. I guessed he was the infamous felon I had read about and heard about from the jailers during the past week. He had already been convicted of armed robbery, and was awaiting sentencing for another similar charge the coming week. He was looking at a minimum of 20 years without parole.

I immediately thought, *I can't let him get one of the kids or parents as a hostage.*

"How can I get out of here?" he demanded tensely.

"Right this way," I said, leading him out of the detention area and away from the others. We entered the foyer with the non-operative main elevator and darkened stairs. As the door locked behind me I pointed to the stairs, which led into the locked main floor public area.

"You first," he said, and we began our descent in the dark down ten flights of stairs.

To further understand the situation: This felon was about 5'10" and skinny at about 145 pounds. I was a former professional baseball athlete in my early 20's. I was 6' 1" and 200 pounds. As we descended, I was taken over by a totally calm yet intensely alert state with an uncanny clear ability to think about the situation even as I gently suggested to the man that it would be unlikely for him to exit the building without a swarm of police around.

"The sheriff's office is in the basement," I observed. "The city police department is three blocks away, and the state police are within minutes of a call."

"Just keep going," he said. So we did.

In this intensely calm yet alert state I began to think about what scenarios might play out in the near future. I had never encountered danger with this attitude before.

Though this was before Star Trek, I felt like Spock—it was like I was totally there, but I also had a total detachment. It surprised me!

The questions I put to myself were these: In an individual "mano a mano" battle, could I prevail?

Answer: clearly yes. I was bigger, stronger and very fit.

On the other hand, was he more desperate than I, and therefore perhaps more dangerous?

Answer: at this moment, probably yes. The outcome would be in some doubt because he had two weapons and I had none.

When, then, would my desperation match his, therefore giving me physical advantage?

Answer: when we got to the main floor. There would be one way out, through very highly placed windows, and he would need my clothes to replace his jail coveralls. He would also need the few dollars I had in my wallet. I figured that at that point I could match his desperation and challenge him. I had noticed that when he began to swing the sap, there was not much weight to it—it was really of little use. The knife was a short blade and I figured I could take one slash and then I would step in and break his neck! None of this boxing footwork or Marquis of Queensbury rules.

At the same time, I didn't really want to challenge him, so I kept up a conversation about his realistic odds, understanding how he must feel looking at a long prison term at such a young age. I said I wondered how he might look at his life differently with the time on his hands, and so forth. The tone of his response subtly changed as we descended and by the time we neared the main floor we were almost like two friendly rivals on a stroll debating the up-coming match.

At the same time I had thought of two more possible responses for myself. First, the main floor was a pretty wide-open area and I could simply run away from him. Second, I could attempt to talk him out of his weapons.

We reached the main floor.

The City Hall had two main entrances, both with thick clear glass doors. Locked, of course. Immediately we could see police at both entries and I heard the sound of someone coming up from the basement. I turned to look at him and said in a matter of fact way, "You see, there really is no way you can get out of here in time, and I don't think you can outrun bullets. Why don't you give me those things and stand very still with your hands in sight?" I was very aware of the need for this to go as calmly as possible, so neither he nor I would be shot by nervous police.

"Yeah, you're right," he said.

I took his weapons, and only then did I see that the knife was really a piece of wood covered carefully with gum-wrapper foil. I slowly walked away as two policeman came onto the main floor brandishing .38s. I wanted to make sure the tense cops made the distinction between jail inmate and juvenile worker. When I came to the nearest policeman to hand him the weapons, I saw that his hands were shaking. I was totally calm, already reviewing this very interesting experience and wondering, "How in heaven's name did I just do that?"

Afterward there was a newspaper interview and a debriefing with the Sheriff's office, and of course an intense questioning by my young wife, but I couldn't really adequately explain the state of mind I spontaneously adopted as soon as the inmate first showed up in the hall on the top floor.

As I reflected later and even now, there was something that triggered an almost benign appreciation of the event. I experienced a complete acceptance: here we are and this is what I must deal with. There were no wishes nor hopes even, just acceptance. Then, very quickly, I saw complete movies of possible futures play out in part of my mind even as I talked with my "captor." I had a strange experience of knowing I had more control of the situation than he did. I just knew. Finally, I came to the conclusion that I didn't want either of us to be hurt. It just wasn't necessary and somehow I sensed I would avoid that outcome as long as we could talk.

When I finally understood what I had done spontaneously in this rather unusual situation, I realized that I could deliberately do something similar in many future situations demanding quick but sure reactions. I began to imagine probable events in my future where some kind of crisis might present itself. Then I literally imagined myself in those situations, experiencing the same resourcefulness that I had recently stumbled upon in the jail. I enjoyed playing these futures out in many different contexts, learning from what happened, but more importantly planting that kind of ability firmly in my future. This rehearsal served me well in many later situations in which I found myself automatically experiencing the same calm acceptance.

Steve Watson

28
Clay Giraffe

Teaching is a delicate affair. Imagine you have a room full of 25 children, all of them six-and-seven-year olds. Your lesson is two hours long. That is a lot of time to fill. And these kids are watching you, eagerly waiting to see what you will do next. And they won't wait for long before they invent something more entertaining to do (such as telling a joke to the kid on the other side of the isle, giving the stink-eye to the girl across the room, playing with a little toy car pulled out of a pocket, or getting up and running around). You don't have a lot of time (or grace) to catch and hold their attention in order to move them as a group to the lesson you have painstakingly prepared.

In my first eight years of teaching grade school, I developed a lot of strategies for quickly catching and then holding children's attention. I learned to be entertaining, humorous, and engaging. I honed my skills as a storyteller and could keep a group silent and spellbound as I unraveled a tale for them. I infused my lessons with humor and welcomed seemingly off-the-wall questions that gave me the opportunity to show the inter-relatedness of every topic.

I had managed to become at least as entertaining as... as a television, with the added feature of being "interactive."

Discipline issues, however, always crop up. I taught in the Waldorf school system where a teacher stays with his or her class for up to eight years. No matter how entertaining I was, over time, the kids came to know my act, and while most appreciated my efforts and cooperated, there were those who wanted something new—as in "change the channel."

I discovered that I resorted to using the teacher's universal cudgel: "I *need* you to sit down right now. I *need* you to stop talking. I *need* you to do your work." The unconscious logic was that if I phrased my request in the form of a *need,* the fundamental urgency intrinsic to the language would prevail and presto, the child would comply, obey, mind, submit, follow, cooperate, and at the very least, *sit down and shut up.*

Every classroom is a community, and the larger the group, the more diversity there is. There are students who follow their teacher's every lead out of an inherent sense of love and respect. Then there are those who go along with the flow as long as you do not push them too far. And always, there are the children who challenge you every step of the way (yes, even among sweet and innocent seven-year-olds). They react to a teacher's "I need you to..." as a bull might react to a toreador's red cape.

After I had finished eight years with one group of children, and five years with another, I came to realize (I'll admit I'm a slow learner) that order in the classroom was not dependent on how entertaining I was or the size of my verbal cudgel. It depended upon the children's good will.

In order to return to the first grade with a new group of children, I knew that I had to find some approach other than the default language of "*I need you to...*" I admitted to myself that I had been imposing my will upon those children who were not interested in my lessons. If I wanted to teach math, and they wanted to play, read a book, or express the turmoil in their soul as a result of an unsettled home life, I had believed it was my position as the authority to force them into at least appearing as if they were doing math. And we teachers have an array of weapons of coercion at our disposal: missing recess, grades, detention, suspension, or a conference with the parents, to name just the most obvious methods. I had convinced myself that it was within the realm of normalcy for me to act this way. In fact, it was my job to act this way, and I was paid for it. Yet the methodology of coercion had become so unsatisfying and painful, that I did not think I could return to the classroom and do it all over again.

I was fortunate to be led by a supportive parent to Non-Violent Communication (NVC) and the work of Marshall Rosenberg. One of the first maxims that stuck in my awareness was the principle: *connect* before you *correct*. It began to dawn on me that in order to gain the children's good will I had to actually take time and get to know them. How foreign this felt from the stance I had held as a teacher for thirteen years! Now, my primary goal was not to *teach*, but to *connect*. Teaching was secondary.

The NVC approach pointed out that any interaction with another human being has to begin with making a connection. Once that connection is made, a world of possibilities opens up. Without the connection, we will most likely experience conflict, particularly if we have different goals. As a teacher, if I have not connected with the students, reluctant or distracted children will experience me imposing my will upon them. Those students then face making one of two decisions: *comply* or *defy*, and either choice is damaging to them. From painful experience, I knew this to be true. I did not want to put that decision before any child again.

This path required me to learn new behaviors when I found myself standing once again before a new class of first graders. The first thing I decided to do was replace "*I need*" with "*I want*." It was a more vulnerable position to come from, but far more honest. I openly discussed with my children what it meant to be in school, and verbalized the fact that their parents sent them to learn all of the skills that lead to taking on adulthood. I found, to my delightful surprise, that even these first graders were aware and appreciative of this. Then, full of trepidation, I asked them what conditions in the classroom would benefit them to learn the best. Their suggestions were surprising and touched me deeply. Many expressed that they wanted our classroom to feel more homey. They wanted pictures on the walls (and even on the ceiling), and they wanted to bring their stuffed animals to school (these were six and seven year olds, after all). They wanted the freedom to get a drink or use the bathroom when they needed to, as well as clearly defined times to talk and equally clear times when everyone is silent and listening to their teacher. The level of respect they defined for one another and toward me was more sincere and detailed than anything I might have imposed upon them.

In particular, the children expressed that because there were so many of them in a small room, they did not want it to get too loud.

"Not me," one boy protested. "I *like* it loud. The louder the better for me." And he *was* a particularly loud child. He was well-intentioned, but loud.

I froze. Here was my first challenge. What was I going to do? My old habit of being the authority wanted to put him down and shut him up. A frantic voice inside of me warned that he would infect all the other boys who secretly also wanted to be louder.

My panic was unnecessary. I was saved by another maxim of NVC: in a stressful situation, connect with yourself first. So I took a deep breath and instead of reacting to his statement, I paused and asked myself what I was feeling. Of course, I was feeling fear that this could all get out of hand. The pause I took was all I needed. In the space where the "old" me would have reacted and the "new" me did not, the boy spoke up again.

"But I see that everyone else wants it quiet," he said. "I don't mind. I can be loud at recess." Who would have expected such perspective and maturity from a seven-year-old? I also learned from this experience that there is magic in remaining silent.

By having given space for connection, this boy had voiced his own preference and at the same time seen the desire of the community, and willingly offered to cooperate. This did not prevent him from time to time speaking very loudly during our lessons. After all, it was in his nature to be loud. But instead of disciplining him and haranguing him to be quiet, all I had to do was remind him of our agreement. "Adam, remember what the rest of the group requested about speaking more quietly?" I would ask, and he would willingly modulate his voice. Instead of creating a conflict between us, it became a cooperative effort.

Borrowing from the NVC movement, we used the giraffe—an animal with a large heart—as our symbol for learning how to get along together. This class taught me many lessons over the coming years. We learned to avoid labeling people (such as, "he's a bully," or "she's mean") and instead talk about what *behaviors* we liked or didn't like. We could be more honest and open in our expression. I was daily faced with the challenge of breaking *my* old habits of behavior. The children grew into it much more naturally.

However, when a new child joined our classroom, I got a reminder of how unique our class had become. In stressful situations, the new child regularly resorted to blaming, name-calling, and even lying to get through the challenges of a day. When there was a misunderstanding, it was always someone else's fault. The new child came to us believing that conflict and negative behavior was "fixed" with simply saying "Sorry." It was in such moments when I realized that in all of my years with this class, I never asked a child to apologize (although some did on occasion out of spontaneous embarrassment). Instead of apologize, I encouraged them to ask, "What can I do to make things better?" The common response was, "Promise me you won't do that again." Once the promise was given, we were finished, and everyone was vigilant to see that the offensive behavior really would not repeat itself. A negative encounter was not something to be "fixed" through an apology. It was an opportunity to discover how we could learn to live with one another with a greater sense of safety and appreciation for our personal boundaries.

This was the only group of children that gave me several endearing nicknames—that is, nicknames they could use to my face. We had become a loving and *industrious* community (This was, after all, school, and after connecting, I did teach). In some ways, we were more of a family than a schoolhouse. We had our spats and disagreements along the way, but what family doesn't?

In my last year with them, when Valentine's Day came around, the children wanted to make something special for me. They conspired with their clay modeling teacher and made the sweetest sitting giraffe about ten inches tall. The clay teacher told me about the conversation she witnessed among them.

"Let's paint hearts on the giraffe," one child said.

"If we do that," another child protested, "then Sammy will think this is only for Valentines Day. And this isn't just for now."

"If we make hearts *all* over," a third pointed out, "then he will know that we *always* love him, not just on Valentines Day."

I have that giraffe sitting on my desk as I write this. I have received their message in my heart and know it is true: by having taken the time to connect with these children, we will always love one another.

Donald Samson

29
Sometimes What it Takes is Trust

In 1972 two quite ordinary young women in Philadelphia walked out one night to pay their rent. They carried neither bag nor purse. After paying the rent, they drifted home penniless, rather obviously penniless. Yet on the dark, empty city street, they were suddenly confronted by a tall youth who held a knife to the throat of the one nearer him.

"I want money. I have to have money."

It does happen on the streets today—the pain-crazed junkie desperate for a "fix." And, having made an approach, quiet retreat becomes for him the certainty of sudden chase by alerted police with screaming sirens and flashing lights and unholstered guns. The stickup is not a business where one can turn from a poor prospect and calmly seek a more promising customer.

What should the two women do? Were either to flee, they recognized at once, the other would fall to the knife.

"I don't want to do this," the junkie said. "I don't like to hurt people. But sometimes I have to!" The knife moved closer. "And if I have to, I will now. If I don't get money, someone is going to get hurt."

"But we don't have any money!"

"I have to have money!"

They began thinking of alternatives for him. None of them would do.

"If I don't get money, you'll get hurt."

"Look," said the smaller one, chin firm over the knife, "I'll stay here with you. Let Mary go back to my apartment and get you the money."

"No way! She'll call the cops."

"No she won't! Really she won't. And I'll be here. She wouldn't call the cops while I was still here."

Still no one on the street. The three stood in an intimate little drama, knife blackened to avoid the light. A strange understanding began to grow in the young women. He really *didn't* like to do this. He really *was* miserable. He was also irrational. And more frightened, really, than they.

"Look, you come back with us. I have some money in my apartment. You come with us."

"No! Your husband will be there. Some man will be there." The jerky threat of the knife again.

"There's no one there. Honestly. The apartment is empty. Look, trust us. We'll get you the money."

"You'll call the fuzz."

"Trust us. Come on, we'll all go."

"It's a trick."

"It's no trick."

Was he weakening? His position was as futile as theirs—more futile. They simply had no money to give him there on the street. Bluster as he might, he could not make them produce what they did not have. And hurting them would not really help. He was in an impossible situation, and that terrible futility added to his crazed frustration.

"Look, trust us." She spoke to him directly, person to person—looked him in the eye, one human to another. "I live just at the corner. Come along to the apartment."

He was wavering.

"There is no one there. Trust us. Come on."

139

Slowly, knife at the ready, he began to move along the dark street with them. The young woman kept talking quietly, normally.

At the outer door, he pulled her nearer to the knife.

"Just upstairs. There's no one there. Just trust us."

Inside the foyer. Up the stairs. Key in the lock. And the other young woman took over the position under the knife while the smaller one went into her apartment and rummaged for her purse. Ten dollars. A ten-dollar bill was all the money she had. She ran back to the door, thrust it at him.

"Is that all you have?"

A sudden sinking feeling. After all this, after the appearance of trust, the seeming solution of their predicament, was he going to demand more? She had no more. And her apartment door stood open behind her.

"That's all. That's really all."

"But I only need five dollars. I don't have change."

"Take it. Take it. That's all right."

"But I only need five." His hands were shaking, his voice trembling.

"That's all right. Take it. Take it."

He looked down at the bill, back into the young woman's eyes.

"Bye," she said. "Bye now."

And he slithered down the steps and out into the night.

Dorothy T. Samuel

Adapted from *Safe Passage on City Streets* by Dorothy T. Samuel (Expanded Edition, 1991) Published by Liberty Literary Works, Providence, RI. Price: $10   Tel. 401-351-9193, E-Mail: libertyliterary@ quakerworks.net. Used with permission.

30

The Drunk Driver and the Businessman

A good twenty or so years ago I worked for the National Council on Crime and Delinquency, which was funded by large foundations interested in corrections reform. I worked as a consultant to communities in Kansas City that were adopting a whole new approach to sentencing called community corrections. Part of this involved getting victim-offender reconciliation programs set up in the city, and once they got off the ground I moved on to other community development projects. Several years later I was invited to a meeting of one of these victim-offender reconciliation programs. It was there that I met a man who was wheelchair-bound, having lost the use of his legs, and he told me his story.

He was a successful businessman and member of the Wichita community. A few years ago he had the full use of his legs. He had been crossing the street at night when a drunk driver ran him over. He managed to survive the horrible accident, but remained paralyzed for life from the waist down.

The drunk driver had his license revoked and spent about six months in prison before he was referred to the

141

victim-offender reconciliation program in its first year of operation. If he hadn't agreed to participate he would have had a much longer sentence, so with that level of coercion he chose to go on early parole under the condition that he participate in the program. Of course, for the program to work, the victim also had to participate. This businessman agreed to come to the initial mediation and meet the man who had crippled him.

The program was set up to start with an open-ended discussion and negotiation process between the offender and the victim. The goal was to take a holistic look at the situation, and find out from the two people involved what they thought would help repair the damage that was done.

In court the businessman learned that the drunk driver had had a lot of hard luck in his life. His family had all left him because of his alcoholism, and he had lost umpteen jobs for the same reason. Yet while in prison he had been forced to become clean and sober for the first time in many years, and he said he was committed to maintaining sobriety. As the dialogue continued, the businessman became convinced that the guy sincerely felt horrible about having hit him and sentenced him to a wheelchair, and that the guy really did want to make a new start of his life.

When they each finished their stories, the businessman decided to offer the drunk driver a job in his machine shop, and not just a dead-end job; it was a good job that paid a decent living wage with benefits and training and an opportunity to progress. The businessman knew that this way he could keep an eye on the man and make sure he wouldn't be harming anybody else. The offender took the job and worked hard for the businessman, eventually advancing to become a supervisor in the company. By then the two men had even become good friends.

Had they never been forced to connect like that, the guy who had the DUI would have had a very hard time. Although he was committed to remaining clean and sober, having the strike of a felony against him would have probably doomed him to repeat the cycle. It's very difficult to get a job with a felony, much less a good job, unless someone gives you a break. The businessman gave him that opportunity, and it totally turned the offender's life around, enabling him to really contribute and move ahead.

On the other end, the businessman was able to feel his power in an incredible way—not by revenge, but by being the agent of change through personally taking ownership of the situation by ensuring that the man got straightened out so no one else would have to suffer a similar accident. Though he was crippled now, what the businessman did proved to himself and the world that he was still a powerful and capable person.

I remember him saying that many people thought what he did was admirable, but it was really just a twist of perspective for him. He told me, "You can go all your life feeling like you're a victim and that someone did you horribly wrong, or you can move forward and say, 'How can I get on top of this situation and take control of it as much as I possibly can? I can't get my legs back, but what can I do to exert my power in this life I've been given?' "

Lynn Knox

31
Firing on the Rabble

During one of the many nineteenth-century riots in Paris the commander of an army detachment received orders to clear a city square by firing at the *canaille* (rabble). He commanded his soldiers to take up firing positions, their rifles leveled at the crowd, and as a ghastly silence descended, he drew his sword and shouted at the top of his lungs: "Mesdames, m'sieurs, I have orders to fire at the *canaille*. But as I see a great number of honest, respectable citizens before me, I request that they leave so that I can safely shoot the *canaille*." The square was empty in a few minutes.

Paul Watzlawick

From *Change, Principles of Problem Formation and Problem Resolution,* by Paul Watzlawick Ph.D., John H. Weakland Ch.E., and Richard Fisch M.D., p. 81. Copyright © 1974 by W. W. Norton & Company, Inc.

32
The Pit Bull

It was Summertime and my boyfriend and I were out barbecuing in our back yard. It was a warm day, so we had the backdoor open and the front door open except for the screen. Even from the backyard we could hear everything that was happening in the eclectic inner-Denver neighborhood. All the houses were single-family houses with nice yards, but they were packed in close together with a diverse mix of ethnicities.

There was only one home on the block that was a rental, owned by an absentee landlord known to rent it out to just about anybody. A month earlier he had rented it out to a small black woman who was rarely there, and she had two dogs. There were rumors in the neighborhood that one of the dogs was a pit bull that had gotten loose and chased one of the neighbors up a ladder. People were afraid of this dog and the landlord wasn't around to talk to about it.

In the middle of our barbecue I heard screaming coming from the street out front, so I ran through the house and looked out the screen door. Immediately I saw the little black woman in a face-off with a large Greek man from the family next door. He had a tire-iron raised above his head in one hand and he was screaming, "Get out of my way! I'm gonna kill your dog! If you don't let me at him I'll hit you!"

The small woman was standing in front of her dog to protect it, screaming back, "My dog didn't do anything! My dog didn't do anything!"

I watched for a second, noticing quite a few other neighbors out there saying, "Calm down, calm down." But the Greek man and the black woman were so engaged with each other that they weren't paying any attention to anything around them. I saw all this and thought, *I think I know what to do here.*

Several years earlier I had taken a training where we learned all about gaining rapport with people through physical and verbal mirroring and matching. I had used it in fairly innocuous situations and found it useful to connect with others, but I hadn't really put it to the big test. *It ought to work here*, I thought. I almost felt obligated to use it. It seemed very clear this was a situation that really needed it.

I said to my boyfriend, "Look, call the police if you need to, but I'm going in."

I ran out and stood next to the Greek fellow, facing the woman, because I didn't want to be in a face-off with a tire-iron. The man was still yelling, "Get out of my way or I'll hit you with this!"

The little woman only kept screaming back.

The two of them were fully engaged with each other, to the exclusion of everything else. I knew they weren't seeing me, so I stood right next to the man and raised my arm to match his body posture. Then I screamed at the woman just like he was, but with a different message: "Get back in your house now!" I yelled. "It's dangerous out here, get back in your house!"

It kind of broke the spell. The little woman looked at me and said, "But it's not my fault, my dog didn't do anything!"

I just screamed at her again. "Go back in your house now! It's dangerous out here!"

She did, she turned around and went back to her house.

146

Then I turned at about a ninety-degree angle to the man and I noticed his mother on the porch holding her arm. There were other neighbors gathered around her with concern, so I screamed at him, "How's your mother?!"

He looked at me for the first time and said, "I don't know!"

I started gradually lowering my voice and lowering my arm. "Let's go find out," I suggested. "Did you call the police? Did you call the ambulance?"

I kept asking him questions while lowering my arm, and as I did he lowered the tire iron. I turned back toward his house, and he turned too. I started walking back to his porch, continuing to talk as he followed me. "Let's let the authorities take care of this," I said. "I don't want to visit you in jail." We both laughed.

It turned out that his mother, who was about sixty at the time, had been outside in the front yard when the dog jumped on her and knocked her down. Her son had grabbed a tire-iron to go kill the dog and protect his mother.

When the police arrived the conflict was already defused.

Jan Prince

33
A Soft Answer

A turning point in my life came one day on a train in the suburbs of Tokyo in the middle of a drowsy spring afternoon. The old car clanking and rattling over the rails was comparatively empty—a few housewives with their kids in tow, some old folks out shopping, a couple of off-duty bartenders studying the racing form. I gazed absently at the drab houses and dusty hedgerows.

At one station the doors opened and suddenly the quiet afternoon was shattered by a man bellowing at the top of his lungs, yelling violent, obscene, incomprehensible curses. Just as the doors closed, the man, still yelling, staggered into our car. He was big, drunk, and dirty, dressed in laborer's clothing. His bulging eyes were demonic, neon red. His hair was crusted with filth. Screaming, he swung at the first person he saw, a woman holding a baby. The blow glanced off her shoulder, sending her spinning into the laps of an elderly couple. It was a miracle that the baby was unharmed.

The terrified couple jumped up and scrambled toward the other end of the car. The laborer aimed a kick at the retreating back of the old lady, but he missed and she scuttled to safety. This so enraged the drunk that he grabbed the metal pole in the center of the car and tried to wrench it out of its stanchion. I could see that one of his hands was cut and bleeding. The train lurched ahead, the passengers frozen with fear.

I stood up. At the time, I was young, in pretty good shape, was six feet tall, and weighed 225 pounds. I'd been putting in a solid eight hours of Aikido training every day for the past three years and thought I was tough. The trouble was, my martial skill was untested in actual combat. As a student of Aikido, I was not allowed to fight.

My teacher, the founder of Aikido, taught us each morning that the art was devoted to peace. "Aikido," he said again and again, "is the art of reconciliation. Whoever has the mind to fight has broken his connection with the universe. If you try to dominate other people, you are already defeated. We study how to resolve conflict, not how to start it."

I listened to his words. I tried hard. I wanted to quit fighting. I had even gone so far as to cross the street a few times to avoid the *chimpira*, the pinball punks who lounged around the train stations. They'd have been happy to test my martial ability. My forbearance exalted me. I felt both tough and holy. In my heart of hearts, however, I was dying to be a hero. I wanted a chance, an absolutely legitimate opportunity whereby I might save the innocent by destroying the guilty.

"This is it!" I said to myself as I got to my feet. "This slob, this animal, is drunk and mean and violent. People are in danger. If I don't do something fast, someone will probably get hurt."

Seeing me stand up, the drunk saw a chance to focus his rage. "Aha!" he roared. "A foreigner! You need a lesson in Japanese manners!" He punched the metal pole once to give weight to his words.

Hanging on lightly to the commuter strap overhead, I gave him a slow look of disgust and dismissal—every bit of nastiness I could summon up. I planned to take this turkey apart, but he had to be the one to move first. And I wanted him mad, because the madder he got, the more certain my victory. I pursed my lips and blew him a sneering, insolent kiss that hit him like a slap in the face. "All right!" he hollered. "You're gonna get a lesson." He gathered himself for a rush at me. He would never know what hit him.

A split second before he moved, someone shouted, "Hey!" It was ear-splitting. I remember being struck by the strangely joyous, lilting quality of it, as though you and a friend had been searching diligently for something and had suddenly stumbled upon it. "Hey!"

I wheeled to my left, the drunk spun to his right. We both stared down at a little old Japanese man. He must have been well into his seventies. He took no notice of me but beamed delightedly at the laborer, as though he had a most important, most welcome secret to share.

"C'mere," the old man said in an easy vernacular, beckoning to the drunk. "C'mere and talk with me." He waved his hand lightly. The big man followed, as if on a string. He planted his feet belligerently in front of the old gentleman, towering threateningly over him. "Talk to you," he roared above the clanking wheels. "Why the hell should I talk to you?"

The old man continued to beam at the laborer. There was not a trace of fear or resentment about him. "What'cha been drinking?" he asked lightly, his eyes sparkling with interest.

"I been drinkin' sake," the laborer bellowed back, "and it's none of your goddam business!" Flecks of spittle spattered the old man.

"Oh, that's wonderful," the old man said with delight. "Absolutely wonderful! You see, I love sake, too. Every night, me and my wife (she's seventy-six, you know), we warm up a little bottle of sake and take it out into the garden, and we sit on the old wooden bench that my grandfather's first student made for him. We watch the sun go down, and we look to see how our persimmon tree is doing. My great-grandfather planted that tree, you know, and we worry about whether it will recover from those ice storms we had last winter. Persimmons do not do well after ice storms, although I must say that ours has done rather better than I expected, especially when you consider the poor quality of the soil. Still, it is most gratifying to watch when we take our sake and go out to enjoy the evening—even when it rains!" He looked up at the laborer, eyes twinkling, happy to share his delightful information.

As he struggled to follow the intricacies of the old man's conversation, the drunk's face began to soften. His fists slowly unclenched. "Yeah," he said slowly, "I love persimmons, too…" His voice trailed off.

"Yes," said the old man, smiling, "and I'm sure you have a wonderful wife."

"No," replied the laborer. "My wife died." He hung his head. Very gently, swaying with the motion of the train, the big man began to sob. "I don't got no wife. I don't got no home. I don't got no job. I don't got no money. I don't got nowhere to go." Tears rolled down his cheeks, and a spasm of pure despair rippled through his body. Above the baggage rack a four-color ad trumpeted the virtues of suburban luxury living.

Now it was my turn. Standing there in my well-scrubbed youthful innocence, my make-this-world-safe-for-democracy righteousness, I suddenly felt dirtier than the drunk was.

Just then the train arrived at my stop. The platform was packed, and the crowd surged into the car as soon as the doors opened. Maneuvering my way out, I hear the old man cluck sympathetically. "My, my," he said with undiminished delight. "That is a very difficult predicament, indeed. Sit down here and tell me about it."

I turned my head for one last look. The laborer was sprawled like a sack on the seat, his head in the old man's lap. The old man looked down at him, all compassion and delight, one hand softly stroking the filthy, matted head.

As the train pulled away, I sat down on the bench. What I had wanted to do with muscle and meanness had been accomplished with a few kind words. I had seen Aikido tried in combat, and the essence of it was love, as the founder had said. I would have to practice the art with an entirely different spirit. It would be a long time before I could speak about the resolution of conflict.

Terry Dobson

From "Epilogue: A Soft Answer," in *Safe and Alive,* by Terry Dobson, pp. 128-132. Copyright © 1982 by Terry Dobson. Used by permission of Jeremy P. Tarcher, an imprint of Penguin Group (USA) Inc.

34
The Homicidal Patient in the Elevator

While working at a psychiatric hospital late at night, I found myself suddenly trapped in a dangerous situation. A homicidal patient had hidden himself in an elevator and I did not see him until after I had stepped in and slammed the door shut. It locked automatically and, although I had a key to unlock it, I did not have the time needed to escape.

The homicidal patient serenely stated, "I've been waiting for you to make the evening rounds. Every one is down at the other end of the ward and I am going to kill you."

My statement was just as simple, "Well, are you going to do the slaughter right there... or over there?"

The patient looked at the first spot I had chosen and then at the second. As he did this, I opened the door and said, "Of course, there is a chair over there that you could sit in afterwards... that is true you know. And at the same time there is a chair down there." And as I spoke, I began walking. "And there is another chair over there and another spot at the other end of the corridor." The patient walked along with me, looking at each spot that he could pick for my demise. Eventually we arrived at the station where the attendants were gathered.

Milton H. Erickson

Story taken from a lecture by Milton H. Erickson, San Francisco, September 11, 1959. Audio Recording No. CD/ EMH.59.9.11 (Phoenix, AZ: Milton H. Erickson Foundation Archives).

NOTE FROM MARK ANDREAS: Rather than contradict or disagree with what the patient said, Erickson's artful response accepted the patient's plan to kill him, simply distracting the patient with the question of which would be the best spot to do the murder. Asking a question is a very effective means of distraction, especially when the question is apparently relevant to the person's goals. Most people have been conditioned socially that when a question is asked, it should be thought about and answered. This technique is used by some sales people, who are taught to use a complex series of questions to maintain control in a conversation. If the sales person is really good at what he does, he will ask relevant questions and actually arrive at a product that the buyer really wants.

35
Making Decisions for Other People

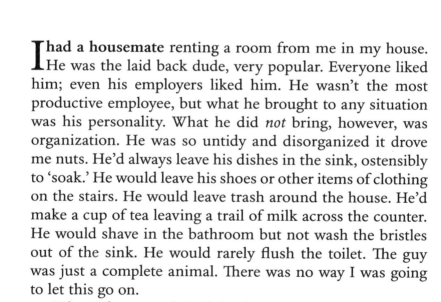

I had a housemate renting a room from me in my house. He was the laid back dude, very popular. Everyone liked him; even his employers liked him. He wasn't the most productive employee, but what he brought to any situation was his personality. What he did *not* bring, however, was organization. He was so untidy and disorganized it drove me nuts. He'd always leave his dishes in the sink, ostensibly to 'soak.' He would leave his shoes or other items of clothing on the stairs. He would leave trash around the house. He'd make a cup of tea leaving a trail of milk across the counter. He would shave in the bathroom but not wash the bristles out of the sink. He would rarely flush the toilet. The guy was just a complete animal. There was no way I was going to let this go on.

When I first complained that he was not cleaning up after himself. He would say, "Yeah, yeah, yeah, I know. Don't worry about it," and he wouldn't change a bit. I started getting more and more uncomfortable with what was going on, and a bit angry. Pretty soon he was doing everything he could to avoid me and my anger, while doing *nothing* to change his behavior. In fact it escalated. His behavior got worse as I got angrier. Now he didn't even want to *think* about any of the issues that angered me, so he put them completely out of his mind.

I soon found out that getting upset with him wasn't going to work. Putting pressure on him to change just made me into the nagging housemate and created greater antagonism. Our communication broke down, making the situation get worse. And not only that, but now I had him pointing out *my* faults, "Well you didn't do such and such… Well you left the front door open…" Instead of my roommate saying, "OK, I'll change my behavior," it became a game of tit for tat. I'd ask him to clean something up, and he'd point out one of my faults. It was not a good situation.

Eventually I realized that I was making decisions about what *he* should do, but I wasn't making decisions about what *I* could do. So I stopped making decisions about how my roommate should behave. Instead I started making decisions only about how *I* would behave, which looked like this: If I found his dirty dishes left in the sink, I put them in his bed. Not on the bed, *in* his bed under the covers. If I found his stuff on the stairs, then I decided to do what I liked with it, like putting it in the trash for example.

After my first day of this new approach, my roommate came home and couldn't find his shoes.

"Have you seen my shoes?" he asked.

"Yes," I said.

"Well, where are they?"

"They're in the trash."

"What are they doing in the trash?"

"I put them there."

"What did you do that for?"

"I did it because they were in my way." What I was sure *not* to say was, "because *you* left them on the stairs." I made sure to delete him out of the transaction. The shoes were on the stairs in my way, so I put them out of my way, which happened to be in the trash.

"You shouldn't have done that!" he said.

"That wasn't your decision to make," I said. "You weren't the one picking them up off the stairs. I was there, so I made the decision. If you want to make the decision where they go, then you can pick them up off the stairs. I'm not going to figure out where you would put them. I only make decisions for me."

It kind of seemed reasonable.

The garbage had already been collected that day, so his shoes were gone. He was already a bit confused by this whole thing when he couldn't find his coffee mug. I could see him start to get pissed off.

"Have you seen my coffee mug?" he asked suspiciously.

"Yes, I put it in the trash with your shoes."

"What did you do *that* for?!"

"It was in the sink in my way when I wanted to wash my dishes."

"You could have just put it on the side!"

"There you go again. You see, you weren't here to make that decision. I was, and I made a decision about what to do with the coffee mug. When you handle the coffee mug, *you* can decide what to do with it. I handle it; I decide what to do with it. What I decided to do was throw it away."

"But that's not fair."

"That's right," I agreed.

Then he said, "How would you behave if I started throwing your stuff away?"

"You start throwing my stuff away and you're going to find yourself homeless," I replied. "I understand now that when I make the rules for you and try to decide things for you it just upsets you, so I'm no longer going to do that. I'm just going to decide what *I* do."

"But that doesn't seem very fair," he said.

"That's exactly right. It's *not* fair. But if you're going to leave stuff around for me to make decisions about, then you can't choose what decisions I make. You decide for you, I decide for me."

After that everything changed. He *completely* changed his behavior. It really worked, and we're still friends now— much better friends because of it.

And one of the interesting things is, the impact on his behavior went beyond just tidying up after himself. Rather than throwing caution to the wind with an attitude of, "well nothing really matters," he actually became much more decisive in general in his life. It was quite amazing what that simple shift in my perspective was able to do.

Andrew T. Austin

36
Two Tribes

I was asked to mediate between two tribes in Nigeria. These tribes had had enormous violence going on between them for the previous year. In fact, one fourth of their population was killed, one hundred out of four hundred people dead, in one year.

Seeing this violence, a colleague of mine who lives in Nigeria worked hard to get the chiefs on both sides to agree to meet with me to see if we could resolve the conflict. After much effort, he finally got them to agree.

As we were walking into the session, my colleague whispered to me: "Be prepared for a little bit of tension, Marshall. Three of the people in the room know that the person who killed their child is in that room."

Well, it was very tense at first. There had been so much violence between these two groups, and it was the first time they had really sat down together.

I started with the question I frequently start conflict resolution sessions with, to focus on people's needs. I said to both sides: "I'd like whoever would like to speak first to say what your needs are in this situation. After everyone understands the needs of everyone else, then we'll move to finding some ways of meeting the needs."

Unfortunately, they didn't have a literacy of needs—they only knew how to tell me what was wrong with the other side. Instead of responding to my question, the chief from one side looked across the table and said, "You people are murderers," and the other side responded: "You've been trying to dominate us. We're not going to tolerate it anymore!" We had more tension after two sentences than we had when it began.

Obviously, just getting people together to communicate doesn't help, unless they know how to communicate in a way that connects them as human beings. My job was to loan them the ability to sense needs behind whatever is being expressed.

I turned to the chief who had said, "You people are murderers," and guessed, "Chief, do you have a need for safety, and to be sure that whatever conflicts are going on will be resolved by some means other than violence?" The chief immediately said to me, "Of course, of course that's what I'm saying!" Well, of course he didn't say that. He said that the other person was a murderer, and made a judgment rather than express his needs. However, we had his needs out on the table so I turned to a chief from the other side and said, "Chief, would you please reflect back what he said his needs were?"

The chief responded to this man by asking in a very hostile way, "Then why did you kill my son?"

That started an uproar between the two groups. After things calmed down, I said: "Chief, we'll deal with your reaction to his needs later, but at the moment I suggest that you just hear his needs. Could you tell me back what he said his needs were?" He couldn't do it. He was so emotionally involved in this situation and in his judgments of the other person that he didn't hear what the other person's needs were. I repeated the needs as I heard them and said: "Chief, I heard the other chief saying that he has a need for safety.

He has a need to feel secure, that no matter what conflicts are present, they'll be resolved in some way other than by violence. Could you just reflect back what that need is, so that I'm sure everybody's communicating?" He couldn't do it. I had to repeat it two or three times before he could hear the other person's needs.

I reversed the process and said to the second chief: "I thank you for hearing that he has this need for security. Now I'd like to hear what your needs are in this." He said: "They have been trying to dominate us. They are a dominating group of people. They think they're better than everybody." Once again, this started a fight with the other side. I had to interrupt and say, "Excuse me, excuse me." After the group settled, I went back to trying to sense the needs behind his statement that the other side was dominating.

I asked: "Chief, is your need behind that statement a need for equality? You really need to feel that you're being treated equally in this community?" And he said, "Yes, of course!"

Now again, the job was to get the chief on the other side to hear, which wasn't easy. It took three or four repetitions before I could get the chief on the other side just to see the need that this human being was expressing. Finally the chief was able to hear the other chief saying he had a need for equality.

After I spent this much time getting both sides to express their needs and to hear each other's needs (this took close to two hours), another chief who hadn't spoken jumped to his feet, looked at me and said something very intensely. I didn't speak his language, so I was very curious what he was trying to express to me with such intensity, and eagerly awaited the translation. I was very touched when the translator said: "The chief says we cannot learn this way of communicating in one day. And he says, if we know how to communicate this way, we don't have to kill each other."

I said to the translator: "Tell the chief I am very grateful that he sees what can happen when we hear each other's

161

needs. Tell him that today my objective was to help resolve the conflict peacefully to everyone's satisfaction, and I was hoping that people could see the value in this way of communicating. Tell him that if people on both sides would like, we will be glad to train people within each tribe to communicate this way, so that future conflicts could be resolved this way rather than through violence."

That chief wanted to be one of the members to be trained, and in fact before I left that day, we had members from both tribes eager to learn this process that would allow everyone to hear needs behind whatever message was being expressed. I am happy to report that the war between the tribes ended that day.

Marshall Rosenberg

From *We Can Work it Out,* by Dr. Marshall B. Rosenberg, 2005, pp. 12-14. Published by PuddleDancer Press. Reprinted with permission. For more information visit www.CNC.org and www.NonviolentCommunication. com

37
The Wall

I was co-leading a backpacking expedition of eight "at risk" adolescent boys in a wilderness therapy program in Colorado. It was the middle of our trip in Rocky Mountain National Park and they had just finished a weekend of therapy. The therapists had left the field that morning and we started out on our six-mile hike to our next camp. The morning sun slanted through the thinning pines, illuminating the steep slopes of the valley as we ascended through the cliffs onto a plateau above tree line.

We had only been underway ten minutes when one of the guys started lagging behind.

"Hold on up there!" I shouted to the kids in front, and they waited for Travis to catch up.

"We need to keep the group together," I said when Travis caught up with the rest of the bunch.

One of the other boys came back to talk to him. Jordan was a super athlete—a competitive skier with the strong muscular build of a wrestler. Frustration showed in his eyes to be slowed down this early in the day. "Hey Travis," Jordan said, "Will you walk up front so we can keep the group together? I don't like stopping and starting all the time."

Travis looked at the ground, also frustrated. He didn't respond.

"Travis, will you go to the front?!"

"Travis," I asked, "Will you respond to Jordan's request?"

He just shook his head.

"Can you at least tell Jordan you need space right now?"

Nothing.

"God damn it!" Jordan cursed.

After a bit more trying it was clear that Travis wasn't going to engage.

"Jordan, he's obviously not in a space to talk about it right now. I appreciate you asking him respectfully and I wish he could respect you by responding. That's clearly not going to happen right now, so let's keep hiking."

"Fuck! Why won't you just go to the fucking front?!" Jordan stormed to the front of the trail. "It's bitches like you that make this take all day. I just want to get to fucking camp!"

In minutes the group was spread out again and we had to stop for Travis a second time. Tensions were rising with Jordan and some of the other boys, and the cursing and angry comments increased.

My co-leader Molly said, "Jordan, I agree with you that Travis is acting inappropriately right now, and that's no reason for you to do the same by calling him names behind his back."

But when we got going again the sideways remarks continued.

"It looks to me like you guys want to have Group," I said. A "Group" was any time the ten of us sat down together to talk about what was up for any of us. We might talk about frustrations or problems, new learnings, things we appreciate, or things we want to improve upon.

"No, you've gotta be kidding," Jordan said.

"Well, you obviously have a lot to say, so let's have a group. What do you think Molly? How about up on the plateau behind those rocks."

"I think that sounds like an excellent plan."

"You've gotta be kidding," Jordan repeated, shaking his head. "I'm not having Group."

At the top of the plateau the rest of the kids stopped, but Jordan kept powering ahead. "Have a nice Group," he said. "I'll see you in camp."

Molly stayed with the seven kids while I dropped my pack and ran after Jordan as he disappeared over a hill. I jogged past him and stood in front of him, blocking his way forward on the trail. My heart was pounding from more than just the jog. I remembered back to a few weeks earlier when he destroyed several aspen saplings in a rage because of what he saw as an unjust consequence.

"We need to keep the group together, Jordan." I said.

"I'm not going back there. I'll see you at fucking camp." He took one step off the path and I mirrored his movement to block his way forward. Then he stepped off in the other direction and I mirrored him again.

"We can't let you go on alone, Jordan. If something happens to you we're responsible."

"Nothing will happen."

"We can't know that."

"Will you restrain me?"

"Maybe," I said. What he didn't know was that we weren't allowed to restrain a kid unless two people were present, and with a kid Jordan's build we probably wouldn't even try a two-person take down.

"Jordan, I don't want to get into a struggle with you." I kept talking, hoping to keep him from trying to solve his problem physically. "I just want to keep the group together and safe. Let's go back, you can leave your pack here and we'll pick it up when we continue hiking."

"If I go back there now I'll look like an idiot."

"I think the group might appreciate you coming back."

165

Jordan shook his head.

"You're kind of stuck, aren't you? Go forward and you have to deal with me, go back and you'll feel like you lost."

"Yep." He bit off the word sharply, still paused in indecision with one foot off the trail. I waited for a bit, but nothing changed, so I decided to try a different tack.

"I can see you're pretty upset," I said. "What's going on for you right now?"

"I want to get to fucking camp."

"Jordan, I know you want to get to camp, but there's more to it than that. What's triggering you so much about this."

He just shook his head.

"I'd really like to know what's going on, but I feel like you've got this big wall up."

"Yep," he said with a defiant glint in his eye. "I'm balancing on that wall right now and I don't know which way I'll fall."

"Which way would you like to fall?

"I think I'll just keep walking until it gets thinner and thinner and I'll be forced to fall."

I took a breath. Jordan was a smart kid. We could trade metaphors all day without making any progress. Our conversation lapsed into silence as we stood there in a standoff. I was out of ideas.

I glanced down at the gold cross hanging on a chain around his neck. Well, if we were going to stand here for a while I might as well learn something.

"Where'd you get that cross?" I asked.

"My uncle gave it to me. He got it on a trip to Spain. It's real gold."

"That's cool. My dad used to bring me back old coins when he went traveling."

"Were they gold?"

"He found a gold coin on an airplane once. It was about that big," I indicated a circle with my finger and thumb. "But he found the owner. It was probably worth about fifty bucks. The ones he brought back to me were silver though. They were old Greek coins. One has the Pegasus on it—the flying horse. They're not even round; they were made so long ago they're all lopsided, and sometimes the printed circle goes off the edge of the coin. They're pretty neat."

Jordan shifted his weight. "Alright, I'll go back but I'm not saying anything."

"That's fine. You can leave your backpack here if you want."

"I'll just leave it on."

"OK."

Jordan turned back down the trail and I followed him back to the group.

It wasn't any clever strategy that worked. By simply connecting with him in a different realm, I was no longer in opposition to him. Instead I was another person who had received something special from a family member. That connection invited him away from the wall where there were no good solutions.

Mark Andreas

38
Bar Fight

I was in a bar once to have a meeting with my friend Richard Bandler. It was the type of place that is typically called a "biker bar," meaning that it was full of pretty rough and unsavory characters. This is not the type of place that I generally liked to hang out, but Richard liked it and wanted to meet there.

We started talking, and pretty soon these two large men came in. They were drunk, angry, violent, and wanted to pick on somebody. I guess they could tell that I didn't really belong in a place like that, because pretty soon they started shouting obscenities at me and Bandler, calling us "queers," and telling us to get out of the bar.

My first strategy was to attempt to politely ignore them, which, of course, did not work. It wasn't long before one of the guys was bumping my arm and spilling my drink. So, I decided to try to be friendly. I looked over at them and smiled.

"What are you looking at?" One of them asked. When I averted my gaze, the other one said, "Look at me while I'm talking to you."

Things were getting pretty bad, and to my surprise, I was getting angry. Fortunately I realized that following this normal pattern of response would only serve to escalate the situation. So, I thought of a different way to respond. I decided to try to discover and address their positive intention behind messing with us. In an even and steady voice, I said to the man nearest me, "You know, I don't really think that you believe we are homosexuals. As you can clearly see, I am wearing a wedding ring. I think that you have a different intention." At this point, the fellow blurted out, "Yeah, we want to fight!"

Now I know that some of you readers are probably sarcastically thinking,

"Wow, Robert, what incredible progress." On the other hand, I had begun to engage in the beginning of a conversation, so that provided an opening for progress.

Seizing the opportunity, I responded, "I understand that, but it really wouldn't be much of a fight. First of all, I don't want to fight, so you wouldn't get much out of me. Besides, there are two of you, and you're each twice my size. What kind of fight would that be?"

At this point, the second fellow (who must have been the "brains" of the two) said, "No. It's a fair fight; we're drunk." Turning to look the man squarely in the eyes, I said, "Don't you think that would be just like a father coming home and beating the crap out of his fourteen year old son, and saying that it was "fair" because the father is drunk?" I thought this was most likely just what happened to this man over and over again when he was fourteen.

Confronted with this way of viewing a fight with us, the two men could no longer continue to be abusive to us. Eventually they went and bothered someone else (a karate expert who took them outside and whipped them soundly).

Robert Dilts

From *Sleight of Mouth: The Magic of Conversational Belief Change*, by Robert Dilts, pp. 57-58. Copyright © 1999 by Meta Publications, Capitola, CA. Used with Permission.

39
Excuse Me!

About three weeks ago I went to the dollar store to get some cheap paper products like Kleenex and paper towels for my work. When I was standing in the checkout line there were two Mexican guys in front of me bantering lightly and joking around with each other. I guessed they were in their twenties. One of them was big, probably six feet tall and overweight by 30 or more pounds. The other guy was probably five nine and about 170 pounds. He reached around his friend to tap him on the far shoulder, revealing a mosaic of tattoos on his hand. His neck and other hand were similarly decorated. His friend glanced the wrong way, looking at me before hitting the tattooed man playfully. They looked very similar, so I guessed they were brothers.

In the other line right next to us was a single guy in his late twenties or mid thirties. He had on a long black overcoat that covered his knees. He had dark hair and skin, so I guessed he was also Mexican.

The brothers and the single man left the store, and soon I paid for my stuff and carried it outside. I walked through the parking lot and just as I reached my car I heard a commotion a little farther down the lot. I turned to see that a car had pulled out of its parking space right in front of a grey van. Everyone had slammed on their brakes and the vehicles avoided a collision, but as soon as the cars jerked to a halt the doors on the van flew open and the two brothers I'd seen in the store jumped out, enraged. The driver of the other car jumped out just as quickly—he was the single man with the long coat. All three ran toward each other, yelling and cursing. They stopped within three feet of each other, shouting in each other's faces.

"I was just looking where I wanted to go!" The single man yelled back at the brothers, holding his ground. He had obviously pulled out in front of the van, but no damage had been done.

I got in my car as the shouting continued. The first thing I thought was, *Men are so stupid. Why do they have to resort to violence over something so small?* Then I told myself, *Just get out of here. Don't even look.*

I didn't want to give any of my energy to watching the altercation, and I also wanted to stay safe. I pictured their coats and tattoos, thinking, *They could have guns or knives; this could really escalate.*

Then as I pulled out to leave, a part of me said, *No. This was just an accident.*

I pulled back in my parking space and reversed the other way, driving toward the argument. I didn't know what I was going to say, I just kept thinking, *This is an accident. We have to be able to cope with that on a day-to-day basis without someone getting killed over it.*

I pulled up alongside the three men and rolled down my window. The single man and the brothers were still posturing and shouting—standing uncomfortably close to each other. I was politely waiting to have my turn to speak and everyone just kept on shouting and shouting.

I remember thinking. *Everyone here is really afraid.* I could feel it. Even though what was being shown was the violence and anger, underneath that was real fear. I could sense it in all three of them, but especially in the single man.

"There's only one of me against two of you!" He shouted in between the cussing.

After about thirty seconds or so, I just said, "Excuse me! I have something to say."

And they actually stopped and turned to me, as if I'd come out of nowhere. I said, "I pray that you will find a way to cope with something that was obviously an accident, in a way that doesn't resort to violence."

They continued to look at me for a few seconds and then without a word they got back in their cars. It diffused just like that. It was kind of surreal.

When it was over I noticed probably three other people who were just standing at their cars watching, but not saying anything or doing anything. I remember the feeling in my heart; it was like my heart was sending out a prayer that everyone would make it home safely, returning to their families without carrying this random violence that can just occur at any time.

I looked in my rearview mirror as I pulled away, and I saw the car and the van drive away too.

Jean Brisson

40
Fixing the Dog

My friend John had just finished consulting with a large company, and the CEO was walking him to the elevator as he was leaving. As they waited for the elevator to arrive, the CEO asked John, "I wonder if you could give some advice on another issue? There's a sales representative from another company who we have to deal with frequently, and he's beginning to be a real problem. His behavior is very close to sexual harassment of our female employees— lewd comments, occasional inappropriate touching... You know the type."

Just as John was about to answer, the elevator doors opened and a man stepped out.

"That's him," the CEO whispered before offering a brief introduction. At that moment, an attractive secretary walked by in the hall. The sales rep. leered and made an inappropriate comment to her.

John smiled and said, "Well I've really got to be going. I need to take my dog to the vet..." He made direct eye contact with the sales rep, saying, "My dog's a misbehaving male trying to mount all the females in the neighborhood. He hasn't changed, so it's time to have him snipped off!"

According to the CEO, the sales rep's behavior changed from then on. John told me this story as an example of how metaphor can be the most respectful form of communication. His metaphor of fixing the dog avoided confrontation, getting the message across without anybody losing face.

Tom Best

41
I Can't Believe I Heard You Right

We were imprisoned in "Stalag IX B." Stalag was a contraction of the German word Stammlager (prison camp). ... There were approximately 6500 POW's incarcerated there, and over 3000 of them were Americans, some held captive since early in the war.... Most of the barracks were of the type I had been assigned to, plain wooden shacks, about eighteen of them. Others were old, crumbling red brick buildings. The GIs were crammed into them, as many as 85 to 160 men in 400 square feet. ... The little food we received each day was more a teaser than real nourishment. After this tiny meal I actually felt hungrier than I had before eating it because it was really nothing more than a reminder of the meal I had missed....

While lying on my bunk in silent thought, my reveries were suddenly interrupted. A soldier in an American uniform with corporal's stripes whom I did not recognize approached me. He was a little taller than I and I immediately discerned a designing expression on his countenance. I wondered what he was doing in our barrack since no NCO's were stationed there. I thought perhaps he was a "dealer" who wanted to trade. I could tell at once I did not like him.

"I am from another barrack," he began, "and I was one of the guys who did not get any bread at all." He hesitated and then said, "I'm very hungry."

I looked at him blankly. We were all very hungry. I had taken one bite of my bread, and to savor its flavor and extend my meal, I was chewing it slowly but holding a half slice of bread in my hands. Maybe the soldier had already eaten his bread; maybe he was double-dipping in our barrack after being fed in his. We had no policy regarding soldiers from other barracks. The soldier looked at the slice of bread in my hands. "I want half of your bread," he said, "and if you do not give it to me, I'll tell the Germans you are a German Jew."*

This was so unexpected, so cruel, and so violent I could not believe he had actually said what I thought I had heard.

"You'll do what?" I spluttered.

"Just don't make any fuss," the soldier said, "and give me half of your bread—or else."

I was initially panic-stricken. Not so much over the possible loss of my bread, or that he would betray me to the Germans, but pure and simple, it was the feeling of being face to face with the enemy. For a good part of my life I had harbored a sense of shame for not taking on those tormentors at *Landschulheim*** who had teased me for being circumcised, and I had been left with a residual gnawing fear and humiliation, even afraid to express myself. I placed the remainder of my slice of bread in my pocket, preparing for a fight. This time I was more than ready to take on this enemy without fear or hesitation, not only to protect myself, but also to make up for all my prior sense of shame. This was my old enemy, and my first impulse was to hit him in his filthy mouth and then, if necessary, to call on my friend Warren.

---

*Beier was from a German Jewish family. He escaped to the United States where he joined the American Army, returning to Germany as a soldier to fight the Nazis, and was taken prisoner by the Germans

***Landschulheim* is German for "a country house used for school classes."

Then I had a change of heart, and I experienced an entirely different emotion. I suddenly felt terribly sorry for this poor asshole, as I realized what the hunger and separation from home had done to him. This thought prevailed for a second.

"I can't believe I heard you right," I said. "You sure look like a decent fellow. I know that hunger can make beasts out of all of us—but so soon?"

My response was rational, even somewhat comic, and I felt good about it. (I obviously had caught him by surprise.) I felt pleased I had not succumbed to panic or given in to his demand. For some reason it actually helped the soldier regain his humanity. He turned without another word and left the barrack, and I never saw him again.

Ernst Beier

NOTE FROM MARK ANDREAS: There is another fantastic account of conflict resolution from Ernst Beier's experience as a POW that was regrettably too long to print here. In chapter thirteen of his book, you will find his account of being called to meet with a Gestapo colonel nick-named Dr. Death by the prisoners, due to the fact that no prisoner had yet returned alive from a "meeting" with the Doctor. Through his love of *Faust,* Ernst creates a tenuous connection with the colonel by reciting Goethe's poetry. From there the two men begin a long "duel" of words through the metaphorical landscape of *Faust,* with which both of them strongly identify—a duel in which Ernst must prove to the Doctor that he is worthy of keeping his life.

42
Not Worth Your Time

In the 1960's I worked for Job Corps as a supervisor in a program that worked with young men off the street, training them in human relations and communication skills. We did this through encounter groups that ran from three to six hours a day. These young men got after each other. I would never run a white middle-class group the way I ran these groups. I really had to get in there with them and get after it. I learned a lot about ethnic diversity and human behavior. We did fantastic stuff.

A position opened up, and I was told I should hire a particular fellow named Gene who was sent to me. In hiring, we were looking for people who were unusually open and who could stand some confrontation and give it back, and do it in a positive and growth-promoting way. When Gene came in, it took me about three minutes to know this wasn't going to work. He was way too rigid, he didn't have the background we were looking for, and his personality was frankly abrasive to me. After I talked with him I said, as kindly as I could, "Gene, I just don't think you're a good fit for this position." After he left, for whatever reason, my supervisor told me I was going to hire Gene, period, or I could forfeit my own job. I reluctantly hired the man.

Now, two or three years later it was time for me to go back to graduate school to get the credentials I wanted in order to go into the mental health field. So I stepped down from my position. Gene, who I'd been coerced into hiring, had left my program and moved up the administrative chain into a manager position of the basic education program. Ironically this was the program I shifted to in order to have part-time work as a dormitory counselor to help pay for school. I ended up working for *him*!

Now I was going to school full time and working in the evenings and weekends. It was just what the current director of the Job Corps center had done when he had gone through school. But not long after I started in my new position, a man under Gene told me, "You can't work this job while going to school full time, Steve."

I knew this guy, and we had no problem with each other. I said, "This isn't coming from you, is it?" He just looked at me, so I said, "I want to tell you that if necessary I'll aggrieve this all the way to the top. You know as well as I do, that the present director of Job Corps did the same thing I'm doing. Why is it all of a sudden not all right for me?"

He knew I was right, so he took the news back that I'd fight it if I had to.

I was really angry, *really* upset. Here I was in a program that I'd just started and half way through the first term someone was challenging me on something that shouldn't have been an issue. I had six kids at home; I couldn't afford not to work. For about a week I went around making myself thoroughly miserable. I had headaches at night, I was yelling at my kids, and I'd grumble about unrelated things. My wife looked at me and said, "What the heck's going on with you?" Of course I told her, and she said, "It's not your fault." I apologized for acting like such a jerk, but knowing that it wasn't my fault just didn't help.

One day I was walking on campus, grumbling to myself as usual, saying things like, "That SOB, I'm ready to take him on and beat the crap out of him; to hell if he's bigger than I am!" I was ready to do anything just to do something. I was *so* angry, which is *not* characteristic of me. Usually I handle things much cooler than that—I can see a situation from perspective and carefully decide what to do. This was different. As I worked myself up, suddenly there was a part of myself, like a voice in my head, that said, *So why are you making yourself so miserable? This is really not doing you much good.*

Well that SOB deserves it, I replied, *He's done this and that and blah, blah blah...*

Well, is he worth making you this miserable?

Of course not! He's not worth... He's not... I must have paused in the middle of the sidewalk as I realized, *My good grief he's really not worth it. Wow, what have I been doing to myself?!*

As I'm standing there having this conversation in my head, I'm sure the young men walking by were looking at me, thinking, *What is that dude over there doing?* I must have looked strange—totally oblivious to the people around me. I had to work this out.

I really need to let this drop right here, right now, I realized. *I'll do what I need to do to take care of myself, and move on.* That's what I decided, and I felt a kind of completion after going through this inner process.

The next thing I did was walk through the central administration area for the dormitories, and walking toward me from the other end of the hallway was none other than Gene. The interesting thing was that now I just saw him as a big, kind of dumb guy who was unfortunately involved with me and he was going to lose. Somehow, somewhere, I knew, *I'm going to be OK.* I just walked by him and said, "Hi Gene, how're you doing?" and walked on.

I swear he must have turned around and stared at me, because previously interactions between us had always been very tense. Now that tension was gone in me. He must have been *very* confused about what was happening, and yet all I'd done was resolve the conflict within myself, which had really been the whole source of my misery. Blaming and giving so much energy to Gene had done nothing to improve my life.

Now that's not the end of the story. The more interesting part to me, and I can't prove any of this, is that when I let go, it allowed other things to happen. I wasn't the only person Gene was messing with. He was also harassing women under his supervision, and he had actually stolen property from the company running the Job Corps center. All of this suddenly emerged, and it began almost the moment I let go. Within a month he was fired. I believe that somehow I was keeping him there with my negative attachment. When I let that go cleanly, it was like he suddenly had no place to hide.

Steve Watson

43
Billy and the Beagles

I met Billy when he was 7 years old. I had taken a graduate internship working as a therapist at a special school for children who were both emotionally disturbed and learning disabled. Each classroom was limited to 6 students with both a teacher and a teaching assistant, and the school had its own full-time crisis team located right within the school. Billy was in the second grade. He had ADHD and a reading disorder. He also had good reason to be emotionally disturbed.

When Billy was 5 years old he was waiting in the car with his pet beagle Barney. His father had gone into the store to rob it. The storeowner had a gun and chased after Billy's father, shooting him on the sidewalk while Billy watched from the car window. Barney the beagle was barking and so protective that when the police and paramedics arrived, the dog would not let them in the car. Fortunately, Billy's grandmother lived nearby and was informed by a neighbor who witnessed the crime. She rushed to the scene and took Billy and Barney home with her. Billy's mother was already in prison serving time for drug dealing, so Billy's grandmother took custody of Billy.

Before his father's murder he had been a likable, talkative little boy who enjoyed the company of others, but after that day Billy no longer spoke. Billy started doing lots of bizarre things. He would bark at his teacher and hide under his desk, refusing to come out. He would attack other children and bite people. The public school he attended at the time deemed him a risk to others and said they could not provide for his needs. Billy suffered from nightmares and stopped eating. He was diagnosed with Selective Mutism and PTSD. Finally he ended up at the "special school," and had been there 2 years when I met him.

Billy's therapist brought me into the classroom to introduce me. "Billy, this is Mrs. Caiton. She's going to be coming to see you while I have my baby."

"Hello Billy," I said in my kindest voice. Billy growled back and refused to look at me. Over the next several weeks I visited Billy during all the sessions his therapist had with him—mostly play and art therapy. In addition to drawing, I noticed that Billy especially loved puppets, so I put in a special order for a puppet that I wanted to use with Billy. It was a beagle.

The day the puppet arrived I brought it to Billy's classroom during his therapy time. I had it on my hand behind my back and told Billy I had someone special who wanted to meet him. Then I pulled out the beagle puppet. He squealed with delight.

"This is Little Barney," I said. "He wants to be your friend. He's a very gentle doggy who NEVER BITES ANYONE. You can give him a little pat on his head if you want." Billy smiled at me and gently patted Little Barney on the head.

Billy's therapist went on maternity leave and, under supervision, I continued my work with Billy. Every time I went to Billy's classroom to get him, I would bring Little Barney with me. Billy finally trusted me enough to let me take him to my office, "where Little Barney lived." We would sit on the floor together and draw. Billy always chose a large black marker and would furiously scribble deep black marks on the page. Following his lead, I would scribble the same way using the same kind of black marker.

As the days progressed, I would spend some of the time scribbling with Billy on the page and then drawing little flowers in one corner of the page in bright colors. Each day, with each drawing, the flowers took over more and more of the page.

Then, on the two-year anniversary of Billy's father's death, I got a call from Billy's teacher. "Billy's having an episode. The crisis team has cleared the classroom. Can you come down right away?" I rushed to his classroom. Billy was under his desk growling furiously at the crisis team members who were trying to calm him. I got down on my hands and knees mirroring Billy's posture, facing him. He growled at me. I growled back…louder. He started to giggle. I started to giggle and then the room was filled with laughter. I said, "Billy, do you want to visit Little Barney at my office? He's worried about you!" Billy nodded his head in agreement and held my hand as we walked down the hall.

Billy started his usual black scribble picture, furiously covering his page. I drew a picture of flowers in a garden with smiley faces, and a big sun in one corner. I drew a little beagle with a larger beagle playing in the garden. Billy tapped his finger on my picture and then shrugged his shoulders, puzzled, as if to ask why I hadn't drawn a picture like his. On the top of the page I printed, "To Billy, We All Love You." Then I told him a story.

"Billy," I said. "Sometimes dark storms can happen in life that can be scary, kind of like your picture." I pointed to it. He nodded his head in agreement. "But storms never last forever. The sun ALWAYS comes out when the storm is over. These flowers are like all the people in your life that love you. They are a beautiful happy garden together. They are there to keep you safe and make you smile, like all of us here at school. This picture is for you."

Billy looked at me with tears welling up in his big brown eyes. "Thank you," he said in a whisper of a voice. He reached out his arms to me as he started to sob. My supervisor heard the crying and knocked, opening the office door. I motioned to her to call Billy's grandmother while Billy continued to cry in my arms. She smiled, nodded her head and left the room.

When Billy's grandmother arrived along with his dog Barney, Billy was still crying. Together we comforted Billy until he finally stopped crying. Two hours had passed. When he was calm I asked him, "Billy, how are you doing?"

"I'm HUNGRY!" he said in a bold voice.

"Billy, you can have whatever you want to eat child!" his grandmother said, hugging him close. Billy patted Little Barney on the head and put him on the shelf. "Night, night Little Barney. I love you." The two walked out the door with Barney the beagle on his leash. It was my turn to cry.

Anonymous

44
Taxi Driver

I was working very hard. I had just come out of a monastery and I had borrowed about $1,500 to continue school. Weekdays I went to class during the day. Then from 6:00 p.m. until 1:00 a.m. I worked at a psychiatric hospital doing my residency. On Friday and Saturday night I drove a cab in New York City to earn some money.

On one of these Saturday nights I picked up the cab in Brooklyn from the Circle Cab Company and drove over to Manhattan where it was easiest to make the most money. It was 1966, and back then the city was pretty close to a segregationist war. Blacks had been so overlooked by political policy and mainstream society that groups like the black panthers were doing their best to segregate portions of Harlem and Brooklyn, so that it was dangerous for a white person to even be in the street in those parts.

I knew all of that because I had run a storefront in Harlem when I was still in the monastery. I was brotha' Frank, and my priest's collar had been the best sign of exception I could have asked for, but even so it had been dangerous. Now, driving the cab, I was lacking even that sign of neutrality.

Early in the afternoon I wound up taking someone near the Bronx Whitestone Bridge, near a psychiatric hospital out on an island across from Harlem. I delivered my charge, and then saw three black female nurses in white uniforms and a black guy dressed in street clothes. They were all waiting at the taxi stand, and they were waving me over.

Now back then black people would drive ordinary cars with flags or painted signs to show that they were working as cabs. These gypsy cabs were illegal, but no white cab driver would go into Harlem, so black people would use the gypsy cabs to get in and out of that part of the city.

I knew the regular medallion cabs didn't go into Harlem, and the problem with this hospital was that the bus transportation was so bad, people who worked there would often have to stand out in the freezing cold for an entire hour waiting for a bus. Often the bus would get so crowded that not everyone could fit on, and some would have to wait for yet another hour.

I decided to pull over, and the three nurses and the man got in the back seat.

"Where do you want to go?" I asked, and of course they gave me addresses in Harlem. We chatted a little bit during the course of the drive, and I told them I was studying during the week and working at another psychiatric hospital on Long Island. One at a time I dropped the three nurses off. When the third nurse was getting out of the car, she stopped and asked the man, "Where are you going?"

He gave an address about ten blocks away and she looked at him a long time before closing the door and walking off. I missed it. It was very cold out, and I was only thinking that I was being a wonderful nice guy driving these people home. I thought for sure they would all recognize I was doing them a favor. On top of that I had only charged them each a portion of the full fare, which I had them split between them. I knew they were probably making fifty cents above minimum wage and supporting kids as well as themselves. I drove forward and made a left-hand turn into a side street.

I got about halfway down the street when I felt something pressed into my neck. The cold metal was the barrel of a gun. I looked in the rearview mirror and saw that he was kneeling on the cab floor behind me. His left hand was behind my head on the back of the seat, and his right hand held the gun pressed into my neck. In a dangerous voice, he told me to pull over. I did so, rolling to a stop in the middle of the disserted block.

He started with a kind of hate "street speak" that went something like, "White man... white devil. Black man... child of God." He spoke in a singsong fashion, and the message embedded in the mantra was, "Death to all white devils." He was clearly in an altered state, moving his head rhythmically as he chanted. I could feel the gun pressing harder into my neck.

I was so filled with terror I had a hard time thinking. I could feel my own death, and my reaction was fear, but I knew that if I showed my fear it would be over right then. I felt my animal intelligence take over, giving me an intense certainty that I couldn't confirm the victim he expected to find in me.

"How can I be a white devil, and also be caring for your sisters?" I asked. My voice sounded unreal in my ears as I went on. "Who else was going to pick them up and take them out of the cold? In actual fact the gypsy cabs are down in lower Manhattan where they get expensive fares, not here taking care of the poor women from the hospital."

At that he came out of his negative altered state and started talking to me in a more ordinary voice, though obvious tension still registered in his words. "Oh, but you don't understand!" He said. "Being a black person here is a dead-end road. You can never get ahead. Everyone's against you."

"I *do* know that," I said. "I helped run the abandoned church of Saint Nicholas here in Harlem at 118th Street for a year and a half. I'm on your side. I don't agree with the things that are going on."

Then his voice changed and he was lost in the hatred again. In this place of anger he kept repeating a segregationist philosophy of building a separate political state. He was clearly back in the thinking of his group church where they would chant hate sayings about white people and what the job of blacks was in the world.

I struggled a second time to lead him back out, maintaining my calm as best I could while at the same time completely fearing for my life.

Whether it was something I said or not, somehow he came back to his normal state of being as a rational man, and when he was there he had much more fluidity. In that part of his mind I could bring his thoughts to many areas— the cab, my driving, his life, where he came from. The other place was almost like a hypnotic state, and the emotion anchored there was hatred. What was terrifying was that I couldn't figure out what kept sending him back into that trance, and every time he went there he was telling himself to pull the trigger! The process was agonizing. Each time I brought him out I would always say something a little later that put him back into his anger again, and the cycle would start over.

We went back and forth between those two states for half an hour. The intensity grew with each switch, and the whole time he never took the gun out of my neck. I was past terror. I thought about half way through, *He's not going to let me out of this cab. I'm dead. He's gonna shoot me in the back of my head.* I wasn't making any assumptions here; he was quite explicit. At one point he said, "I'm compelled to offer you some time to pray, if you have any godliness in you." Which of course I didn't because I was white, but he was being a good black person and preparing me to go to God.

Still, every time I'd say *something* in an effort to bring him out again, based upon something he said. "And why would a white devil be sitting here with a cab driving you home? Why would this cab stop and pick you up if I'm not a nice man?" I never gave up trying to confound his belief that I was evil.

Had I known more of the actual church he was in, and what he had been told, perhaps I could have made more meaningful connections, but I just had to do the best I could with what I knew. I was hanging on by a thread.

I just *couldn't* figure out what was firing the hatred. It would just suddenly trip, and he would be gone—like another person took over. It got to the point where his eyes would actually roll back up into his head when he went into the anger. The switches became an internal war, so that at the juncture points between anger and the more rational side of himself, he was no longer talking to me, but actually arguing out loud with himself:

"How can you think of letting this bastard go when you have him here dead to rights!?"

"But he drove you home, he drove you home."

"He's the white devil."

In these conversations with himself I started chiming in with the rational side.

"All this would do is add to the evil," I'd say. "When you treat love with more evil you've become what it is that you're fighting against."

"Bullshit!" His angry side would kick in, reciting his religious chant of hatred proclaiming all white men to be the devil, and that the black man's destiny was to overcome and succeed the whites.

As his personal battle of love vs. hate raged on, I added my own voice to the love side whenever I could. "What are you going to have in this black political state?" I'd question. "Where is the love in it? It's all just built on hatred and aggression. This isn't an alternative life, there's no love in it. There's nothing. The whole thing is posited on killing the whites, rather than building anything worthwhile."

In the end he got so agitated that his internal battle actually manifested itself physically in the two sides of his body. He held the gun to my neck in his right hand as he argued for my death, then his left hand started struggling to actually pull the gun back from his right as he questioned the violence of murdering me. Finally his left hand got the gun away and rested it on the top of the seat right behind my head. The man yelled, "Go, go! Go now! Just go!"

I didn't argue with that. I jumped out of my own cab and ran up the street, stopping to wait on the street corner about fifty yards from my cab. After two or three minutes he got out of the back seat and retreated down the block the other way. I returned to my cab and drove away in a daze, amazed that I was still living.

Looking back on it, my life depended upon speaking from the part of me that could remain emotionally calm and reasonable and loving, even in such a terrifying situation. I think all of us have different "persona" and "multiple personalities." I had spent years imagining myself being Christ-like in possible real-life situations, and also redoing angry or selfish scenarios from my past in my mind until I could go through them lovingly. That "work" is far from over, but the fact that I had been doing it regularly allowed me to say and believe with matching emotional intensity that I was a good person. Had it not been real, I believe he would have seen straight through me, and even as it was he had a difficult time letting me go. I simply continued projecting the complete honesty and congruence that came from my loving persona, despite the abject terror I felt underneath. If I hadn't been able to do that, I sincerely believe I would have been killed, and that man would have become a murderer that day.

Frank Bourke

45
Sweet Fruit from a Bitter Tree

When the war in Europe ended in May 1945, the 123rd Evac entered Germany with the occupying troops. I was part of a group assigned to a concentration camp near Wuppertal, charged with getting medical help to the newly liberated prisoners, many of them Jews from Holland, France, and Eastern Europe. This was the most shattering experience I had yet had; I had been exposed many times by then to sudden death and injury, but to see the effects of slow starvation, to walk through those barracks where thousands of men had died a little bit at a time over a period of years, was a new kind of horror. For many it was an irreversible process: we lost scores each day in spite of all the medicine and food we could rush to them...

And that's how I came to know Wild Bill Cody. That wasn't his real name. His real name was seven unpronounceable syllables in Polish, but he had long drooping handlebar mustaches like pictures of the old Western hero, so the American soldiers called him Wild Bill. He was one of the inmates of the concentration camp, but obviously he hadn't been there long: his posture was erect, his eyes bright, his energy indefatigable. Since he was fluent in English, French,

192

German and Russian, as well as Polish, he became a kind of unofficial camp translator.

We came to him with all sorts of problems; the paperwork alone was staggering in attempting to relocate people whose families, even whole hometowns, might have disappeared. But though Wild Bill worked 15 and 16 hours a day, he showed no signs of weariness. While the rest of us were drooping with fatigue, he seemed to gain strength. "We have time for this old fellow," he'd say. "He's been waiting to see us all day." His compassion for his fellow prisoners glowed on his face, and it was to this glow that I came when my own spirits were low.

So I was astonished to learn when Wild Bill's own papers came before us one day, that he had been in Wuppertal since 1939! For six years he had lived on the same starvation diet, slept in the same airless and disease-ridden barracks as everyone else, but without the least physical or mental deterioration.

Perhaps even more amazing, every group in the camp looked on him as a friend. He was the one to whom quarrels between inmates were brought for arbitration. Only after I'd been at Wuppertal a number of weeks did I realize what a rarity this was in the compound where the different nationalities of prisoners hated each other almost as much as they did the Germans.

As for Germans, feeling against them ran so high that in some of the camps liberated earlier, former prisoners had seized guns, run into the nearest village and simply shot the first Germans they saw. Part of our instructions were to prevent this kind of thing and again Wild Bill was our greatest asset, reasoning with the different groups, counseling forgiveness.

"It's not easy for some of them to forgive," I commented to him one day as we sat over mugs of tea in the processing center. "So many of them have lost members of their families."

Wild Bill leaned back in the upright chair and sipped at his drink. "We lived in the Jewish section of Warsaw," he began slowly, the first words I had heard him speak about himself, "my wife, our two daughters, and our three little boys. When the Germans reached our street they lined everyone against a wall and opened up with machine guns. I begged to be allowed to die with my family, but because I spoke German they put me in a workgroup."

He paused, perhaps seeing again his wife and five children. "I had to decide right then," he continued, "whether to let myself hate the soldiers who had done this. It was an easy decision, really. I was a lawyer. In my practice I had seen too often what hate could do to people's minds and bodies. Hate had just killed the six people who mattered most to me in the world. I decided then that I would spend the rest of my life—whether it was a few days or many years—loving every person I came in contact with."

Loving every person ... this was the power that had kept a man well in the face of every privation.

George G. Ritchie

46
A Little Preparation

One woman who had a job that required her to walk home late at night through a rough neighborhood always made special preparations before leaving work. First she put half of her hair in a ponytail sticking straight up from one side of her head, and the rest of it in another pony tail sticking out horizontally on the other side. Then she painted her mouth in a very exaggerated "cupid's bow" smile with bright lipstick. Finally, she put a couple of alka-seltzer tablets in the palm of her hand. When a man approached her suspiciously, she would turn to face him, and smile broadly, with wide-open eyes, which was usually enough to discourage him. On the one occasion when that didn't work, she put the tablets in her mouth and started foaming, and he ran away.

Steve Andreas

From *Transforming Yourself*, by Steve Andreas, pp. 251. Copyright © 2002 Real People Press, Boulder CO.

47
Opening Presents

From the moment of my birth I had come into a really chaotic family situation. My mom and dad were separated, and my dad would go out drinking with other women. My mother's brothers often had to track him down and sometimes take him to the hospital after the trouble he would get into. My life started out like that, exposed to a lot of the world's harsher realities.

When I was about nine or ten, I was living with my grandmother in a fairly small house in Albuquerque New Mexico. I called her mother, because she essentially raised me. It was Christmas eve, and I remember lying awake in my bed thinking about the presents I would get the following day. The tradition was that Santa Clause wouldn't come unless I'd gone to sleep, but of course I was wide awake with thoughts of Christmas morning. There were two or three things I had asked for that I was really looking forward to getting, especially the high-powered microscope with slides. But it was more than excitement for the next day that kept me awake in bed that night.

My grandmother had recently taken up with a guy named Frank, who was an alcoholic. This particular night he'd been drinking quite a lot, and I could hear the conversation from the other room. My grandmother was instigating a fight with Frank, telling him about all the boyfriends she had had who were better than him.

"You don't measure up to any of them!" She said loudly from the other room.

I grew more and more apprehensive. I knew they were both drunk, and the conversation just kept escalating and escalating, growing louder and more violent. I lay there tensely in the dark, growing more and more anxious, remembering when Frank had come home drunk a couple months previously. He had woken us up late at night and when my grandmother and I walked into the living room, he kicked me hard in the leg for no reason whatsoever.

Now I heard my grandmother threaten to call one of her boyfriends. Frank shouted and began calling her a string of names. Then from her broken screams I knew he was hitting her. I wanted to do something, but I was terrified. I was really afraid that if he saw me he would start taking his anger out on me.

But I couldn't just lie there and wait to see what happened. That was a scarier thought. I felt I needed to take initiative and at least see what was going on. I got up in my PJ's and crept into the living room where the Christmas-tree lights cast a cheerless glow in patterns on the walls and carpet. She was in the middle of the floor with Frank sitting on her chest. He had ripped the phone out of the wall and was using it to beat her. I remember the phone was beige. He had the phone receiver clamped to the phone, swinging it back and forth like a rock, hitting her head from side to side like he was reaping grain.

It was utterly terrifying. I was scared to the bone. I had no idea how badly she was hurt, or what he was going to do to me. In that moment I don't remember making any conscious decision, or choosing between several scenarios in my mind. I just found myself walking up to Frank. I remember his white shirt all covered with my grandmother's blood, and the Christmas presents set out neatly beneath the tree. I stood right next to him and put my arm around his strong shoulder.

"Frank, do you want to open up your Christmas presents now?" I asked.

That seemed to disconnect him from what he was doing, and I could feel him relax a bit under my hand. He mumbled something and just walked back into the kitchen. I didn't know if he was fixing up another drink, or what, but he seemed to kind of disappear. I don't know what it did for him, but his aggressive behavior stopped immediately after my question. He could have easily pushed me down or taken a swipe as he walked off, but he didn't respond to me with any violence.

When he was gone my grandmother reached up with a horribly bloodied arm and took my hand. I could see white where her scalp had opened up.

"Get out, get out, as quick as you can," she whispered. "Go call the police."

I ran next door and knocked on the door. I didn't know them that well. I told them that my grandmother had been beaten up and to call the police.

The rest of the night is pretty fuzzy. I'm sure they took Frank away and my grandmother must have gone to the hospital to get stitches. I must have stayed at the neighbor's until dawn. By mid-morning my grandmother was back in her bedroom, sedated and recovering. There was nobody else around. I remember opening Christmas presents all by myself—things that I'd looked forward to so much. The day was grey and cloudy and I had this feeling of total sadness. I couldn't really enjoy the things I'd been looking forward to getting the night before, because something else was stirring inside me. My sense of what was important had shifted dramatically. It was one of the major experiences in my life that propelled me to find meaning and purpose in the midst of a lot of chaos and violence; and through my own pain, I gained a depth of empathy for the suffering of others.

While I've had a hard time enjoying Christmas after that, I am forever grateful for the ability that emerged in me that night out of my apparent powerlessness. Somehow, as small as I was, something prompted me to act in a way that kept us all three alive. Sadness didn't leave the world that Christmas, but neither did my grandmother, nor did I.

David Clark

48
Lilly

L illy was a very heavy-set 200 lb. black woman who had a high school equivalency diploma and worked as an aide during the evening shift in the catholic psychiatric hospital where I did my residency. Lilly had the most incredible presence. Whenever I was near her my response was almost physical; I couldn't stand next to her and be my normal intellectual self, and others seemed to react to her in similar ways. She moved in a way that projected about four feet from her body in all directions. Her aura, or energy, or body language carried with it an encompassing calmness and "in-chargeness" that affected everyone within its broad boundaries. Her main impact upon me when I came into that circle, was a complete sense of caring.

She would often tell little jokes, and had favorite observations. "You get there yet?" She would often say as she chased after the Indian psychiatrist who was always rushing somewhere. She had similar adroit observations of all our personalities, delivering them with humor and sincerity difficult to ignore.

Lilly was the lowest person in the pecking order on our shift. Starting at the top there were the head nurses in charge of the whole hospital who would come through every couple hours. Then there was the psychiatrist who was legally in charge of the unit of about twenty patients, the registered nurse on the floor, and myself, the psychological intern. Lilly was staffed as an aide. After I was there for about a week, however, it became quite clear to me that clinically, Lilly ran the floor. The entire staff on our shift revolved around her persona.

This was fascinating to me. Lilly's grandparents had been slaves who had lived in wooden sharecropper's cottages in the Carolinas. Lilly had only come north into New York State in the last twenty years or so, where she got a high-school equivalency from the local high school, and then got her job at the psychiatric hospital as an aide. Yet here she was, the de facto leader of our shift!

Being a student, I was curious as to how she did what she did. She saw that I was watching her, and she took an interest in me. One day she stopped and said, "Why don't you come ta my home. You're a student; you're starvin' ta death. Let me introduce you ta my family an' come ta Sunday dinner with us." I visited her several times and soon I got to know her pretty well.

At one point we had a catholic priest in the unit who had been stripped of his right to say mass. He had been drinking and chasing women for a number of years and got caught. Back then they considered that a psychological problem, and this being a catholic hospital, he was sent to us until they could put him someplace out of the way to serve as a chaplain where they could still keep an eye on him—like an out-of-the-way army post or in a prison.

Late in the evening the nurse was walking by and she saw him starting to cut his wrists with a large butcher knife he had somehow managed to smuggle in with him. She immediately rang the alarm and soon the psychiatrist and I joined her. Lilly was somewhere else in the hospital running an errand. The three of us clustered outside the priest's door, desperately trying to talk him out of hurting himself.

He was on the edge of his bed about fifteen to eighteen feet from the door. His wrists were already bleeding from the knife cuts, and I guessed his agitation was only heightened by the alarm and our sudden presence. I was quite athletic and trying to time a run at him for a football dive, but he lifted the knife and pointed it toward himself, holding the point tensely a few inches below his left collarbone. He was too much on his guard, full of grief that just welled out of him. He said he knew we'd stop the blood flow from his wrists if we jumped him, so he threatened to take his life by stabbing himself in the heart.

Any attempt we made to get him to change his mind was met with an overflow of his pain and shame, and any attempt we made to move through the doorway was immediately met with the point of the butcher knife held rigidly at his chest. It was one of the longest half hours of my life. It's hard to describe what happens to time in those situations. He was in complete despair—a catholic priest who had been called a mental patient and put in a mental hospital. Life was over for him.

The Indian psychiatrist didn't speak English very well, and he was just flabbergasted at the situation. The nurse was managing to control herself, but I could see that underneath she was hysterical with the horror that someone was going to commit suicide on her watch. I was talking as nicely and in as many different directions as I could think of, and making no real contact with the man whatsoever.

In the midst of all this, none of us noticed that Lilly had come back on the floor. She grasped my shoulder and the nurse's shoulder and pushed us apart with no effort whatsoever. She probably could have lifted me over her head if she wanted to. Lilly walked straight into the room.

"What's goin' on heah?" She demanded kindly. "What's all this heah fuss about?" She didn't walk at the priest, she walked beside him, fluffing the pillows on his bed with that presence she had. Her body language communicated, *I'm here to care for you.* Even more, it was as if every movement carried with it the absolute, deep, deep, implicit assumption that you would know she cared for you, and that she would have your respect for that.

She turned around and told the three of us, "Go on back ta the nursin' station, I'll be out in a while. I'd like ta talk ta him." I can still remember the way she sat down on the bed next to the priest, squeezing his knee with an affection that melted him. He just broke down sobbing and latched on to Lilly both physically and emotionally.

In those thirty seconds Lilly had walked into an emotionally charged hydrogen bomb space and diffused the situation as easily as popping a soap bubble. Just like that. It was something purely kinesthetic. I realized how profoundly the way we walk and move and smile and project ourselves affects our relationships and what we communicate to each other. There are a whole set of assumptions in there that are expressed with all the people we meet.

Afterwards we talked about it, and Lilly's philosophy was simple. She did very little analysis. She said, "I was just walkin' my talk." She was a Christian and morally bound to love all people and do good whenever and wherever she could. During my recent time in the monastery I had taken a vow of poverty, but she lived the underlying principles easily and naturally, always giving freely of her "excess" money to people in more need than herself. "Here's five dollah," she'd say to me. "You buy some gas an' go visit your wife in that hospital an' tell 'er how much you love 'er, and that Lilly says, 'Hi.' "

I did cognitive therapy with the priest for the next two weeks, helping him through his despairing belief that he no longer had a life worth living. As his caseworker I was able to develop a connection with him, since I had recently spent time in a monastery. I helped him work out a plan to transition out of the priesthood, with an eye toward becoming a teacher, and Lilly was very supportive and complimentary of my work with him.

At about the same time I remember reading a treatise about saint Francis of Assisi. It talked about his incredible presence that alone was enough to communicate his mission of peace and assistance to the poor, so that people trusted him without ever speaking a word to him. I remember saying to myself, "I think I've met an American saint."

I'll remember Lilly that way for the rest of my life.

Frank Bourke

49

A Letter From Norway

Thank you for messages of condolence and sympathy regarding the bombing in Oslo and shooting in a youth camp on a small island near Oslo.* It warms to have you thinking of us.

I have been able to reach almost all co-counselors living in Norway. They have not been so close as to be injured by the bombing and they were not present on the island during the attack. But many people here know survivors or victims or their relatives or friends. We are a small nation and youth delegations from all parts of Norway were present at the camp.

I guess you know most of the cruelty from the news. I will not repeat.

But I would like to share some hopeful and deeply moving things happening here.

The prime minister, the head of police in the municipality of the attacked island, the king, the queen, leaders of

---

*On July 22, 2011, Anders Breivik bombed government buildings in Oslo, Norway, causing eight deaths, and then killed 69 more people, mostly teenagers, at a camp of the Workers' Youth League of the Labor Party on a nearby island. This attack on his countrymen was an attempt to protest against Islamic immigration.

different political parties—they have all cried on national television. The leaders of the nation encourage people to hug, hold hands, be close, cry, tell their stories and listen to each other with love and respect.

There is very little demand for revenge against the anti-Islamic offender. Instead a collective agreement has been reached to embrace the values that the offender wished to destroy by creating a more open, friendly and inclusive society. A young woman said, "If one person can hate this much, think of all the love we are able to show together."

There has not been so many people out in the streets since the celebration of the end of World War II. On Monday in my town, there were Muslims and Christians, young and old—thousands and thousands of people hugging, giving flowers to each other, putting flowers on buildings and fences. A wonderful appeal was given: "Tonight the streets are filled with love."

This atmosphere of sister and brotherhood will probably fade as society goes back to normal. But something special and precious happened these days. It showed us what is possible and there are many, many who will make an effort to have this as a permanent part of society. It will definitely have an impact on the upcoming elections. Racist statements and extreme right wing sympathies will be very unpopular.

Myself, I can't help smile at every person I meet. Thinking, "You precious person, I am so glad you are alive." I am proud of my people.

Anne Helgedagsrud

50
He's the Asshole

My girlfriends and I had just moved to Boulder Colorado in 1973. We were out one night at a bar in North Boulder, where a band was playing. To give a sense of the scene, there were a lot of transient street-people in Boulder at that time, and a lot of people were taking a kind of speed drug called STP. Everyone was pretty drugged up; we'd smoked a bunch of pot ourselves.

My friends and I are dancers, so we were all out on the dance floor when two guys got rowdy on the floor and started going at each other. I don't remember if they'd bumped into each other, or if it was over a woman, but soon they were swearing at each other and throwing punches.

Immediately I backed away because I wasn't going to get caught in that. There was no way I was going to try to break that up. I was thinking of my own safety. Everyone backed away and there was this little circle around the two men as they swung at each other. Petty soon there was a bloody nose, and it became clear, no question, that one man was the aggressor. He was really out of it and he just kept whaling on the other. It was awful!

Then to my utter surprise, my friend Sheila just walked right out into the space where this man was getting beaten! She was fearless. She was physically like an Earth Mother, really wide hips, overweight, large breasts, long hippie hair, big beautiful eyes. She had a way about her that you could just melt into—a Mother Theresa kind of energy. You could tell her anything and just trust her.

What is she doing? I thought, as Sheila went right up to the fight, but she was so grounded with her stature that somehow I wasn't terribly concerned. It was like no one could hurt her. She got between the two men and pulled the attacker aside just a few feet. With heavy-lidded eyes she said, "Hey, forget it man, *he's* the asshole." I could see the aggression just drain from him.

And that was that. What she said completely defused the situation and the men went their separate ways.

Mamie Kakes

51
The Mosque of Ali

*"For, to win one hundred victories in one
hundred battles is not the acme of skill. To subdue
the enemy without fighting is the acme of skill."*

~Sun Tzu

I didn't know it then, but my battalion—nicknamed *No
Slack*—was the 31ˢᵗ foreign army in the last 4,000 years to
find itself at this intersection on the verge of taking control
of the ancient city of An Najaf.

To do it by the book meant we would have to push into
each home, detain everyone in the house, search the house,
and move to the next. But I had no intention of doing this.
I wanted to move only through the streets, overtly letting
the citizens know we were here to kill or capture Saddam
Hussein's *Fedayeen** fighters, not to hurt or embarrass them

---

*Fedayeen Saddam was a paramilitary organization loyal to the former
Ba'athist government of Saddam Hussein. The name was chosen to mean
"Saddam's Men of Sacrifice." Fedayeen Saddam was one of the most
unpopular Iraqi paramilitary groups to have sprung up after the 1991
Gulf War, a notoriously violent security unit with little formal training
that was mostly used to crush domestic dissent, and also employed to
resist the American invasion alongside Iraqi regular forces.

by entering their homes and violating their religious and cultural norms. I was determined to avoid contact, both physical and visual, with local women. These people were not the enemy, and using traditional US urban fighting techniques would only alienate them, bringing us down to the level of the *Fedayeen* in their eyes.

Respecting and understanding the Arabs' cultural norms was paramount in taking control of Najaf. Any violation of these closely-held beliefs would only fuel the resistance, and I felt I needed to stop the violence as quickly as possible in order to control the city in support of the march to Baghdad. Since our battle the previous day we hadn't received any hostile fire, so conditions seemed ripe for restraint—a risk I was prepared to accept.

I was struck by how the people of Najaf reacted when I smiled at them—it seemed to ease their fear. As the infantry companies pushed into the city, they managed to maneuver without taking enemy fire, and the streets were starting to fill with dozens of curious and friendly Iraqis. As I walked toward the rear of Charlie Company, I could feel the anxiety bubble in my stomach starting to ease.

But I still wondered, *Where were the Iraqi regular soldiers we had fought the day before?* In addition to the *Fedayeen*, there had been dozens of Iraqi regulars in Najaf, as evidenced by the large numbers of dead in their former battle positions and command posts along the road to the city. I had also seen abandoned Iraqi uniforms strewn amongst the dead. It appeared that many regulars had taken off their uniforms and faded into the population. I could feel them everywhere, watching us and trying to determine our next move as we set up our command post in the city.

That evening I met with two US groups that had covertly operated in and around Najaf for over two months prior to our arrival. One was a US Special Forces team, the other a curious group of men called "OGA," which I later learned is an acronym for "Other Governmental Agencies"—CIA ... I think. Both groups were convinced that we should seek an audience with the senior Shiite cleric in Najaf, the Grand Ayatollah Sistani. They believed that Sistani's cooperation with the Coalition would be decisive not only in Najaf but in winning over public opinion within the entire Shi'a community, which would essentially stop the fighting in southern Iraq.

Because Sistani was the Grand Ayatollah, he was legally capable within the Islamic community of issuing a formal *fatwa*, a form of religious proclamation similar to a Papal Bull or Encyclical. To the Shi'a, it would be a legal order as well as a religious injunction. It was hoped that such a proclamation could convince the Shiites to support the Coalition and assist in the overthrow of Saddam Hussein. Initial reports from the OGA's informants and emissaries were hopeful, but loyalists of Saddam's Ba'ath party were still holding Sistani under house arrest at his residence near the Mosque of Ali, making our plans to seek his support even more difficult and dangerous. At the end of this first meeting we agreed to launch a patrol into the heart of Najaf to facilitate a meeting between our emissaries and the Ayatollah.

I had already decided that this mission required an overt display of military might—tanks, infantry, heavy weapons, and the critical OH-58D Armed Reconnaissance and Light Attack Helicopters that had so effectively helped us fight our way into Najaf. However, our secret weapon was a man named Abdul Majorid al-Khoei. Khoei was the son of Sistani's predecessor, and as an Iraqi dissident, he had left the country and lived in the United Kingdom since 1991. I didn't know much about Khoei, but the OGA team offered to fly him into Najaf and have him available to act as our intermediary with Sistani.

For three straight days we found ourselves seeking an audience with the Grand Ayatollah Sistani. Movement through the inner city of Najaf was very restrictive and uncomfortable as we worked our way ever nearer to the famed Imam Ali Mosque—named for the founder of the prophet of Shi'a Islam. As I walked between the infantry and the hummers, I would hold my right hand over my heart, nodding at the elder men and saying *marhabba*, or hello. I was doing everything I could to read their reactions to our presence.

On the third day, as we moved downtown, the crowds grew, the waving increased and the worrisome smiles of the elders began to lose their dull look. *No Slack* stayed focused while scanning each window, gate, alley and roof as we moved closer to the Mosque. Constant scanning in a city quickly overwhelms a soldier's senses, adding to his stress and overall fatigue. This same stress and the spikes in adrenaline raise the body's core temperature, radically increasing a soldier's need for water and food. The deeper we probed into the city, the more and more I noticed the *No Slack* sergeants prodding their men to drink water and eat small foods like crackers, candy, and peanut butter from their MREs. As I worked my way toward the front of the column, I passed a young stud who looked up at me and said, "Hey sir, when ya gonna let us kill someone?"

I shot back with, "If you shoot your rifle, I've failed. Let's give everyone else a chance to shoot these bastards before we have to."

He looked confused. I was OK with that. He would soon learn that war was not a game. Killing humans, even your enemy, was nothing I wished on anyone with a good conscience. I would shoot all the artillery, drop all the Air Force's bombs and strafe the enemy with the division's attack helicopters before I would see one of my young soldiers in a street fight with the enemy at close quarters. I had to think, innovate—can I win without a fight? Should I even try? Yes, it was my sacred responsibility as their commander to try.

We had reached the main intersection south of the Mosque of Ali. The Golden Dome was visible down a cobblestone road lined with multi-storied buildings and cinderblock houses. It was a bullet shooting gallery waiting to happen I walked the line of troops so I could gauge their physical condition while also trying to get a feel for the route to the mosque. I also never stopped working the crowd to the best of my ability. I returned to my small John Deere tractor—called a Gator—and sat down in the front seat to wait for a platoon of Bravo Company that was searching an empty school on our flank. The school would provide me an excellent position for the snipers to cover our advance to the Ayatollah's residence. Once the Bravo platoon was in the school, I went in and had a look at the city from the roof to study the route we would have to negotiate if Sistani decided to meet with Khoei. When I returned to my "Gator," I decided to take my own advice and eat something.

As I picked through my MRE, First Sergeant Ron Gregg, the top sergeant in Bravo Company, told me that the Special Forces team wanted me to move to the front of the column. Once there I was summoned over to the hood of a vehicle to discuss strategy. The OGA team was waiting for one of their primary emissaries who was meeting with Sistani. They were optimistic as we discussed how to get Khoei through the crowd and up to Sistani's residence. Sistani's house was 150 yards up the road and we needed to try and keep the move low key while providing Khoei adequate security. The plan was for the SF team to take him in as *No Slack* secured the route and provided a quick reaction force in case the SF team and OGA got into trouble.

When the emissary returned he told us Sistani's demands. First, Sistani wanted US protection since he was concerned for his safety after his Iraqi guards had left in the middle of the night, leaving him and his students unprotected. Second, he wanted to meet with Khoei and the American commander who had allowed his people to go to prayers during the fighting.

"He wants to meet with *me*?" I asked in surprise.

"Yes, he was impressed with your actions this week and your words—he wants to meet you," said the elder emissary.

213

Now it was clear to me that Mr. Kadhim al-Waeli had proven himself to be the most effective combat system at my disposal.

Deployed as my cultural and linguistic advisor, Kadhim was from St. Louis, Missouri, but he'd been born an Iraqi national who fled his country after the failed Shi'a uprising against Saddam Hussein in 1991. After working his way through numerous refugee camps, Kadhim had ended up in the United States and become an American citizen. For nearly ten years Kadhim had worked his way from one odd job to the next in search of the American dream. He had gone from dishwasher to waiter to college student to political consultant, the latter a position he lost when he decided to join the "Bush War" in Iraq.

The previous week Kadhim had been riding in my hummer as we navigated the desert to what would be our first sight of the city of Najaf. Kadhim was alive with excitement. After hours of rambling on about the possibility of seeing the Mosque of Ali, Kadhim was on the verge of realizing his dream. I must admit, up to this point, his promises to bless my children's children for a hundred years if I allowed him to see the mosque had seemed a bit pretentious and overenthusiastic. However, I was not prepared for what would happen next.

After clearing the last fold in the ground at the edge of the desert, it appeared out of nowhere—the glistening golden dome of the Mosque of Ali and the white façade of the city of An Najaf. The sudden mosaic of color—the golden mosque, the huge green palm trees, the deep pools of blue water lining the road, and the fields of bright yellow flowers—was awe-inspiring against the dull backdrop of the open desert.

Even more overwhelming was Kadhim's reaction in the passenger seat of my hummer. First, he said a quick prayer and then fidgeted in childlike anticipation—scrambling inside our vehicle trying to get a better look at the Mosque. When the vehicle stopped, he burst out the door and ran in front to pray. I was happy for him and I was proud that I'd helped make his dream possible.

Days later, during our battle to enter the city of Najaf, *No Slack* fought the most intense combined arms fight the 101st Airborne Division had seen since Vietnam. In the thick of our assault I was about to decide whether or not to bring the infantry forward when Kadhim came over to me and quietly tugged on my sleeve. I didn't notice him at first and then he yelled, "Colonel, it's almost prayer time." I didn't know him well enough yet to pay him much attention and shrugged him off. He then pulled at my arm a second time and made eye contact, "Colonel, it's almost prayer time. The people want to go to the Mosque."

My first instinct was to pull out my sidearm and tell him to step back. Then I noticed the pain in his eyes. This was the mosque that had made this American from St. Louis, Missouri throw himself in the dirt and bless my family for ten generations. He was right; the Mosque was the key to taking Najaf. Kadhim's insights were the next weapon I needed to employ against the enemy along the escarpment.

I quickly ordered the tanks to disengage. Delta Company would cover their withdrawal and the artillery would shift from high explosive rounds to smoke rounds to mask the movement. I withdrew the attack helicopters and staged them to our rear. I did not want to completely release them in case the plan didn't work.

I ordered Kadhim to get in the speaker trucks and move to Delta Company's forward positions to announce to the people of Najaf that out of respect for Ali and Islam we would not fight the enemy during prayer time. I gave him the following message to read to the people over the speakers:

"We are the 101st Airborne Division and our mission is to destroy Saddam Hussein and his brutal regime. We respect your religion and the Mosque of Ali, and we do not wish to hurt the people of Najaf. You are free to go to prayers. May Allah be praised."

Kadhim continued the announcement as our tanks withdrew and the enemy guns went silent. Moments later, without warning, the escarpment at the edge of the city became covered with makeshift white flags. The families and children of Najaf were carrying them as they walked across the escarpment to the Mosque of Ali for prayers.

Now, listening to this emissary tell me that the Grand Ayatollah wanted to meet with me—I was stunned. Never for one minute did I think Sistani would allow an audience with an "infidel." This was an opportunity to stop the fighting in the south and possibly gain the support of the Shi'a in Iraq and the Middle East.

As I looked at the men of Bravo Company, the crowd and the ever-present reporters, including Al Jazeera, I knew this was quickly becoming an international strategic event. I had a chance to make a huge difference and there was no time for hesitation. I accepted Sistani's terms but offered one demand of my own. I wanted to send my speaker trucks forward so he could come out of his residence and tell the world he was inviting my battalion to protect him and asking me into his residence to talk. The man had been under house arrest for over fifteen years and the last thing I wanted to do was make it look like I was arresting him— live on Al Jazeera and CNN.

Later I would learn that Sistani had a number of secrets that prevented him from addressing the crowd in Najaf that day, including the fact that he received most of his religious training in Iran and spoke with a heavy Iranian accent. This is a little known fact that to this day has left him isolated and hesitant to vocally counter the radical rantings of Muqtada al-Sadr, a mere layman with no Islamic credentials.

The emissary understood my concerns, and after conferring with Khoei he returned to Sistani's residence to pass on my request. When the emissary returned from Sistani's quarters, he told me Sistani agreed that the crowd needed to know he was inviting us to his compound, but he was too afraid to move out of his compound and use the speaker trucks. Sistani had recommended a compromise. He would have his students file out into the streets and let the crowd know he wanted us to come to his compound and meet. Concerned that Sistani's patience was wearing thin, I agreed with the OGA leader that it was a fair compromise. The emissary left again and moments later returned with a huge grin on his face, "His eminence has agreed and his students are moving into the crowd to announce your invitation."

I waited long enough to see these "students" of Sistani's; they were not what I expected. They were older men with white and black turbans, long robes and neatly groomed beards. They swiftly moved into the crowds on the road to the mosque, outside Sistani's compound and around my battalion. The sudden and euphoric actions of the crowd reminded me of Pope John Paul's first appearance in Vatican Square in 1978. The people of Najaf hadn't publicly seen their Ayatollah for years, and the possibility of him making an appearance spread like wildfire through the streets of Najaf. Window shutters were banging open, and people were running toward us from every alleyway, street and rooftop. The intensity of the situation was reaching a fever pitch and we needed to take action before we lost control. The overwhelming force of *No Slack* was growing relatively weaker by the second.

The senior cleric from Sistani's office approached our emissary and told him we were clear to move to Sistani's compound. The Ayatollah's wishes were clear to the crowd and the students would act as escorts.

"Good, we need to move. Captain New," I ordered, "Get the men up. Let's go!"

The entire patrol picked up and started to slowly proceed down the Golden Road to the Mosque of Ali. I started to make my way back to my Gator when suddenly there was a huge crash to my left rear. As I turned to see where the sound came from, something hit me in the left corner of my sunglasses. As I staggered back, something else hit me in the back of the helmet.

What the hell was that?

Someone behind me yelled, "They're throwing rocks!"

"Rocks? No, Sistani invited us. Where the hell are those fucking students?"

I looked back to the front of the column in time to see a large vegetable cart being pushed into the street and turned on its side by a large and angry mob.

Now I was pissed. I put my head down and started to briskly walk to the front of the column. This is a mistake, I thought. These people don't understand we were invited! Closer to the quickly growing riot, I took my M-4 rifle off safe and prepared to shoot a couple of rounds into the air to get their attention. OK, so you get their attention, then what—what do you say? How long will the pause last—will it be a pause or will it be an excuse for someone in the crowd to shoot back? I put my M-4 back on safe as I neared the front of the column. The SF team and my lead platoon were already intermixed with the crowd and beginning to push and shove. This was about to erupt out of control. Someone was either going to accidentally shoot their weapon, or feel threatened and shoot into this crowd. I knew someone was causing this riot and I had to stop it—NOW.

I had to do something visually that couldn't be mistaken for a hostile act by the crowd, the bad guys, the media or my men. Reasoning with the crowd was futile—I could barely hear myself think over the growing riot. Trying to speak would only pull me into the chaos. So I turned my M-4 rifle upside down and yelled, "Take a knee! Everyone take a knee!" It was all I could come up with. I needed the men to stop entering this mob and "taking a knee" is what infantrymen do when they stop. It lowers a soldier's profile, stops them from making noise, and lets them rest. The moment the column of *No Slack* soldiers stopped and took a knee, the mood of the crowd softened, almost as if it became confused and curious. I had learned in Haiti that crowds have personalities. This crowd paused, a safer and surer pause than one that would have come if I had chosen to fire warning shots.

"*No Slack*, point your weapons toward the ground—show no hostile intent!" I shouted. The crowd paused again and people in the front began to smile and sit down with my soldiers. *OK, I'm thinking, so most of these people don't know what the hell's going on, someone is pushing and agitating them from behind.*

Taking advantage of the lull in the crowd's mood, I quickly walked over to the speaker truck, stuck my head in the driver's side window, and told the sergeant inside to get a linguist and tell these people we were invited. He pointed outside the passenger side of the hummer at the Iraqi colonel that the SF team had brought with them. He was a defector, and before I could get his attention he began to speak to the crowd on the loudspeaker. The moment he began to speak, the crowd erupted back into an angry mob. I don't know what he said, but the crowd quickly pinned him against the side of the hummer in protest. I told the sergeant to unplug his ass and lock the doors. Screw him!

Realizing that the crowd was going in the wrong direction, I walked back to the front of the column and, pacing behind the wall of *No Slack* soldiers, I gave the order that Jim Lacey of Time Magazine would later say "may have been the most unusual directive of Gulf War II."*

"Smile, men," I shouted, "they have to know we were invited—SMILE!"

Slowly but surely the men began to smile. They were short, awkward and forced smiles, as would be expected from young men facing down an out-of-control mob. Running out of options, I turned my rifle upside down and tried to work the crowd, shaking hands and smiling my ass off. The people nearby started smiling again, but the rabble rousers

---

*"With The Troops: Armed with Their Teeth" by Jim Lacey; Simon Robinson; Alex Perry; Terry McCarthy Monday, Apr. 14, 2003, Time Magazine. http://www.time.com/time/magazine/article/0,9171,1004634,00. html#ixzz1OoD9Ztfk

were still yelling. We had managed the situation well, and now I needed to break this off. The Iraqi colonel had ruined it for us, and it was obvious that there were agitators in the crowd who wanted us to fire on them. It didn't make any sense to muscle through this crowd to meet with Ayatollah Sistani. To do so would feed right into the hands of Saddam's *Fedayeen* fighters and Ba'ath party officials who were surely in the crowd. They wanted me to screw this up, not just for the people of Najaf, but for the world. Thanks to the press, the world was watching. *No Slack* would maintain the moral high ground today; I walked back to the speaker truck.

"*No Slack*," I shouted into the microphone, "We're going to pull back and let them sort this out themselves. Everyone pull back. You will keep your guns pointed at the ground and you will smile at everyone." As the soldiers stood up and began to walk backward, smiling, the Iraqis began smiling again too, patting my men on their backs and giving them thumbs-up signs. But seeing the men walking backward bothered me ... it looked like we were defeated and withdrawing. There was no way the world or the *Fedayeen* were going to get a picture of *No Slack* retreating.

"Just turn around and move—just turn around, men, and walk away," I yelled across the column and the street. T.E. Lawrence had learned 85 years earlier that Arabs respect a man who turns his back on an aggressor without fear. It was a risk, but so was each unexpected action we had taken up to this point. It was another curveball to throw at the instigators of this now obviously staged riot—something else to make them think twice. I wanted them to know that *No Slack* was not the least bit afraid of them. So the men turned and walked away for the whole world to see. This move allowed me to speak to the Arab world with actions that could not be twisted or manipulated. We were leaving as men and were not the least bit afraid. If we had continued to back off facing the crowd as we had been trained, the Arab press and those who wished us to fail could have used this visual against us as we neared Baghdad, with headlines like "The Americans retreated from an unarmed crowd, they are afraid to fight." It was a chance I could not take.

As we cleared the crowd and started to get some distance between us, I remembered something Kadhim had taught me. He had told me to place my right hand over my heart and slightly bow to show respect. The gesture meant, "Allah be praised" or "God bless your heart," and had worked well for me up to this point in the city. So, as *No Slack* turned the corner toward our compound, I turned back to the stunned crowd, stopped, placed my right hand over my heart and slowly bowed.

Later that evening, when we were waiting for the emissary to return to the headquarters, we got word from our informants that Ayatollah Sistani had issued a formal *fatwa* to the people of Najaf: "Do not interfere with the American forces entering Iraq, Praise be to Allah, Grand Ayatollah Sistani of the Mosque of Ali."

Colonel Christopher P. Hughes

Adapted from Chapter 3 of *War on Two Fronts, An Infantry Commander's War in Iraq and the Pentagon* by Col. Christopher P. Hughes. Copyright © Christopher P. Hughes 2007. Used with permission.

52
He Just Sat Back Down

In 1973 Boulder Colorado was to be the host of a four-day international festival called World Invocation Day—supporting human unity and diversity. An organization that I co-founded, called World Family, was organizing the event. We were bringing together teachers and other organizations from all over the world to address spirituality, ecology, and education, as related to human unity and diversity.

As part of planning the event, we brought together various organizations to meet here in Colorado. One of these organizations was called Cooperative Consciousness, the head of which was a man named Carl Wright. Carl turned out to be my Achilles' heel, because every time we had a meeting he would oppose me, telling me I wasn't doing things right.

We had to go through all kinds of bureaucracy to get approval from the city regarding the locations where we would hold our events, and where and how we would organize our parade. When the county didn't let us have the site we had originally requested for the festival, Carl wanted to fight the county. I thought it would work best not to spend our energy that way, and instead to be more flexible, and look for the unseen opportunities in not getting what we had originally wanted. I was coming from a spirit-driven place of, *We just have to be patient with the way this unfolds and it'll work out for the best.* Carl, on the other hand, reacted to every bump in the road by wanting to confront the government bureaucracy. We were at opposite ends of the spectrum, which kept us in a constant power struggle around how to proceed.

In the end, the festival took place in Chautauqua park, which was not where we had originally wanted to be, but it was where we could make it happen. It was a beautiful place—the holy grounds of the indigenous people at the foot of the Rocky Mountains. I felt a certain reverence for the history of the site.

But as the festival proceeded, Carl and I continued to have this constant conflict between us. Since I was one of the key organizers of the festival, he held me responsible for having "given in" to having the festival where the county told us to have it, instead of fighting for our original plan. He just couldn't let the issue go.

On the second day of the festival, I went to dinner in downtown Boulder with my friend Ben, one of the other organizers. When we finished dinner, we had to walk through the bar to get outside, and as we did I heard a booming, forceful, voice say, "Roske, COME HERE!"

I looked over and saw Carl sitting at a table with about six other guys from his organization, Cooperative Consciousness. They had all been drinking, and Carl had an aggressive tension visible all through his body. The irony of it all was a bit surreal.

As soon as I heard Carl's shout coming at me, I could feel the beginning of a physical reaction inside my chest. As a kid growing up I was taught to fight. My dad always told me that if somebody slaps you and you don't slap them back, then they'll slap you again and so will everybody else. He put the boxing gloves on me when I was six years old, and started teaching me self defense. I grew up to be a boxer and a street fighter. I fought in what they call smokers, fought in the navy, was chosen the best boxer out of 10 bouts at Boot camp, and I fought middle weight on the USS Boxer aircraft carrier.

Normally, in this kind of situation I would have gone up to Carl and gotten into a confrontation ending in some kind of physical exchange. But I didn't want to do that here, with this man who was a part of this festival of *unity*.

I had a spiritual practice that I'd been doing for years, and part of it involved a simple Hindu chant: *Om mani padme hum*. Like other mantras, it can be interpreted in many ways, or even as mere sequences of sound whose effects lie beyond strict meaning. As I walked over to Carl, I began repeating this mantra inside my own head. It calmed me, guiding my focus to my breathing. When I reached Carl, he began confronting me with angry argument. I just kept the chant going on internally as he dumped his negative energy and his projections about me. Then he yelled, "Sit down!"

I sat down at the table, and so did my friend Ben, who had come along beside me. The energy in the room was tense, like "What's gonna happen? A fight?"

Carl dumped some more, and I just kept my chant going inside, staying calm and listening. When Carl finished, I spontaneously got up without reacting to what he had said. Ben got up with me and I said simply, "Let's go."

Carl leapt up out of his chair. "I want a response!" he demanded.

His six buddies were all staring at me, wondering what I would do now. Everyone in the bar had their eyes riveted on what was about to take place. I just looked into Carl's eyes, continuing to say the mantra inside my mind, staying silent and centered.

Then the strangest thing happened. In the moment that I didn't react, it was like an energy threw Carl back into his seat. He'd stood long enough to shout his demand for a response, and then he was just back down in his chair again, his face white. His expression was like a cold, blank, energy-drain. I turned away and just walked out the door with Ben. It was the weirdest thing I've ever experienced. It was almost like a Gandhi kind of move. All of a sudden he was just back in his seat, and I didn't *do* anything.

But that wasn't the last of it. The next day I was coming out of the festival grounds at Chautauqua Park, walking towards my car, when I heard a loud voice once again hollering my name.

"ROSKE!"

I turned around to see Carl coming towards me like a lion. My instincts kicked in and I went into a fighter's stance. He came at me aggressively, and as he did, something happened spontaneously within me. I was in this fighter's stance, and then, without thought, I just opened my stance. When I did Carl came right into my arms into a fierce embrace and started crying. I'd never experienced anything like it; it was amazing. We embraced for several minutes. Then we just started sharing, and a heartfelt feeling began emerging between us. We went down to a restaurant and had tea and talked more. That was when we really started creating together, rather than being closed to each other's perspectives. After that we became friends. It was a very profound experience.

To this day I don't know what it was that happened in that moment of going from a fighting stance to an open embrace. It was one of the most interesting experiences in my life—so different from anything I'd ever experienced in terms of encountering conflict. I used to have a lot of confrontation and fighting in my life. I never have it now. It just doesn't show up in my reality anymore.

Makasha Roske

53
Yer Momma

I **work** **as a** professional counselor in a Mental Health clinic that works with the school system in a rural county outside Baltimore. Recently I was assigned a 16-year-old boy named Sam. He was on probation from High School because he'd gotten in two fights. In one of them Sam beat the crap out of another kid, giving him a black eye and a broken nose.

The first time I met with Sam I mainly filled out paperwork, but I also got to know him a bit. He told me that in the last fight he had only gotten in a few swings before the principal stepped in. "I stopped 'cause I respect the principal," he said. "But I still yelled to the guy, 'I'm not just gonna fuck you up. You better watch out. I'm gonna kill you!'"

In this county a lot of the kids hunt and have weaponry at home, so I knew that kind of a threat was taken very seriously.

In our second meeting we were talking and I asked Sam, "Why do you get in these fights?"

"I'll beat anyone who says something bad about my mom or my girlfriend."

Of course at the age of 16, that kind of poking fun is just what kids do, so Sam was getting baited all the time. I asked him more about his home life and he quickly confirmed that he had a very close relationship with his mom, and his girlfriend was also very important to him.

I asked about past incidents and found that they were all similar: kids would taunt Sam about his mom or girlfriend and he would view that as disrespect, feeling the need to defend them.

"When you get in these fights what are you focusing on?" I asked.

"Well, the other guy is disrespecting. I've got to teach him, and protect my mom or my girlfriend."

"You're on probation now. Have you ever thought about how much *you're* disrespecting your mom and girlfriend by taking away their ability to be with you? Get in a fight again and you'll be locked up. What would happen to your mom and girlfriend if you were locked up? How disrespectful would that be to them given how much they care about your future?"

He just sat there looking as if smoke were coming out of his ears. "Oh my God, I have hurt them," he said. He continued to process silently for a good 10 minutes as he expanded his understanding of disrespect to include himself. "This changes everything," he said, "Everything has been flipped." It was the weirdest thing to watch. Every once in a while he'd shake his head and make some comment, "It was so stupid what I did... like a little kid." Eventually he looked up and said, "I can't believe that all those times I was disrespecting my mom!"

To further his experience I asked, "How much heartache did your mom have when she found out you were on probation?"

"Oh, man," he said. "She was *so* upset."

He started talking about other fights in the past where he was trying to protect his mom or girlfriend against insults. "Now I realize I was such a clown!"

When I saw Sam the next week he said several people had tried to bait him in the last seven days, but he just ignored them, when in the past he would have fought them. He told me he just looked at them and realized how immature they were. He gave me three or four specific examples of this, telling me his thought process when one kid in his neighborhood got in his face to start a fight: "I thought, *If I fight this kid, what will happen long-term?* I knew fighting would risk my future for some kid who's just a clown, so I just walked away."

Sam now sees his old behavior as childish and views folks who want to fight as silly. Wow. There is still work to do with this young man, but this was incredibly powerful for him. I wish it was always this easy. I'd help a lot of delinquents retire!

Jesse Kessinger

54
I Just Stopped Walking

I'd been out drinking with some friends in Southampton in the UK, first at a bar and then at a club. As I was walking back through town it was really late, or early, depending on how you look at it. I was heading through the main precinct, which is a type of walking Mall that goes on for a ways without any side streets. At some point I noticed three men up ahead going in the same direction as me, but much slower. They were swaggering and clearly drunk, taking their sweet time. Everything about their body language suggested that they could really pose a problem. I thought to myself, *Well, my options are to walk past them, or to walk really slowly.* It was still a long stretch before there were any turnoffs. If I decided to walk slowly it would look like I was lurking behind them; I might draw their attention and that could be a risk. Of course if I walked past them I also risked incurring their attention.

I decided to get it over with and just walk past them, but I didn't go way around them, because that could send a message of fear. Instead of altering my course, I simply walked forward as *outwardly* confident as I could bring myself to appear. As I passed them, one of the guys started making a few comments, throwing out a few insults. He was spoiling for a fight, trying to trigger something off in me. His friend started laughing and jeering as well, trying to get me to respond. I just carried on walking, hoping they'd break it off. Then the one making all the comments started getting *really* aggressive and nasty.

"I'll 'ave you, you cunt! Fucking come here, I'll 'ave you!" He just kept escalating and wouldn't stop.

Now I was absolutely scared. This was quickly feeling like a very serious problem.

My first thought was, *Run. These guys are fairly drunk.* But I've seen people with adrenaline suddenly sober up remarkably fast. This was not a pretty picture. I decided not to run. Instead, I simply stopped walking. I didn't turn around, I didn't say anything. I just stopped, and waited. It was the most unpredictable thing I could think of to do.

As soon as I stopped I heard all three sets of footsteps behind me immediately stop as well. My heart was pounding, but I forced myself not to look back. I just stood there.

One of them—a different voice from the other two—said, "Knock it off you two, you're gonna get us in trouble." The jeering of the other two went quiet. Then I heard the voice of the most aggressive of the three say, "It's alright mate, I'm only messin' around."

Still I didn't move. I just stood there waiting a bit longer…

By now I was aware of my knee caps quivering up and down underneath my trousers from my own adrenaline. But I'd had a few beers, and I still had a bit of the beer courage. Finally, I carried on walking *slowly*, still never looking back. I heard nothing more from the three men. When I got to a place where there were once again multiple directions to go, I turned off on a side street and got myself home as quickly as possible.

Looking back on my experience in Southhampton, I'm sure my inspiration must have come from an incredible thing I saw on a TV nature program once. The program showed a leopard walking across the African plains with three or four little baby cubs. A group of hyenas started closing in. The voice-over explained that the mother could run off easily enough, but if she did that, she'd lose her cubs. So what did the mother do? The mother stopped walking and the cubs followed her example. Then the mother dropped to the ground and rolled over in the sun like she was sunbathing. The camera cut to the hyenas at this point, and they all grew suddenly tense. It was as if they were thinking, *How can she afford to be so calm? Where are the rest of them?* Very quickly the hyenas backed way off. The moment the mother was aware that they were all gone, she got her cubs out of there.

In the moment that I stopped walking, there was never a conscious plan in my head, but I'm sure that what I did had the same intention behind it. The unconscious logic was to provoke the question, "How can he afford to be so relaxed in the face of aggression?" And that's quite a nice principle.

It's not easy though! My God. If it hadn't been nighttime… If I'd had to turn around, or make verbal contact… Any of those things and they would have seen that I was terrified.

Andrew T. Austin

Introduction to Bank for the Poor

The following story is told by an economics professor, Muhammad Yunus, who looked at crisis and famine at a *system* level. By interviewing the very poorest people in his home country of Bangladesh, one of the poorest countries in the world, Yunus saw a clear pattern underlying their suffering. The poor taught him "an entirely new economics," prompting him to challenge the most fundamental assumptions of banking, which would eventually lead to a global movement known as micro-credit. Since its inception, Yunus' Grameen Bank (Village Bank) has helped poor people by giving them a way to help themselves instead of resorting to charity.

Yunus' story is particularly inspirational to me because of how carefully he created an institution that is self-reliant and self-sustaining—something that its poor patrons could always rely on. The Grameen Bank is based on community and trust that is not assumed, but rather *supported* by the structure of the institution, which is fueled by the self-interest of each individual struggling for a dignified and decent life.

In 2006 Yunus and the Grameen Bank received the Nobel Peace Prize for their success in creating economic and social development from below. As the Nobel Committee said in its citation, "Lasting peace cannot be achieved unless large population groups find ways in which to break out of poverty. Microcredit is one such means."

This is Yunus' story of how it all began, and the many obstacles he and his bank-workers faced in creating this new reality in Bangladesh...

Mark Andreas

55

Bank for the Poor[*]
The Greatest Conflict Of All

I have found from personal experience that the greatest conflict a person faces is the struggle for life over death simply from a lack of food.

In the year 1974 Bangladesh fell into the grip of famine.

The university where I taught and served as head of the Economics Department was located in the southeastern extremity of the country, and at first we did not pay much attention to the newspaper stories of death and starvation in the remote villages of the north. But then skeleton-like people began showing up in the railway stations and bus stations of the capital, Dhaka. Soon this trickle became a flood. Hungry people were everywhere. Often they sat so still that one could not be sure whether they were alive or dead. They all looked alike: men, women, children. Old people looked like children, and children looked like old people. The starving people did not chant any slogans. They did not demand anything from us well-fed city folk. They simply lay down very quietly on our doorsteps and waited to die.

I used to feel a thrill at teaching my students the elegant economic theories that could supposedly cure societal problems of all types. But in 1974, I started to dread my own lectures. What good were all my complex theories when people were dying of starvation on the sidewalks and porches across from my lecture hall? My lessons were like the American movies where the good guys always win. But when I emerged from the comfort of the classroom, I was faced with the reality of the city streets. Here good guys were mercilessly beaten and trampled. Daily life was getting worse, and the poor were growing even poorer. Nothing in the economic theories I taught reflected the life around me. How could I go on telling my students make-believe stories in the name of economics? I wanted to become a fugitive from academic life. I needed to run away from these theories and from my textbooks and discover the real-life economics of a poor person's existence.

So that is what I did.

In 1976, I began visiting the poorest households in the village of Jobra to see if I could help them directly in any way. My colleague, Professor H. I. Latifee would often accompany me. One day as Latifee and I were making our rounds in Jobra, we stopped at a run-down house with crumbling mud walls and a low thatched roof pocked with holes. We made our way through a crowd of scavenging chickens and beds of vegetables to the front of the house. A woman squatted on the dirt floor of the verandah, a half-finished bamboo stool gripped between her knees. Her fingers moved quickly, plaiting the stubborn strands of cane. She was totally absorbed in her work.

On hearing Latifee's call of greeting, she dropped her bamboo, sprang to her feet, and scurried into the house.

"Don't be frightened," Latifee called out. "We are not strangers. We teach up at the university. We are neighbors. We want to ask you a few questions, that is all."

Reassured by Latifee's gentle manner, she answered in a low voice, "There is nobody home."

She meant there was no male at home. In Bangladesh, women are not supposed to talk to men who are not close relatives.

Children were running around naked in the yard. Neighbors peered out at us from their windows, wondering what we were doing.

In the Muslim sections of Jobra, we often had to talk to women through bamboo walls or curtains. The custom of *purdah* (literally, "curtain" or "veil") kept married Muslim women in a state of virtual seclusion from the outside world. It was strictly observed in Chittagong District.

As I am a native Chittagonian and speak the local dialect, I would try to gain the confidence of Muslim women by chatting. Complimenting a mother on her baby was a natural way to put her at ease. I now picked up one of the naked children beside me, but he started to cry and rushed over to his mother. She let him climb into her arms.

"How many children do you have?" Latifee asked her.

"Three."

"He is very beautiful, this one," I said.

Slightly reassured, the mother came to the doorway, holding her baby. She was in her early twenties, thin, with dark skin and black eyes. She wore a red sari and had the tired eyes of a woman who labored every day from morning to night.

"What is your name?" I asked.

"Sufiya Begum."

"How old are you?"

"Twenty-one."

"Do you own this bamboo?" I asked.

"Yes."

"How do you get it?"

235

"I buy it."

"How much does the bamboo cost you?"

"Five taka." At the time, this was about twenty-two cents.

"Do you have five taka?"

"No, I borrow it from the *paikars*."

"The middlemen? What is your arrangement with them?"

"I must sell my bamboo stools back to them at the end of the day as repayment for my loan."

"How much do you sell a stool for?"

"Five taka and fifty poysha."

"So you make fifty poysha profit?"

She nodded. That came to a profit of just two cents.

"And could you borrow the cash from the moneylender and buy your own raw material?"

"Yes, but the moneylender would demand a lot. People who deal with them only get poorer."

"How much does the moneylender charge?"

"It depends. Sometimes he charges 10 percent per week. But I have one neighbor who is paying 10 percent per day."

"And that is all you earn from making these beautiful bamboo stools? Fifty poysha?"

"Yes."

Sufiya did not want to waste any more time talking. She set to work again, her small brown hands plaiting the strands of bamboo as they had every day for months and years on end. This was her livelihood. She squatted barefoot on the hard mud. Her fingers were callused, her nails black with grime.

Sufiya Begum earned two cents a day. It was this knowledge that shocked me. In my university courses, I theorized about sums in the millions of dollars, but here before my eyes the problems of life and death were posed in terms of pennies. Something was wrong. Why did my university courses not reflect the reality of Sufiya's life? I was angry, angry at myself, angry at my economics department and the thousands of intelligent professors who had not tried to address this problem and solve it. The existing economic system made it absolutely certain that Sufiya could never escape her miserable situation. The trader made certain to pay Sufiya a price that barely covered the cost of the materials and was just enough to keep her alive. She would never save a penny, and so she could not break free of her exploitative relationship with him. Her children were condemned to live a life of hand-to-mouth survival, just as she had lived it before them, and as her parents did before her. I knew that the slightest ill fortune could push Sufiya and her family beyond the edge of subsistence to join the multitude I had already seen dying in the streets.

I had never heard of anyone suffering for the lack of twenty-two cents. It seemed impossible to me, preposterous. Should I reach into my pocket and hand Sufiya the pittance she needed for capital? That would be so simple, so easy. I resisted the urge to give Sufiya the money she needed. She was not asking for charity. And giving one person twenty-two cents was not addressing the problem on any permanent basis.

With the help of Maimuna, one of my university students, I made a list of people in Jobra, like Sufiya, who were dependent on traders. Within a week we had a list of forty-two people, who borrowed a total of 856 taka—less than 27 dollars! We were both sickened by the reality of it all.

I handed Maimuna the twenty-seven dollars and told her, "Here, lend this money to the forty-two villagers on our list. They can repay the traders what they owe them and sell their products at a good price. They can repay me whenever it is advantageous for them to sell their products. They don't have to pay any interest. I am not in the money business."

Usually when my head touches the pillow, I fall asleep within seconds, but that night sleep would not come. I lay in bed feeling ashamed that I was part of a society that could not provide twenty-seven dollars to forty-two skilled persons to make a living for themselves. I knew that what I had done was drastically insufficient. My response had been ad hoc and emotional. What was required was an institution that would lend to those who had nothing. An institution they could always rely on.

The next morning I drove my white Volkswagen beetle to my local branch of the Janata Bank and asked the manager to lend money to the poor villagers of Jobra.

His jaw fell open and he started to laugh. "I can't do that!"

"Why not?" I asked.

"Well," he sputtered, not knowing where to begin with his list of objections. "For one thing, the small amounts you say these villagers need to borrow will not even cover the cost of all the loan documents they would have to fill out. The bank is not going to waste its time on such a pittance."

"Why not?" I said. "To the poor this money is crucial for survival."

"These people are illiterate," he replied. "They cannot even fill out our loan forms."

"In Bangladesh, where 75 percent of the people do not read and write, filling out a form is a ridiculous requirement."

"Every single bank in the country has that rule."

"Well, that says something about our banks then, doesn't it?"

"Look, the simple truth is that a borrower at any other bank in any place in the world would have to fill out forms."

"Okay," I said, bowing to the obvious. "If I can get some of my student volunteers to fill out the forms for the villagers, that should not be a problem."

"But you don't understand, we simply cannot lend to the destitute," said the branch manager.

"Why not?" I was trying to be polite. Our conversation had something surreal about it. The branch manager had a smile on his face as if to say he understood that I was pulling his leg. This whole interview was humorous, absurd really.

"They don't have any collateral," said the branch manager, expecting that this would put an end to our discussion.

"Why do you need collateral as long as you get the money back? That is what you really want, isn't it?"

"Yes, we want our money back," explained the manager. "But at the same time we need collateral. That is our guarantee."

"To me, it doesn't make sense. The poorest of the poor work twelve hours a day. They need to sell and earn income to eat. They have every reason to pay you back, just to take another loan and live another day! That is the best security you can have—their life."

The manager shook his head. "You are an idealist, Professor. You live with books and theories."

I ended up talking to officials higher up, who talked to officials even higher up. Finally they were willing to grant a small loan of 10,000 taka ($300), but only with myself as guarantor. At the end of the year I succeeded in taking out a loan from the Janata Bank and passing it on to the poor of Jobra.

That was the beginning of it all. I never intended to become a moneylender. All I really wanted was to solve an immediate problem. Out of sheer frustration, I had questioned the most basic banking premise of collateral. I did not know if I was right. I was walking blind and learning as I went along.

A BANK FOR THE POOR

In January 1977, with the help of some of my university students, I started the pilot project that was to become Grameen Bank, (Village Bank). Without knowing how we would succeed, we were starting a bank for the poor.

If Grameen Bank was to work, we knew we would have to trust our clients. From day one, we recognized that there would be no room for policing in our system. We never used courts to settle our repayments, and we did not involve lawyers or any outsiders. We assumed that every borrower was honest and completely avoided the cost and nuisance of legal instruments between lenders and borrowers. We were convinced that the bank should be built on human trust, not on meaningless paper contracts. Grameen would succeed or fail depending on the strength of our personal relationships. So we began by walking the streets, getting to know the communities. We believed that the only way we could truly develop trust and reach the poorest of the poor was to bring our services to the doorstep of the most disadvantaged, rather than expect them to come to us.

I was also strongly committed to granting at least 50 percent of our experimental project loans to women. In Bangladesh, even a rich woman could not borrow money from a bank without her husband's authority. I was angry about this on principle, but we soon discovered compelling socio-economic reasons to focus all our loans on women. The more money we lent to poor women, the more I realized that credit given to a woman brings about change faster than when given to a man.

In Bangladesh, women experience hunger and poverty more intensely than men. If one of the family members has to starve, it is an unwritten law that it will be the mother. The mother will also suffer the traumatic experience of not being able to breast-feed her infant during times of famine or scarcity. Poor women in Bangladesh have the most insecure social standing. A husband can throw his wife out any time he wishes. He can divorce her merely by repeating, "I divorce thee," three times. And if he does, she will be disgraced and unwanted in her parents' house. Despite these adversities, we saw that destitute women adapt quicker and better to the self-help process than men. Though they cannot read or write and have rarely been allowed to step out of their homes alone, poor women see further and are willing to work harder to lift themselves and their families out of poverty. They pay more attention, prepare their children to live better lives, and are more consistent in their performance than men. When a destitute mother starts earning an income, her dreams of success invariably center around her children. A woman's second priority is the household. She wants to buy utensils, build a stronger roof, or find a bed for herself and her family. A man has an entirely different set of priorities. When a destitute father earns extra income, he focuses more attention on himself. Thus money entering a household through a woman brings more benefits to the family as a whole.

If the goals of economic development include improving the general standard of living, reducing poverty, creating dignified employment opportunities, and reducing inequality, then it was natural for us to work through women. Not only do women constitute the majority of the poor, the underemployed, and the economically and socially disadvantaged, but they more readily and successfully improve the welfare of both children and men. Studies comparing how male borrowers use their loans versus female borrowers consistently show this to be the case.

It was not easy to focus our efforts almost exclusively on lending to women. The first and most formidable opposition came from the husbands, who generally wanted the loans for themselves. The religious leaders were also very suspicious of us. And of course the moneylenders saw us as a direct threat to their authority in the village.

In the beginning, we were unsure how to attract women borrowers. 85 percent of poor women in rural Bangladesh cannot read, so advertising on signs was out of the question. To make things more difficult, women are rarely free to come out of their houses without their husbands. At first, those of us who were men never dared enter a woman's house because of the rules of *purdah*—a set of practices that uphold the Quranic injunction to guard women's modesty and purity. In its most conservative interpretation, *purdah* forbids women to leave their homes or to be seen by any men except their closest male relatives. Even where *purdah* is not strictly observed, custom, family, tradition, and decorum combine to keep relations between women and men in rural Bangladesh extremely formal.

So when I would go to meet with village women, I never asked for a chair or any of the bowing and scraping that usually accompanies figures of authority. Instead, I would try to chat as informally as possible. I would say funny things to break the ice or compliment a mother on her children. I also warned my students and coworkers against wearing expensive dress or fancy saris.

Instead of asking to enter a woman's house, I would stand in a clearing between several houses, so everyone could see me and observe my behavior. Then I would wait while one of my female students entered the appointed house and introduced me. This go-between would then bring me any questions the women might have. Sometimes she would shuttle back and forth for over an hour and still I was not able to convince these hidden women to seek a loan from Grameen. But I would come back the next day. And again the go-between would shuttle back and forth between the village women and me.

One day, as I sat in a clearing between the houses of a village, it clouded over and started to rain. As this was the monsoon season, the rain turned into a heavy downpour. The women in the house sent an umbrella out so I could cover myself. I was relatively dry, but the poor go-between got rained on every time she shuttled back and forth. As the rain increased one of the elder women in the house, said, "Let the professor take shelter next door. There is no one there. That way the girl won't get wet."

The house was a typical rural Bengali hut—a tiny room with a dirt floor and no electricity, chair, or table. I sat alone on the bed in the dark and waited. Wonderful smells of simmering *atap* rice seeped into the hut from next door. A bamboo wall and cabinets divided this house from the neighboring one, and every time my go-between talked to the women in the adjoining house, I could hear some of the things they said, but their voices were muffled. When the go-between returned to tell me what they had said, the women next door would crowd against the bamboo divide to hear my answers. It was far from an ideal way of communicating, but it was certainly better than standing outside in the rain.

After twenty minutes of this—hearing each other's voices, but talking indirectly through a go-between—the women on the other side of the wall started bypassing my assistant and shouting questions or comments directly at me in their Chittagonian dialect. As my eyes grew accustomed to the darkness, I could make out human shapes staring at me through the cracks in the partition.

There were about twenty-five women peeking at me through the cracks in the bamboo when suddenly the pressure on the partition grew too great and part of it collapsed. Before they knew what had happened, the women were sitting in the room listening and talking directly to me. Some hid their faces behind a veil. Others giggled and were too shy to look at me directly. But we had no more need of someone to repeat our words. That was the first time I spoke with a group of Jobra women indoors.

Progress was still very slow that day, as it was slow on many that followed. Very early on we realized that having female bank workers made it a lot easier to convince village women to become Grameen Bank borrowers. Our female workers found it easier to establish rapport with the village women, but faced many obstacles of their own. The nature of a bank worker's job requires that he or she walk alone in rural areas, sometimes for distances as long as five miles in each direction to reach the poor. The parents of many prospective female bank workers found this demeaning— even scandalous. In some places female workers were even attacked by villagers for riding bicycles from place to place, which is considered improper for a woman. Even when arriving on foot, a female worker often faces criticism from the villagers who are not used to seeing women anywhere but in the home.

So our fight against the ill-treatment and segregation of women took place not only on behalf of our borrowers. My students and I tramped around the village all through the monsoon and through the month of Ashar, when people eat the lush leafy greens of *kalmi* and *puishak*. My favorite smell came from the delicious *kachu shak,* a sort of long asparagus, simmering with bay leaves, ground cumin, and turmeric.

We learned many things along the way—constantly refining Grameen so that the structure of the institution would naturally support the poorest of the poor to raise themselves out of poverty using their own ample ingenuity and skill. As we continued to adapt and learn, to my great surprise I was soon to find that the repayment of loans by people who borrowed without collateral would prove to be far higher than commercial banks—over 98 percent! We had challenged the most basic banking premise of collateral and not only proved it wrong, but turned it on its head.

A STRUCTURE THAT NATURALLY SUPPORTS SUCCESS

Early on we discovered that requiring support groups of five borrowers was crucial to our success—significantly reducing the work of the bank while creating strong incentives for honesty and self-reliance among group members. Subtle and at times not-so-subtle peer pressure keeps each group member in line with the broader objectives of the credit program, and if any member of a group gets into trouble, the rest of the group usually comes forward to help.

It is not always easy for borrowers to organize themselves into groups. A prospective borrower first has to take the initiative and explain how the bank works to a second person. This can be particularly difficult for a village woman. She often has a difficult time convincing her friends—who may be terrified, skeptical, or forbidden by their husbands to deal with money—but eventually a second person, impressed by what Grameen has done for another household, will take the leap of joining the group. Then the two will go seek out a third member, then a fourth, and a fifth. Once the group of five is formed, we extend loans to two members of the group. If these two repay regularly for the next six weeks, two more members may request loans. The chairperson of the group is usually the last borrower of the five. Often, just when the group is ready, a member changes her mind and the group falls back down to four or three, or even back to one.

It can take anywhere from a few days to several months for a group to be recognized or certified by Grameen Bank. To gain recognition, all the members of a group of five prospective borrowers have to present themselves to the bank, undergo at least seven days of training on our policies, and demonstrate their understanding of those policies in an oral examination administered by a senior bank official. Each of the members must be individually tested. That night before her test, a borrower often gets so nervous that she lights a candle in a saint's shrine and prays to Allah for help. She knows that if she fails she will let down not only herself, but also the others in the group.

The pressure provided by the group and the exam helps ensure that only those who are truly needy and serious about joining Grameen will actually become members. Those who are better off usually do not find it worthwhile. And even if they do, they will fail our means test, which ensures we reach only the poorest of the poor.

Once all members pass the exam, the day finally comes when one of them asks for a first loan, usually about twenty-five dollars in the 1980's. How does she feel? Terrified. She cannot sleep at night. She struggles with the fear of failure, the fear of the unknown. The morning she is to receive her loan, she almost quits. Twenty-five dollars is simply too much responsibility for her. How will she ever be able to repay it? No woman in her extended family has ever had so much money. Her friends come around to reassure her, saying, "Look, we all have to go through it. We will support you. We are here for just that. Don't be scared. We will all be with you."

When she finally receives the twenty-five dollars, she is trembling. The money burns her fingers. Tears roll down her face. She has never seen so much money in her life. She never imagined it in her hands. She carries the bills as she would a delicate bird or a rabbit, until someone advises her to put the money away in a safe place lest it be stolen.

This is the beginning for almost every Grameen borrower. All her life she has been told that she is no good, that she brings only misery to her family, and that they cannot afford to pay her dowry. Many times she hears her mother or her father tell her she should have been killed at birth, aborted, or starved. To her family she has been nothing but another mouth to feed, another dowry to pay. But today, for the first time in her life, an institution has trusted her with a great sum of money. She promises that she will never let down the institution or herself. She will struggle to make sure that every penny is paid back.

By 1994 we were operating Grameen Bank on purely commercial terms, having decided to give up the grants and low-interest loans we had been receiving during our early years. We were now completely self-sustained, paying our bankworkers decent wages. Our operations were funded entirely by the deposits we received from the rural poor whom we served. Two years later we extended our one-billionth dollar in loans to one of our 2 million borrowers. It was a thrilling moment. A project that had started with a spontaneous twenty-seven-dollar loan from my own pocket had reached its billionth dollar. In a little over two more years, we loaned our two-billionth dollar. Grameen was picking up steam. When I went to the villages I saw how many of our borrowers had not only crossed the poverty line but left it far behind. I met borrowers whose weekly loan repayments were now larger than the entirety of the original loan they borrowed from Grameen 10 years earlier—a fifty-fold increase.

One such wonderful success story comes from Murshida Begum. Murshida was born into a poor family of eight children. Neither her father nor grandfather owned any farmland. At fifteen she was married to a man from a nearby village who worked as an unskilled laborer in a factory.

The first few years of the marriage went relatively well, but things turned sour when Murshida began having children. Just as their family expenses went up, her husband started bringing home less and less money. Finally it became clear that he was a compulsive gambler. During the 1974 famine, he was given a company bonus of 1,800 taka. He lost it all gambling. When Murshida complained, her husband beat her.

To earn some extra money, Murshida took up spinning raw cotton into yarn. She worked on contract for other people and was paid very little, sometimes no more than a handful of broken rice. Still the work prevented her from starving. She considered other options—working as a domestic servant for a rich family or begging. But what would happen to her children?

One day Murshida's husband came home after a week's absence and complained that there was not enough food for him. Murshida had cooked up something modest and had not eaten the entire day. Angry, her husband beat her and then left, saying he would return later in the morning. That day there was a thunderstorm, and as her husband had sold the roof of their house to pay gambling debts, Murshida and her three children were soaked. at that moment Murshida decided that something had to change. When her husband returned at midnight, Murshida confronted him.

"You have only brought a small quantity of flattened rice for your daughter," she remembers saying, "but nothing for me. Yet everyone in the village says you earn a lot of money." Her husband flew into a rage and beat her. Then he divorced her on the spot and told her to leave the house.

"What about the children?" Murshida asked.

"You can throw them into the river and let them drown, for all I care," he responded.

Murshida sent word to her brother, who offered to take her into his home. Once she had moved in, Murshida found some more work spinning on contract. She heard about the Grameen Bank when it came to her village. She stopped a bank worker on the village path and begged him to give her money. "I told him I would swim across a river to attend Grameen Bank meetings if necessary. I told him that I wanted to follow him to wherever he was going to form a group, so I could join. I told him that he must give me money, otherwise I would not be able to survive with my children.

At first Murshida borrowed 1,000 taka to purchase a goat and she paid off the loan in six months with the profits from selling the milk. She was left with a goat, a kid, and no debt. Encouraged, she borrowed 2,000 taka, bought raw cotton and a spinning wheel, and began manufacturing lady's scarves. She now sells her scarves wholesale for 100 taka with tassels and 50 taka without. Murshida's business has grown so much that during peak periods she employs as many as twenty-five women in her village to manufacture scarves. In addition, she has bought an acre of farmland with her profits, built a house with a Grameen Bank housing loan, and set up her brothers in businesses that include sari trading and raw cotton trading.

Though Murshida's story may strike some as exceptional, it really is a microcosm of what goes on in Grameen—how people are able to reach their full potential much more easily after accessing credit.

I always believed that charity was not the answer to poverty. Charity only helps poverty to continue. It creates dependency and takes away the initiative of individuals to support themselves through offering their talents to the world. Instead of offering charity, Garmeen Bank offers a way for poor families to help themselves overcome poverty. Grameen Bank is as self-reliant as its members, funded entirely by the deposits repaid on its low-interest loans to the poor. This ensures that Garmeen Bank will always be there for its members. Since it's inception, Grameen Bank has made profits every year except for three—the year the bank was founded and still getting off the ground, and two years during and directly after one of the worst floods in our country's long history of natural disasters. This is an incredible record of profitability when compared with many other successful traditional businesses. And since Grameen Bank is owned by the rural poor whom it serves, its profits go directly back to its members. Today, borrowers of the bank own 95% of its equity, while the remaining 5% is owned by the government.

I never imagined that my micro-lending program would be the basis for a nationwide "bank for the poor," providing its services in 81,379 villages—97% of the total villages in Bangladesh. I never imagined that Grameen would one day serve at the door-steps of 8.36 million people—a number still growing today—68 percent of whom have clearly lifted themselves and their families out of extreme poverty. I never imagined that the concept of micro-lending would be adapted in more than one hundred countries spanning every continent. I was only trying to relieve my guilt and satisfy my desire to be useful to a few starving human beings. But it did not stop with a few people. Those who borrowed and survived would not let it. And after a while, neither would I.

After more than thirty years, Grameen is living proof that poverty is not created by the poor; it is created by the institutions and policies that surround them. In order to eliminate poverty, all we need to do is to make appropriate changes in existing institutions and policies, or we need to create new ones. If we continue to do this, I have no doubt that there will be a day when the intense struggle to preserve one's life will never be fought over the lack of basic necessities. Poverty will be a thing of the past, a cautionary tale left to history books and museums.

(Read more about the conflicts overcome by Grameen Bank in the next story, *The Women and the Mullah.*)

Muhammad Yunus

56
The Women and the Mullah[*]
(A continuation of the previous story)

Despite our incredible success in Jobra village with the Grameen Bank pilot project, people refused to see Grameen for what it was—a truly sustainable bank boasting a repayment rate of over 98 percent despite the fact that we lent to only the very poorest individuals. People had a hard time believing it could really be true, so they came up with reasons to explain away our success. They argued that borrowers were repaying their loans simply because I was a highly-respected university professor and that micro-credit worked in Chittagong because I was a native of that city. I tried to explain that the poor did not go to my university, that none of their families could read and write, and that my academic reputation was meaningless to them, but it became clear that if I was to demonstrate to the banking establishment that Grameen was replicable by any other bank, I would resign my professorship, become a banker, and set up a Grameen branch in another district.

In the end, I did just that. The University of Chittigong granted me a two-year leave of absence. On June 6, 1979, before I knew what had happened, I had officially joined the Grameen Bank Project in the District of Tangail.

Tangail District was in the throes of a warlike situation. Armed gangs in an underground Marxist dissident movement called the Gonobahini ("The People's Army") terrorized the countryside. These guerrillas killed with little compunction. They simply pointed a gun and fired. In every village we came across dead bodies lying in the middle of the road, hanging from trees, or shot by a wall. The countryside was awash with arms and ammunition left over from the War of Liberation. To save their lives, most of the local community leaders had run away, hidden with neighbors, or moved into hotels in Tangail City. There was neither law nor order.

What could we, a fledgling bank project, achieve in the face of this bloodshed and killing? We worried about the physical safety of our newly recruited branch managers and bank workers who would be working and living by themselves in distant villages. To make matters worse, many of the young workers we were hiring were ex-students with radical sympathies, who could easily be swayed by the armed leftist guerrillas. (In fact, we later found out that some of our workers had been active Gonobahini members up until they began working for us.)

It was the hottest part of the year. Even the slightest effort left one completely exhausted. During the day the roads were deserted and people stood under trees praying for a *kalbaisakhi*, a sudden summer storm. The villages we passed through seemed so godforsaken and the people so poor and emaciated that I knew I had come to the right place. This was where we were needed most.

We soon discovered that the ex-Gonobahini turned out to be excellent workers. These underground fighters were young (usually between eighteen and twenty years old), hard working, and dedicated. They had wanted to liberate the country with guns and revolution, and now they were walking around those same villages extending microloans to the destitute. They just needed a cause to fight for. We channeled their energies toward something more constructive than terrorism. Provided they gave up their guns, we were happy to hire them as bank workers.

But there remained another significant challenge in Tangail.

Our branch managers and bank workers were used to facing skepticism from religious and political leaders in the villages. But it was in the District of Tangail that we first encountered large-scale opposition from conservative clerics. In numerous cases these figures tried to scare uneducated villagers by telling them that a woman who takes loans from Grameen is trespassing into an evil area, forbidden to women. They warn her that as punishment for joining Grameen, she will not be given a proper Islamic burial when she dies—a terrifying prospect for a woman who has nothing.

Other rumors, which can be as frightening to a poor woman as they seem ludicrous to Grameen staff, often surfaced in the villages. Maharani Das, age thirty-five, from the coastal region of Pathuakali, was told that contact with Grameen would turn her into a Christian. Her family beat her repeatedly to prevent her from joining. Musammat Kuti Begum, age twenty, from Faridpur, joined Gramen in spite of being warned that the bank would take her to the Middle East and sell her to a slave trader. Mosammat Manikjan Bibi, age thirty-five, from Paipara, said, "The moneylenders and the rich people told me that if I joined Grameen, I was a bad Muslim, and the bank would take me out to sea and drop me to the bottom of the ocean." Manzira Khatun, age thirty-eight, from the Rajshahi District, heard she would be tortured, have a number tattooed on her arm, and be sold into prostitution. Grameen was said to convert women to Christianity, to destroy Islam by taking women out of *purdah*, to steal houses and property, to kidnap women borrowers, to run away with any repaid loans, and to belong to an international smuggling ring or a new East India Company that would recolonize Bangladesh as the British had done two and a half centuries ago.

As soon as such rumors start—and the above list is by no means exhaustive—the situation can become tense very quickly. In one particular village in Tangail, for example, our Grameen manager was physically threatened by a religious leader. When the manager saw there was no way to reason with the mullah, he quietly closed the branch and left the village. He told potential members that his life had been threatened and that they would have to go through orientation meetings in the neighboring village. Some women made the daily trek to the neighboring village to form groups and join Grameen. But others, inspired by the way Grameen had bettered the lives of their neighbors in other villages, visited the religious leader and argued with him.

"Why did you threaten that Grameen manager?" they asked. "Grameen was coming here to our village to do nothing but good."

"Do you want to go to hell?" answered the mullah. "Grameen is a Christian organization! It wants to destroy the rules of *purdah*. That is why it has come."

"The Grameen manager is a Muslim, and he knows the Quran better than you! Besides, Grameen allows us to work at home, husking rice, weaving mats, or making bamboo stools, without ever going out. The bank comes to our house. How is that against *purdah*? The only one who is against *purdah* here is you, by making us travel miles to a neighboring village to get relief. You are the one who is destroying our lifestyle, not Grameen."

"Go to the moneylender, he is a good Muslim," answered the confused mullah.

"He charges 10 percent a week! If you don't want us to borrow from Grameen, then you lend us the money."

"Leave me alone. I have had enough of your harassing me day and night."

"It is you who harasses us by not letting Grameen come here," answered the women. "We will only go when you let Grameen into our village. We will come every day and harass you until you let the bank in."

Eventually the mullah relented, "Oh, okay then, to hell with you all. If you want to damn yourselves to perdition forever, go ahead, join Grameen. I have tried my best to save you. No one can say I didn't try my best to warn you. So go, borrow, and be damned!"

The women were overjoyed. They rushed in a group to the neighboring village and told the Grameen manager that he could come back now that they had talked to the mullah and that he no longer had any objection. The manager thanked them for their persistence on his behalf but said that he would return only if the man who threatened him came and requested his return. He did not want any misunderstanding or any physical threats hanging over him and his Grameen colleagues.

And so the women returned to their village. Again they went and confronted their mullah. Again they argued with him, until he was so disgusted and tired of the whole matter he wished he had never gotten involved. Finally, at his wit's end, he agreed to invite the manager back into his village. It was not an extremely courteous invitation, but everyone heard it. That was the important part.

The women who are the most desperate, who have nothing to eat, who have been abandoned by their husbands and are trying to feed their children by begging, usually stand by their decision to join Grameen Bank no matter who threatens them. They have no other choice. In some cases they must either borrow from us or watch their children die. And those on the sidelines who watch but dare not ignore the terrible rumors about us soon find out that the Grameen managers' understanding of religious issues is often deeper than that of most of the people who accuse them of being anti-Muslim.

We believe that Islam is not at all a hindrance to the eradication of poverty through micro-credit programs. Islam does not inherently prevent women from making a living for themselves or from improving their economic situation. In 1994, the adviser on women's affairs to the president of Iran came to visit me in Dhaka, and when I asked her what she thought about Grameen, she said, "There is nothing in Shariah law or the Quran against what you are doing. Why should women be hungry and poor? On the contrary, what you are doing is terrific. You are helping to educate a whole generation of children. And thanks to Grameen loans, women can work at home, instead of sitting around."

Many Islamic scholars have also told us that the Shariah ban on the charging of interest cannot apply to Grameen, since the Grameen borrower is also an owner of the bank. The purpose of the religious injunction against interest is to protect the poor from usury, but where the poor own their own bank, the interest is in effect paid to the company they own, and therefore to themselves.

With any social change there is often resistance. but with change that makes a fundamental kind of sense, that accounts for each human individual in the most comprehensive way, there will naturally arise the solution to those conflicts. Such was the case in Tangail, where these brave women confronting their mullah represent just one of many stories of the poor women of Bangladesh taking hold of their own power and insisting on participating in a better life. All that the Grameen Bank does is give them an opportunity to do just that.

Muhammad Yunus

57
Kicking the Car

I was driving my little Fiat in the middle of a six-lane inner-city street, taking my mentor Nathaniel Branden from the airport to his hotel. I was Nathaniel's Rocky Mountain representative, promoting his Denver Colorado workshops on *Self Esteem and the Art of Being*. I was both excited and nervous as we talked about the upcoming workshops. I really wanted everything to go as well as possible.

Just as we passed through a large intersection I heard an ambulance behind me and saw its lights flashing in my rear-view mirror. To get out of his way I flipped on my right turn signal and changed lanes. As soon as I did I hit something! To my surprise a large Lincoln Continental had pulled into my blind spot from the side street. In my mirror I saw that I'd clipped the car's front bumper, thankfully nothing worse. I pulled over and the Continental pulled over behind us.

Immediately four large, young, 18-year-old men jumped out of the Continental and the driver ran and started kicking my car anywhere he could. He was screaming and cursing at me using words I won't repeat, telling me how stupid I was for what I'd just done. His three friends were yelling too, nearly as angry as he was.

Still sitting in the driver's seat, my heart was pounding in my chest. I started to get out of the car, but Nathaniel got out of the passenger side much faster. He walked straight up to the driver and said very loudly over the yelling, "That was a really stupid move on her part, wasn't it?!" I was shocked. I didn't know what he was doing. Here he was *agreeing* with these men who were attacking my car! The kicking faltered for a moment as they turned to him. Nathaniel gestured toward the car where the continental's fancy red fiberglass bug-shield hung at an odd angle from the hood, broken from the incident. "We're gonna make sure *this* gets corrected!" He said emphatically.

"I just got this God damn windscreen on my car!" The driver yelled. "Brand *new*. Now it's ruined!" The other three men joined in again, continuing to shout about what a stupid move I had made.

"It was *all* her fault!" Nathaniel yelled back, "We'll make sure *this* is paid for!" He pointed at the broken bug-shield.

As I watched him interact with the men I was very scared, but also fascinated. Something was happening here that I wasn't used to. I was observing something that was outside of my awareness of what could work, but as I watched I saw it working.

Nathaniel didn't waste a moment in directing the situation: "We will get your name and phone number to make sure this is all paid for!" he said. He got out a pencil and paper and thrust it into the man's hands. The four men started to calm down as the driver wrote down his information, and we made sure he had mine. "Great, we're gonna get this solved." Nathaniel reached out and shook the guy's hand.

They seemed OK with that. We all just got back in our cars and drove off. My heart was still in my throat. I didn't even talk to Nathaniel about what had just happened. I was just feeling lucky to be alive and unhurt and leaving.

The next day, with some trepidation, I called the fellow. When he answered he was so kind and apologetic that he calmed me down right away. "I am *so* sorry I screamed and yelled at you," he said, "but I had just gotten that bug-shield and I was so upset to see it ruined…" Through the whole conversation he was *really* nice to me.

My insurance paid for the damage. It was no problem.

What was amazing was the really good resolution between the man and me. It was a huge shift. They were actually great guys, it's just that in the moment they had been outraged, and strongly caught up in it.

Only much later did I come to understand what Nathaniel had done instinctively in that unusual moment. His swift meeting of the volume and energy of the men's anger, while simultaneously agreeing with their basic complaint (that I had done something stupid), communicated an understanding of the situation that the men could both *hear* over their shouting and also *agree* with. When he had their attention, Nathaniel kept the negative part of the situation at a distance by gesturing to their car whenever he spoke of the problem. At the same time he associated both of us with the solution by saying, "*we're* gonna make sure this gets corrected … *we'll* make sure this is paid for … *we* will get your name and phone number … *we're* gonna get this solved." These short proactive statements were congruent with his actions as he handed the driver a pencil and paper and shook the man's hand. Together, Nathaniel's words and actions communicated a *complete* assumption that everyone would cooperate to resolve the problem in a nonviolent way.

It was an inspiration to see him do all this in an intuitive reaction to the moment. His natural response to the circumstances saved us both from what could have become quite a confrontation!

Jan Prince

58
Internal Garden

Iwork as a therapist, and my experience is that all successful therapy is the resolution or transformation of conflict within the self.

One day I got a call from a man asking me to go to the local hospice and work with his wife. She had cancer, and they said she would be dying any day. He just wanted me to do anything I could for her, so I said of course I would go.

I don't remember the exact kind of cancer, but when I arrived the nurse told me that it had metastasized to such a degree that the woman had areas in her buttocks where the cancer had eaten away so much that you could put your whole fist in it. That image stuck with me.

This woman was in a fairly delusional state. She didn't make much eye contact, always looking off in other directions. The cancer had progressed so far and she was so ill, that I just did what I could to be supportive. I was very gentle about it, giving her a lot of choices, such as not needing to talk to me—there was very little that she could say anyway. I just talked to her, doing my best to make good contact and give her the sense that she was cared for, even while she was mostly off in her own world. When I left, I figured it would be the last time I saw the woman.

A couple weeks later I was surprised to get another call from her husband. He told me that his wife had lingered longer than expected, and so hospice had thought it better to send her home where she could spend her remaining time with her husband. Over the phone her husband asked me, "Could you come in and meet with her again? She appreciated the last time you came."

So I agreed to come, and figured it would be more of the same.

When I arrived at their house, I went in to where she was in bed in her room. She was much more lucid this time. We began talking, and in our conversation it became very apparent to me that for a long time she had really been holding people away from her. Other people felt like a threat and an imposition to her, and very unsafe. The more she interacted with me, the more clues I got telling me that this issue was very significant for her. I got the sense that there was no place at all where she felt safe to just be herself.

So I suggested that we do a visualization. I asked her to imagine some place that she felt very, very safe, and that felt comforting and inspiring to her.

She said, "A garden." But it was interesting, because even there she was hesitant.

"What's the problem?" I asked.

"Well, other things could come into the garden," she said. "It's too open."

"What if we put some kind of force-field around the garden so nothing else can come in?"

At that suggestion, her whole face and body relaxed.

I asked her about the garden, and from what she told me it was pretty bare, pretty sparse. It had some flowers and that was about it. There wasn't much there.

I said, "OK, you've got some flowers with a force-field around it." We talked about that for a bit, and what that was like for her. Eventually I asked her, "Are there any other plants you'd like to have in the garden?"

"I like roses," she said.

I told her that it was her garden, and she could plant roses there if she liked. She did.

Then I asked, "What about some fruit trees? They might provide nice shade for some of the flowers that don't do well in direct sun." It was a slow process, but gradually, in a way that was safe for her, we built up the sense of a true garden, always keeping that force-field around to protect it. We added nut trees, and some other plants that she liked. Plants seemed to be the one kind of living thing around which she could still feel safe.

Then, being a little bit pushy, I asked her, "Are there any earth worms in there?"

"No!" she said.

"Well do you think it would be a benefit for the plants to have some earth worms to loosen the soil?"

She had a lot of hesitation with the idea that letting in worms might be a good idea. It was a big deal. I took the plant's point of view—what would be good for the plants. I appealed to her kindness and consideration for the plants. After a bit more discussion, she finally said, "I guess worms might be good for the garden."

I said, "Now would that be safe for you? Would that be alright for you?"

After more exploring she eventually said, "I guess I can't imagine that worms would be a problem."

So I had her design some way that the worms could get into and out of the garden through the force-field, and that seemed pretty good to her.

"What about beetles?" I asked next. "Are there any beetles in there?"

"NO!"

"Well, do you think it might be good for the plants to have some beetles in there to eat the old dead leaves and help turn them into good compost for the garden?"

Eventually she agreed it would be a beneficial thing for the plants, and that beetles would not really pose a problem for her.

Next I asked, "Well are there any bees? Do you want bees to be able to pollinate the plants?"

She said, "huh?"

I asked, "Do you have any allergies to bees?"

"No, no, I like bees," she said.

So she figured out a way to let bees in and out, and we went through a few more beneficial insects—praying mantises and spiders. Each time we introduced something new we had to really work through, metaphorically, all her issues of engaging with any other kind of life beyond plants, and how she could do that in a way that was safe.

Then I said, "This garden sounds so beautiful with the fruit trees and the flowers and the insects, how about birds? Would birds be nice? To have birdsong—you know, to be able to share such a beautiful place with a bird—that might be nice."

"Oh yeah," she said, "I hadn't thought about that; that does seem nice and I do like birds."

So she designed a way for birds to come in and out of the force field that worked for her. One by one we went through all these things that can help a garden grow well, becoming a whole, balanced ecosystem. We added squirrels, and even let in a fox or two. The whole time she was safe and in control, and every time she let in another critter, I could see something light up in her a little more.

Finally I thought, *I'll push it even farther.*

I said, "You know, this sounds like such a *beautiful* place. What would you think if we let somebody come in and see what a beautiful thing you've created?"

It was very interesting, because I could see on her face that, after having created such a beautiful place, a part of her longed to let somebody else see it.

"But I don't want them to always be there," she said. "I want to have the garden to myself."

262

"Hey, you're in charge," I said. "You could set it up so that nobody comes in, or maybe only one day a week, or maybe for just a little time during each day—however you'd like to do it."

We talked about it for quite a while, and finally she decided that it sounded like a good idea. To be able to share her garden with other people—something beautiful that she'd created—really appealed to her. As long as she got to choose when, and whether or not she was even there at the same time.

So she set that up in a way that felt safe for her, which involved building an airlock through the force-field—two pressurized doors so the visitor would have to come through the first one, which would then close behind the visitor and seal before the second door opened. She wanted that level of control. She didn't want anything else or anyone else getting in by accident.

By this point it had probably been about 2 ½ to 3 hours. It was a *long, slow* process. So we closed with that. I really thanked her, both for sharing her garden with me, and for being open about it, and for letting me spend this kind of time with her. I left her room and walked down the hall and past the kitchen where her husband was cooking up a bunch of food to have on hand for himself, since his wife was due to die any day. He and I talked for probably fifteen, twenty minutes. Then we heard this pretty big noise come from the back room where his wife was staying.

We both were thinking, *What is that? Did she fall out of her bed? Is she calling out?* We heard another couple bangs, and around the corner the woman appeared, rolling herself in her wheelchair! The banging had been her getting out of bed into her wheelchair, which she hadn't done in weeks and weeks. She looked at her husband and said, "I'm kind of hungry." I knew she hadn't asked for food in a long time. I talked to them a couple minutes more and then I left, because I realized this would be one of their last real times together.

Three months later I ran into the woman's husband downtown. I was a little cautious, because I figured his wife had died, and so what do you say? But I went over to him and asked, "How are you doing? How did your wife's passing go?"

He said, "Well, she didn't pass."

I said, "What?"

He pointed down the street, and I saw her sitting there on a bench right next to where a bunch of kids were playing. There were people all around her. She was just sitting there watching everyone with a big smile on her face, clearly delighted at being out in public.

I walked over and talked with her, and she told me that the doctors said the cancer was gone. All these big sores—everything had healed up. It was the last thing I would have expected, but there she was, talking to me.

I had direct follow-up with her six months later, and indirect at least a year later through reports from other people. At that time I know for sure that she was still healthy and cancer free, and that's quite a lot of time given the nature of the cancer that she had.

When I had met with her in her home, it was clear that she had retreated from other people and didn't think she had anything to offer. Yet at the same time it became obvious that she *wanted* to have connection with people. She had this huge internal conflict of wanting something to offer, yet feeling that she had nothing. The garden was something that *she* had created that was really beautiful. There was clear value in the garden, enough value that it was worth letting someone else in to see it. Before this, I don't think she'd ever had a sense that there was something of value in her.

The garden also represented something that she had to take care of, and something that was *worth* taking care of. The framework was: "This is your garden, and whatever you decide, is up to you. As the caretaker for the garden, what do you want for the garden?" She was in charge, and that also allowed her to create and have control over her own safety. That was hugely important. Without that safety, none of it would have been possible.

I think there are so many things that were important for her about the garden, and who knows exactly how that affected her cancer, which is the body's own cells growing out of balance—the body's "ecosystem" going out of balance. I wondered about how that related to her experience of creating a garden that was no longer just flowers, as it had started out, but a whole network of plants and bugs and animals all working together. Whatever is the case, I never imagined that creating one story of a garden might have such a profound impact. The whole thing was a very powerful experience to be a part of.

Mark Hochwender

59
Welcoming the Enemy

It was **midnight**. Before retiring I walked out on the screened porch where my 15-year old son was sleeping. I was leading a team of 17 young people, including two of my own children, on a three-month work assignment in a jungle area 200 miles from the nearest city in a South American country. Four years before, my husband and I with our four children had first come to this area at the request of the village people to help them start a church, build a fish hatchery, and develop other forms of appropriate technology to meet basic human needs. After the church and appropriate technology center had been established we moved to work in another country. This summer the village had asked us to return to experiment with a vegetable protein project.

When we received the invitation, my husband was already committed to a project in Haiti for the summer. We decided to divide up for three months in order to work in both projects. My husband took our 14-year-old Karen with him to Haiti while our 15-year-old Tommy and 16-year-old Kathy went with me, leaving our 19-year-old Chris to take care of things at our headquarters in Alabama.

The air on the porch was chilly, so I laid a blanket across Tommy's cot, then stood a moment looking out across the fishponds that were bringing hope of more food to our village. The light from the moon made a rippling path of white across the water.

Suddenly I heard a crash. Turning quickly I could see in the moonlight that a soldier had slid into our water barrel. I was paralyzed with shock as I looked out over the clearing that separated our temporary home from the jungle. About 30 soldiers were rushing our house.

Our host country had just held elections, not the usual custom, and the military did not agree with the results. The military had taken over one week before, exiling the newly elected president and repressing any resistance, real or imagined. Since we were in such a remote frontier village, I had not expected the fighting to reach us.

While I stood there, frozen in fear, watching the soldiers surround our house, the message a neighbor woman had brought me that day flashed through my mind.

"Sister, keep your team in the house," she had urged. "I just came from the market over near the military camp. I overheard two soldiers saying the Americans were to blame for the resistance to their takeover. They said they would not rest until they had exterminated every American in this zone."

Since we had not been involved in political activities in their country, I thought that she had misunderstood. I did not think that we could be suspected of participating in such resistance, but now what the neighbor woman had warned me about was taking place before my eyes. Evidently, the soldiers were intent on carrying out their threat. If they wanted to kill us, there was no way we could stop them.

My heart was beating so fast, I thought my blood vessels would burst. It felt as if I was about to have a stroke. I knew I had a responsibility for the team members inside the house, but I could not even call out to them. I was paralyzed with fear.

I had only a split second to pray before the soldiers found me: "God, if I have to die, take care of my family. And God, please take away this fear. I don't want to die afraid. Please help me to die trusting you." I was suddenly aware of the presence of God.

We do not always feel God. Usually we trust God by faith. However, at that moment God's presence was very real, seemingly touchable. I still thought I was going to die, but I knew God had things under control. I remember thinking that maybe our deaths would accomplish things that we had not been able to accomplish with our lives.

I found myself stepping up to the closest soldier and speaking words I could never have thought to say. "Welcome, brother," I called out. "Come in. You do not need guns to visit us."

At that the soldier jumped, dropped the bullet he was putting in his gun, and shouted, "Not me. I'm not the one. I'm just following orders. There's the commander over there, he's the one."

I raised my voice and repeated, "You're all welcome. Everyone is welcome in our home."

At that the commander ran up to me, shoved the muzzle of his rifle against my stomach, and pushed me through the door into the house. Thirty soldiers rushed into the house and began pulling everything off the shelves and out of the drawers, looking for guns. They herded the team members into the kitchen, where they sat quietly by the glow of the two candles we used for light.

The soldier who led the attack turned his gun on me and demanded angrily, "What are you Americans doing down here—trying to stop our revolution? Seventeen Americans would not be living in this poverty if they did not have political motivation."

"Sir," I responded truthfully, "we have had nothing to do with your revolution. We are here for two reasons. We are teaching self-help projects to the hungry and we are teaching the Bible."

"That tells me nothing," he responded. "I have never read the Bible in my life. Maybe it is a communist book, for all I know."

"You have never read the Bible in your life? Oh, sir, I am so sorry for you. You have missed the best part of your life. Please let me tell you what it says."

He made no objection. He had to stand there with his gun on us while the other soldiers ransacked the house looking for the guns we did not have.

I picked up a Spanish Bible and turned to the Sermon on the Mount. "We teach about Jesus Christ," I said, "God's Son who came into this world to save us. He also taught us a better way than fighting. He taught us the way of love. Because of him I can tell you that even though you kill me, I will die loving you because God loves you. To follow him, I have to love you too."

In that particular Bible there were paragraph captions. He glanced at them and read plainly, "Jesus teaches love your enemies," and "Return good for evil."

"That's humanly impossible!" he burst out.

"That's true, sir," I answered. "It isn't humanly possible, but with God's help it is possible."

"I don't believe it."

"You can prove it, sir. I know you came here to kill us. So just kill me slowly, if you want to prove it. Cut me to pieces little by little, and you will see you cannot make me hate you. I will die praying for you because God loves you, and we love you too."

The soldier lowered his gun and stepped back. Clearing his throat, he said, "You almost convince me you are innocent—but I have orders to take everyone in the house and the ham radio. I will let you get some warm clothes and a blanket—you will be sleeping on the ground."

They marched us two by two at gunpoint down a trail to where a truck was waiting on the one little road that came into our village. We saw that others in our town had been taken prisoner also. The district superintendent of the church, the leader of the youth group, and other leaders were lined up at gunpoint, ready to be loaded on the trucks with us.

Suddenly the soldier changed his mind: "Halt!" he said. "Take only the men. The women will come with me."

He led us back to our home, saying, "I don't know why I am doing this. I was about to take you into a jungle camp of over a thousand soldiers. I know what they do to women prisoners. You would be abused many times. I cannot take you.

"In our army no one breaks an order," he continued sternly. "I have never broken an order before, but for the first time tonight I am refusing to obey an order. If my superior officer finds out that you were in this house when I raided it, and that I did not take you, I will pay for it with my life." He strode to the door, stopped, and looked back again.

"I could have fought any amount of guns you might have had," he said, "but there is something here I cannot understand. I cannot fight it."

Then the hard part began—waiting to hear what had happened to the men of our team and the leaders of the village. The waiting, the uncertainty, seemed endless. If a twig snapped outside our window everyone jumped, thinking the soldiers were back again. The people of our village were as distressed as we were. They stood around in our house all day—some weeping, others coming to offer their sympathy. No one knew what would happen next.

The local people insisted we could not have a service in the church on Sunday because the soldiers considered any meeting held to be for the purpose of political agitation. "Soldiers will be there if you have a service. They will take more prisoners," they told me. We all agreed to pray at home on Sunday.

But on Saturday night a messenger came to our door. "I bring a message from the man who commanded the attack on your village Thursday night," he said. "He says he will be at your service Sunday. However, he has no vehicle on Sundays so you are to bring the church's jeep and get him. He said to tell you that if you don't come he will be there anyway, even if he has to walk the 10 miles." It sounded like a threat.

I sent a message to everyone in the town that night. "We will have the service after all," I told them, "but you are not obligated to come. In fact you may lose your life by coming.

No one knows what this soldier will do. Do not come when the church bell rings unless you are sure God wants you to come." I knew that the villagers feared the military and stayed out of sight when soldiers were around. I did not expect any of them to come.

The next morning I took the jeep and went to get the commander. He came with a bodyguard. The two of them marched coldly into the church and sat down, still holding their rifles. The women on our team came in, the bell was rung, and we began to sing. The church was packed before the first hymn was over. The people came pale and trembling, but they came. They had felt that their faith was at stake, and they were determined to attend, even if it meant imprisonment.

Since the leaders of the church had been taken by the military, I led the service. I tried to do just what I would have done had the soldiers not been there. It was church custom to welcome visitors by inviting them to the platform, singing a welcome song, and waving to them. Everyone would then line up to shake the visitors' hands, hug them, and say some personal words of greeting.

How could I ask these people to hug the very man who had taken their husband, son, or brother prisoner? That was asking too much. I decided that I would ask them to sing a welcome song but that I would stop there and leave out the hugging.

The soldiers were surprised when I asked them to the platform to let us welcome them. "Welcome us?" they asked in amazement. "Well, all right," they shrugged. They came forward and stood very formally with their guns across their backs.

The people stood, singing weakly and waving their hands timidly. I expected them to sit back down, but no. The first man on the front seat came forward and put out his hand. As he bent over to hug the soldier I heard him say, "Brother, we don't like what you did to our village, but this is the house of God, and God loves you, so you are welcome here."

Everyone in the church followed his example, even the women whose eyes were red from weeping for their loved ones whom this man had taken prisoner. They too said words of welcome. The looks on the soldiers' faces became ones of surprise, then incredulity.

When the last person finished greeting them, the head soldier marched to the pulpit and said in a very stern voice, "Now I will have a few words. Never have I ever dreamed that I could raid a town, come back, and have that town welcome me as a brother. I can hardly believe what I have seen and heard this morning. That sister told me Thursday night that Christians love their enemies, but I did not believe her then. You have proven it to me this morning," he said to the congregation.

"This is the first church service I have ever been to," he continued. "I never believed there was a God before, but what I have just felt is so strong that I will never doubt the existence of God again as long as I live."

He turned from one side of the congregation to the other. "Do all of you know God?" he asked. "If you know God, hang on to him. It must be the greatest thing in this world to know God." As he spoke in an urgent voice he motioned with his hand, clenching it as though to hold on to something, while in his other hand he held a gun.

"I don't know God," he confessed in a low voice, "but I hope someday I shall, and that someday we can once again greet each other as brothers and sisters, as we have done this morning."

He came home with us for lunch. The men caught fish from the ponds to cook for his meal. The women helped me cook, even those who had lost a loved one. While we prepared lunch, the men took him around to see the brick project for dry housing, the chicken and vegetable protein project, and the clean water project. At last he said, "I have taken innocent people, but I did not know it when I did it. Now it is too late. If any of you need anything since you do not have your men, please tell me, and I will pay for it out of my pocket." He left, planning a return visit that was never to transpire.

Seven days later the bishop of our church sent a message for all Americans to come immediately to the capital city. He urged us to return to the United States as soon as possible, since he feared that our lives would be endangered by a possible countercoup.

Once in the capital, we learned that the American men who had been taken from our house at midnight had been taken by dump truck to a military camp 10 miles from our village. There they had been loaded on a plane with many other prisoners from the local area and flown to the capital, where they were held in a basement cell.

Three days later the US embassy was successful in negotiating the release of the Americans and helping them leave the country. The local men, however, were not released for two weeks. Some, particularly the religious leaders, were tortured.

Often I think of the soldier and his 30 men who stormed out of the jungle ready to kill us. Within 15 minutes he had changed his mind and risked his life to save us. I thank God for putting divine love in my heart for a person I could not love on my own.

I cannot forget the last thing the soldier said to us as he left: "I have fought many battles and killed many people. It was nothing to me. It was just my job to exterminate them. But I never knew them personally. This is the first time I ever knew my enemy face to face, and I believe that if we knew each other, our guns would not be necessary."

Sarah Corson

Reprinted with permission from *Sojourners*, (800) 714-7474, www.sojo. net.

60
Words Save Lives

After my training to become an Emergency Medical Technician (EMT) I was given an opportunity to further my learning. I would participate in a 120-hour unpaid internship riding with Chicago Fire Department Paramedics to learn further crisis intervention techniques in the field.

One of the paramedics who mentored me during my field internship said some things on my first day that I will never forget. "You are going to be seeing and meeting people who may be very different than you. They may not look like you, may not act like you, they may not share the same values as you, they may use foul language, and they may not have the same personal hygiene habits that you have. They may be homeless or living in poverty. They may have had horrible life experiences that have shaped the way they act and what they do. They may be deaf or blind. They may be from another country and not speak English. You must treat every person you come in contact with, regardless of who they are, with RESPECT."

He continued, "The words you use and how you use them convey many things in this work. First, they must always convey respect. Next, you must be able to communicate with others in terms that they use and understand. You will have to learn to be very flexible and change with the circumstances. In any situation, you must always protect yourself and protect your patient. When you take a person onto your stretcher, their life becomes your total responsibility. It makes no difference if you're in a hospital or in the projects; if a person is on your stretcher, that person is your responsibility.

"When you are here with us in the field," he said, "I want you to keep your mouth shut and watch everything we do, listen to what we say, and especially observe people's expressions as we interact with them."

During the months that followed, I watched hundreds of faces. Each transport provided a wealth of knowledge regarding human behavior, and taught me to choose my words with care. All that training prepared me for the day that was to change my life...

I had taken a job working for a private ambulance company that had contracts with hospitals and nursing homes all over the Chicago area. Each ambulance was assigned a two-person team that included a driver and an attendant, both certified EMTs. Long before the era of cell phone technology, the ambulances were equipped with stationary CB radios. (The only portable radios available were carried by the paramedics who staffed the four mobile intensive-care ambulance units.) This meant that when we left the ambulance to get a patient, we had no radio contact with dispatch.

My partner and I that day were assigned a routine transport that was dispatched as a "patient pick up" at one of the housing projects, Cabrini Green. The patient was to be transported to a local hospital for physical therapy. I had been to Cabrini Green many times during my internship with the fire department. As part of my training, I had a crash course on gangs and gang violence. In effect, I had learned to "speak gang."

The cement walls of the high-rise buildings were covered with gang graffiti, much of it dominated by The Vice Lords and The Latin Kings. Graffiti was one way the gangs claimed their territories, letting others know that this was their turf. The hallways were also cement and open to the air, being covered by chain-link fencing from the first floor to the top floors to prevent people from falling to their deaths. The elevators were in poor repair. We never knew beforehand if the elevator we needed would be working or not. Today we were lucky. The elevator doors opened. I pulled the stretcher in and my partner Joe pushed the button for the 14th floor. The doors closed. As we lurched upward the light in the elevator kept flashing on and off, and the elevator would stop all together and then jerk upward again. Perhaps the wiring had been gnawed on by rats, which were a common problem here.

When we arrived at the 14th floor we both cautiously stuck our heads out to see if the scene was safe. It looked clear so we pulled the stretcher out of the elevator and proceeded down the hall to apartment number 1407. Joe stood on one side of the door and I stood on the other side. We knew not to stand directly in front of the door because you never knew if there was a person on the other side with a gun. Joe pounded hard on the door. A voice came from the other side.

"What the hell you want?"

Joe said, "We're EMTs here for Jessie."

The door opened and a little boy of about 10 was standing there. "C'mon," he said, "Jessie's in here."

We followed the boy with our stretcher in tow, passing through a small living room and into a bedroom. Sitting upright on the bed was a young man with thick white casts on both legs. He was wearing shorts that had been cut up the sides to make room for the casts that started at his hips.

"Jessie can't move himself at all," the little boy said. "You have to lift him up."

"What's your name?" I asked

"I'm Henry, Jessie's my brother."

Jessie told his brother to go next door and stay with a neighbor while he was at the hospital. After Henry left I asked Jessie what had happened to him. He said that the Lords had broken both of his legs with baseball bats because he would not join their gang. He and his family were Jehovah's Witnesses. He said that due to his religious beliefs he would never join the gang. He asked that I give him his Bible so that he could read at the hospital while he waited for his physical therapy appointment. When we had Jessie safely secured on the stretcher, we headed back out into the hall.

I was at the front of the stretcher as we pulled Jessie along to the elevator. I pushed the down button and again the elevator doors opened. This time three men were standing there. The man in the middle was holding a gun. He looked down at me and said, "WHAT THE HELL do you think you're DOING with MY BOY?"

I glanced back at Jessie and saw sheer terror on his face. In that split second I knew that these were some of the men that had done this violence to him. I straightened to my full height of exactly five feet, looked up at the man with the gun, and said, "He's NOT your boy, he's on my stretcher, he's on MY TURF. He's MY boy!"

Shocked, the man looked at the gun he was holding, looked back down at me, and said, "SAY WHAT?"

So I said, "Now I can see that you're a man that demands RESPECT."

"YOU GOT THAT RIGHT."

"I give you that RESPECT." I said. "Now let me tell you about my gang."

He said, "YOU in a gang?"

"Yeah! All these EMTs and Paramedics that come here when you call 911 are all part of MY GANG. Now, let me ask you, has there ever been a time when you called 911 and someone from MY GANG didn't come to help you?"

"No, they be there," he said.

"THAT'S RIGHT. If you mess with me or you mess with anyone on MY TURF," I pointed to Jessie, "or you mess with anyone in MY GANG, WHAT THE HELL DO YOU THINK'S GOING TO HAPPEN THE NEXT TIME ONE OF YOUR BOYS IS BLEEDIN' OUT BAD AND YOU CALL 911?"

He looked back down at the gun, then looked back at me and said, "DAMN, YOU A BITCH!"

"YOU GOT THAT RIGHT," I yelled at him, "AND WHILE I GIVE YOU THAT RESPECT, I DON'T HAVE ALL DAY TO BE STANDIN' HERE SHOOTIN' THE SHIT WITH YOU!"

"Let the lady pass on by," he said with a nod of his head.

I pulled the stretcher into the elevator, praying that he wouldn't change his mind. Tears were streaming down Jessie's face as the elevator doors closed. Joe and I took some deep breaths, doing our best to prepare for whatever might meet us on the ground floor. Thankfully, when the elevator doors opened again the scene was safe enough to proceed to the ambulance. We notified our dispatcher that an incident had occurred but that no injuries resulted and we would call him from the hospital. En route, I asked Jessie who the men were. He said he didn't know their names. I asked him if they were some of the men that had broken his legs. He nodded and said, "If I tell anyone who they are, they will kill my family. I already talked to the police. What you don't understand is that I have to live there."

When I called my dispatcher, a meeting was arranged with the supervising field paramedic and the owner of the company to discuss what to do. Because the man with the gun did not actually point the gun directly at me and say he was going to kill me, and I did not know who the men were, filing a police report was not recommended. Thousands of people live in Chicago Housing Projects and many have guns. Paramedics and EMTs across the country face dangerous situations every single day. They continue to do their job. We were there to safely transport Jessie to physical therapy and back, not try to hunt down gang members. Following the meeting, I was promoted to become one of the company's EMT trainers.

As a trainer, I went to pick up Jessie three times a week for the next six months with trainees under my charge. Every time I pulled up to Cabrini Green and got out of the ambulance, the gang scouts that were watching over their turf would say, "Hey, it's that little white MEDIC BITCH again!" And then the call would come back, "He says let the lady pass on by." I was never bothered by anyone there ever again.

Rosemary Lake-Liotta

61

Closing Together

It was the summer of 1992, the last day of a residential personal change seminar in the Rocky Mountains in Winter Park, Colorado. The group of 75 people had bonded very strongly over the past 20 days, and one thing they did as part of their group process was to create a piece of visual artwork representing "our community" or "who we are." The group started with a big 4' x 8' sheet of plywood which they covered with a collaborative painting symbolizing their experience together. It was painted with red, white, black, and yellow to symbolize all the peoples of the earth, and it was filled with a collage of handprints, spirals, a yin-yang, and the individual contributions of every participant. The finished piece was very meaningful to everyone.

Now we were at the very end of a packed three weeks and the group was about to finish their time together and head home. Only one thing remained to be done. The question before the group was, "What are we going to do with this piece of art that is 'us'?" The group discussion started, and since I was the closing trainer I was somewhat involved with helping facilitate this process. Soon it became clear that most of the group's opinion was that it should be kept safe and given to somebody who would be the custodian. But the question remained, "How the heck are we going to do this?" We had people from all over the world, and it was not a small piece of plywood. Who was going to take it and how were they going to get it there?

Then one man spoke up.

"Well," he said, "because this is so challenging, and because we're spread out all over the planet—we've got people from Europe and Asia—my proposal is we destroy it. If we burn it, it will be like *everybody* has it."

I could feel the tension in the room mount instantly. It was clear that the group was generally very opposed to the idea of destroying it. It was the end of 20 days, and everyone was tired and ready to leave. I could see in their faces that to most of them, burning the artwork would seem like a great offense to what it represented. The man who had offered the suggestion was thinking on a more abstract level, but almost everyone else wanted to keep this piece of art that represented the close-knit community they had formed over the past weeks. They did not want it destroyed.

I was trying to facilitate the conversation and I was not particularly effective. After about 15 minutes we hadn't made any progress toward a solution. I had my eye on the clock because we were already going overtime, and I needed to get everybody out of the room. It was obvious to me that this was not going to resolve quickly. Even on the "keep it" side there were *many* different opinions, but that side was becoming more and more polarized against this guy who was saying, "destroy it." People were getting frustrated and upset, and the prospect of a satisfying group closing was unraveling by the second.

At this point somebody in the group stood up and proposed to have a vote so that we could at least get past the "keep it" or "destroy it" alternatives. But before I could respond, a Native American from the Mi'kmaq tribe in eastern Canada stood up and faced me directly.

"Gerry, can I take over?" he asked. "I have an approach, and if you give me ten minutes by the clock, I'll have it solved."

I had *no* idea what he had in mind, but I was more than glad to let him take this problem off my hands. I was tired and the discussion wasn't going anywhere useful, so I told him to go ahead.

He came up to the front of the room and first he asked, "Everybody's agreeing that we're ready to get a resolution?" People nodded, so he continued. "I have the solution if you're all willing to go along."

Everyone said, "Yeah, yeah, go ahead."

Then he turned to the man who wanted to destroy the artwork, and gesturing to him he spoke in a soft, deep voice that seemed utterly unconstrained by time.

"In my Native American tradition, when we have a group which is all on one side, and we have one person who is on another side, we would never have a vote to overrule him, because it's obvious that the majority will win, making him isolated.

"We would never do that to someone.

"The solution is we're going to turn over the responsibility for the decision to you—the one who's the isolated person. We're going to let you decide for all of us."

There was no mistaking that the words of the Native American were wholeheartedly genuine and sincere. He was really *completely* giving over the decision to this man.

I could hear people's jaws hitting the floor, and as I looked around the room I saw eyes wide with surprise. It was an amazing thing to watch the wave of shock move through the room. But then very quickly I began to see that certain people started to understand the wisdom in what the Native American had done, and they relaxed a little.

The man who had been given responsibility to make the decision went through his own initial shock. Right at first there was a little bit of a glint in his eye, which I'm guessing was his self-interest side, but then I could see a change taking place inside of him as well. His face went through several emotional swings, though I couldn't tell exactly what they meant. Pretty soon he stood up to speak.

"Well I think it's obvious that we need to find a way that satisfies all of us," he said.

I could feel the tension in the room disappear. Earlier it had been clear in the man's argumentative tone that he had set himself against the rest of the group, but as soon as the responsibility was completely in his hands, his opposition simply melted away. It was wonderful. He immediately started moving in the other direction.

"My objection was that there wasn't a place where we could put the artwork," he said, "And I want to honor the spirit of what we all did together. Is there a place where we could put this piece of art where everybody would have access to it, and it would feel fair to all of us?"

Very quickly someone who had not been involved in the earlier discussion spoke up.

"I have a place," she said. "It's a big barn in the central US where I could hang it. I also have a truck here; we could cut the piece in half to transport it, and once it's hanging up I can take a picture of it and send it to everybody, and anyone can drop by and visit it at any time."

Immediately it was done. The shift was profound. The emotional ripple through the room was huge. You can tell the difference between people who are just agreeing because they want an argument to be over, and people who are deeply satisfied. It was quite a wonderful moment. Everybody was really pleased, including the man who had originally objected. The whole group was suddenly aligned and there was a powerful sense of completion.

I think part of the reason it worked so well was because the guy who was given the responsibility had such a strong relationship with the group. The wisdom of the Native American in trusting so much responsibility with this one man made me imagine a culture in which that kind of approach was a common practice. That conception of community would create a profoundly different way of working together.

My Mi'kmaq friend glanced down at his watch. Looking up again he met my eyes and said, "Seven minutes."

Gerry Schmidt

Closing

I hope you have been nourished by these stories in the same way that I was when I first heard them. While they continue to inspire me with each reading, there's something special about the first time a new realm of possibility is opened up—the feeling of one's personal world becoming that much more expansive and rich.

I remember uninspiring days when out of nowhere I'd find an unfamiliar email waiting—another story sent by a friend or acquaintance, or a friend of an acquaintance. As I began to read, I would feel myself once again coming fully alive. I remember showing up at the doorsteps of people who said they had a story to share, being invited in to a table or couch where I'd pull out my mini-disc player and press record. With the sound of their voice I would gradually be transported into a place of such richness it felt like remembering an important reason for living. I felt how these stories filled me and warmed me—I could literally feel my chest and heart opening more fully with each new inspiring example of connection over conflict. It was as if each new story woke me up just a bit more to the true range of what is possible in life, like a veil lifting away to reveal a world where the old, rigid rules no longer apply. Oliver Wendell Holmes Jr. said, *"A mind, once stretched by a new idea, never regains its original dimensions."* The same is true of the heart and spirit when nourished by new experience. What a gift it is that we can share these experiences through the magic of written words.

These stories have taught me that extraordinary solutions are not beyond any of us. No situation, no matter how dire, is completely beyond hope or possibility. In our darkest moments, when we pause in the face of our complete inability to know what to do… when we simply *give up*—somehow even out of this void, a solution can spring forth.

Of course this doesn't mean we'll find the best way forward every time. Far from it. We'll continue to stumble and make mistakes—often huge ones—and that's all a part of life. But as Wendell Castle said, *"If you're not making mistakes, you're not making anything."*

Also, just because a certain pathway worked in a story from this book, that doesn't mean the same exact approach will necessarily provide the right way forward in another place and time with someone else. As many problems as there are, there are at least that many solutions. I hope this book will serve as inspiration to finding more of them.

The stories in this book are just a small sample of the stories out there in the world—just the few that have found their way to me over the last seven years. I am continuing to collect more for a second book, so if you have a story to share with me, please send it to wovenwords@gmail.com. I look forward to reading it.

If this book has touched you, please pass it on to someone you care about, or keep it around to share with the people who pass through your life. As Barry Lopez says in one of my favorite quotes from *Crow and Weasel:*

"The stories people tell have a way of taking care of them. If stories come to you, care for them. And learn to give them away where they are needed. Sometimes a person needs a story more than food to stay alive. That is why we put these stories in each other's memory. This is how people care for themselves. One day you will be good storytellers. Never forget these obligations."

Mark Andreas

Afterword

In a word: *connection*

For me, the greatest gift I've received from these stories is the skin-prickling truth of each real-life example. These are stories that I will read again and again to keep them present in my mind and body and spirit. If you prefer to let the richness of each story speak for itself, feel free to read no further. However, if you're interested to hear more of what I have personally learned from these stories, read on.

I never intended to write this afterword. Then I got encouragement from a friend to share the conclusions that I had taken away from gathering, writing, and re-reading this collection of stories. As I looked more closely for the underlying patterns emerging from this collection, I found several that might serve as a useful guide to having more of the kinds of relationships we want in our lives.

When I first began this project, I was looking for stories of resolution of the obvious conflicts between people. These range from the threat of physical violence such as crime and war, to the less acute but no less important disputes over how to work together, whether in a relationship, a family, a work environment, or a community. But as the project unfolded I became aware of other kinds of conflict just as important to focus on—one at such a small scale, the other at such a large scale, that both can be easily overlooked.

The small-scale conflicts are those that take place within the self. There are several stories in this book that I found particularly fascinating because they began with conflicts that seemed to have everything to do with the outside world, and yet when conflict within the person was resolved, the external conflict completely dissolved *(Seeing Each Other 23, Why Did You Look Up? 40, Not Worth Your Time 178, Internal Garden 259).*

The large-scale conflicts are those that are inherent in the structure of a society, such as Muhammad Yunus' description of the poor of Bangladesh, where so many people found themselves up against nearly impossible odds no matter what positive efforts they made. In some instances like this, it is necessary to create new cultural norms or social institutions before more people can have the opportunity to live decent lives.

So within this expanded range of conflict resolution and transformation, what conclusions have I drawn from these stories as a whole? In answer to this question there are countless elements that I could discuss, so I'll leave the finer distinctions to other books and speak only of broader themes. In a word, my answer is *connection.*

In every story in this book, rather than run away or separate from the conflict, people stayed *connected* with the difficulty, maintaining a relationship through which they could bring about a more positive outcome. If we are disconnected, we have no way to influence events. Staying connected gives us an opportunity to have an impact on the course that the conflict takes.

On the other hand, clearly there are times when people do their best to connect in a positive way, and don't succeed. If you have a choice about involving yourself in a conflict and you're not prepared for the risks involved, your wisest choice may be to simply ignore or leave the situation. However, many of the people in these stories did not have this choice.

If you're like me, you may be wondering at this point, is it really true that *every* story in this book is about connection? Certainly many are, but *every* one? Let me share more of what I mean by connection, and the different kinds of connection demonstrated by these stories.

First, connection to *self* is just as important as connection to *others*. Many, if not all, of the people in these stories were only able to successfully connect with others because they maintained connection with themselves—with their own present experience as well as their deeper beliefs and values. Rather than getting lost in fear or helplessness, maintaining connection with our full range of experience gives us access to all our resourcefulness and creativity (*Jail Break 127, Excuse Me! 170, I Can't Believe I Heard You Right 175, Taxi Driver 186, Defense Through Disarmament 27, and many if not all the others*). Trying to control other people is difficult and doesn't work very well, while taking responsibility for ourselves and our own actions is always within our control and can bring about great results (*Making Decisions for Other People 155*). And as noted earlier, sometimes the entire conflict can be maintained within the self. When we can connect with all the different aspects of our experience, this can achieve a new alignment and integration in which the conflict simply dissolves away (*Seeing Each Other 23, Why Did You Look Up? 40, Not Worth Your Time 178, Internal Garden 259*).

There is a great story about a three-year-old girl who was given a puzzle of the world. The world was so big and complicated that she had no idea how it went together. But she noticed that on the backs of the puzzle pieces was an image of a person. She knew how people went together, so she finished the puzzle this way and then turned it over to see the world. When her father came back he was surprised to see that she had managed to put this puzzle of the world together so quickly. When he asked her how she did it, she told him, "It was easy. When I put the person together, the world comes together."

Some of the themes I noticed in these stories made me realize that *time* is an important element in connection, whether with *self* or *others*. Connection happens not only in the *present* moment, but also in relation to the *past* and the *future*.

Forgiveness is a connection between people despite the damage or violence of *past* events. Forgiveness allows the "victim" to move forward rather than remain burdened by something that can't be changed *(Sweet Fruit from a Bitter Tree 192, One Question 45, Only if my Mother Tells Me 104)*. As Nelson Mandela said, *"Resentment is like drinking poison and then hoping it will kill your enemies."* True forgiveness often also heals the perpetrator, allowing him to more easily see that it is possible to come back into peaceful alignment *(Soul Force 11, The Imam and the Pastor 66, The Drunk Driver and the Businessman 141)*.

A significant element of other stories is *trust*: not a blind trust, but a trust that is worth making—a trust that forges a connection with people about the *future*. Actually, all these stories include an element of trust, because *connection* is about relationship, which happens over time and thus demands a certain degree of trust. But some of these stories rely particularly on trust *(The Imam and the Pastor 66, Sometimes What it Takes is Trust 138, Bank for the Poor 232, Closing Together 280)*.

From these stories I've noticed six primary ways of connecting with *others*.

The first is quite straightforward and basic—simply understanding and relating on the same level as another person. This alone is often enough to dissolve previous conflict, even when the conflict was quite extreme *(The Wall 163, The Mosque of Ali 209, Defense Through Disarmament 27, Guests in the Night 48, Gratitude 116, Neither Violent Nor Victim 120, Jail Break 127, Clay Giraffe 132, A Soft Answer 148, Excuse Me! 170)*.

Similar to this is *connecting* and then *leading*, often referred to as *pacing and leading*: first connecting with the other person or persons in a conflict by matching their experience, and then once in rapport, actively leading them to somewhere more useful *(The Dork Police 85, The Pit Bull 145, The Homicidal Patient in the Elevator 153, Billy and the Beagles 182, Kicking the Car 256).*

Interestingly, the third kind of connection works by specifically *not* connecting with or pacing the experience of the other person in the conflict, but instead responding with a different and stronger frame. Many of these stories worked out well because the "victim" refused to accept the frame or context with which he or she was presented (such as a "violence" frame), and instead created a *new* frame that was more to his or her liking (such as a "friends" frame). In the new frame, it is then possible to connect, rather than conflict *(You Have My Wallet?! 8, Defense Through Disarmament 27, Size Matters 43, Guests in the Night 48, Flex Cop 76, The Dork Police 85, Neither Violent Nor Victim 120, A Soft Answer 148, Bar Fight 168, I Can't Believe I Heard You Right 175, A Little Preparation 195, Opening Presents 196, The Mosque of Ali 209, I Just Stopped Walking 229).* This principle is demonstrated by the following short accounts: *

A woman was in bed one night, when suddenly there was a man on top of her. She reached over to the night stand, picked up a quarter and offered it to him, saying, "Excuse me, would you please call the police; there's a strange man in my bed." He left.

Another woman who was being held hostage with a shotgun taped to her throat kept telling her captor jokes, "Have you heard the one about the—" After about an hour of this, he released her unharmed.

An attendant in a mental hospital was grabbed from behind in a choke-hold by a patient who was not only much stronger, but who had a lot of martial arts training. The attendant knew that struggling to release himself would be useless. Just as he began to lose consciousness, he reached up

---

* From "Transforming Yourself" by Steve Andreas, pp. 250-251. Copyright © 2002 Real People Press, Boulder, CO.

to where the patient's arm was clamped tightly around his neck. Lovingly, the attendant began stroking the patient's arm. At that the patient stopped choking him. As the patient later said, "That was just too weird, so I had to stop and figure out what was going on."

Another woman was walking down the street in a rough neighborhood late at night, when she noticed a man who seemed to be following her. She crossed the street, and he followed her. She speeded up her walking and he did, too. She was starting to get a little worried, so she turned around and walked up to him and said, "Excuse me, I'm feeling scared. Would you escort me home?" The man held out his arm and escorted her home. She found out later that he had gone on to rape someone else later that evening.

In all these examples, by creating a context that was much better than the one they originally found themselves in, these people acted in a way that drew the conflicting person into the new frame, eliciting a different response, and through that, a new reality.

Other stories in this book arrive at a solution not by creating a new reality, but by recognizing and returning to (connecting with) the reality already existing but forgotten—the reality of the basic values of each party in the conflict. This is the well-known method in conflict resolution of getting away from conflicting positions and returning to fundamental interests and needs, then finding a solution that meets everyone's interests and needs. Often it turns out that the same underlying interests and needs are held in common by each party to a conflict (*Muslim Extremist Encampment 17, Doggedly Determined 121, Third Grade Bully 93, Clay Giraffe 132, Words Save Lives 274*). Other times, interests and needs may be different, even very different, but they can still easily coexist with one another (*The Imam and the Pastor 66, Firing on the Rabble 144, Two Tribes 159, The Farm Culture 55, The Living God Inside You 58, Kicking the Car 256*).

In fact, sometimes this difference in needs makes it *easier* to coexist. This is illustrated by the story of the last orange in the supermarket: Two people arrive at the same time and both need an orange, so they start to argue over who got there first and who should get to buy it. Someone passes by and suggests that they split it, to which they each say, "I need the whole thing, a half orange won't do!" A second person walks by and asks, "What do you each need the orange for?" One responds, "I need the rind to flavor a cake." The other replies, "I want a cup of fresh-squeezed juice." After learning each of their needs or interests, it now becomes clear how, with a little cooperation, they can both get exactly what they want from the same orange.

The fifth kind of connection is not as clever or skillful as the previous methods, and not as easy, but may be more powerful than any of them. It is to sincerely offer deep love and compassion for someone in turmoil, who may harm himself or someone else. *(Lilly 200, Sweet Fruit from a Bitter Tree 192, Navajo Handshake 29, The Ranch 37, It Was Like a Spring Thaw 123, A Soft Answer 148, Billy and the Beagles 182).*

Finally, there is the connection to others that comes through a connection to God or Spirit or "The whole." This is a connection that some say is impossible from the standpoint of our individual egos, but *is* possible through the transcendent nature of God, Allah, Shiva, the Holy Spirit, or the Higher Self *(Navajo Handshake 29, Guests In The Night 48, The Living God Inside You 58, The Imam and the Pastor 66, Only If My Mother Tells Me 104, The Ganges River 111, It Was Like a Spring Thaw 123, The Mosque of Ali 209, He Just Sat Back Down 222, Welcoming the Enemy 266).*

The last element of connection that I think is important to mention is the role of a larger *community*. Some of these stories ended well because someone from outside the conflict took it upon themselves to step in and offer help and guidance *(A Soft Answer 148, Excuse Me! 170, The Decision Has Been Made 98, The Pit Bull 145, The Third Hand 20, The Farm Culture 55, Gratitude 116, Doggedly Determined 121, Two*

Tribes 159, Fixing the Dog 173, He's the Asshole 207, Yer Momma 226). This was common practice among the smaller, closely-knit tribal groups and communities to which all humans of the past belonged. In the large societies most of us live in today, it can be easy to simply sit by the sidelines and watch violence occur between people whom we've never met, and most likely will never see again. Yet there are ways that we can continue to offer this kind of support from the outside.

Beyond these individual responses of help and concern, we can also foster a community culture that supports the resolution of conflict *(The Imam and the Pastor 66, Clay Giraffe 132, Two Tribes 159, Welcoming the Enemy 266, One Question 45, Only If My Mother Tells Me 104, Gratitude 116, Closing Together 280)* as well as a societal structure that supports the resolution of conflict *(Bank for the Poor 232, The Women and the Mullah 250, The Imam and the Pastor 66, The Drunk Driver and the Businessman 141, A Letter from Norway 205, Closing Together 280)*. I find the final story in this book to be a particularly interesting example of a community practice for resolving conflict: giving all the power to the most isolated member of the group.

But now, how can we actually cultivate the ability to be able to connect in these different ways?

Spontaneity is one key ingredient of many of these successful stories *(Opening the Door 5, You Have My Wallet?! 8, The Third Hand 20, Defense Through Disarmament 27, Navajo Handshake 29, Size Matters: part one 43, Guests in the Night 48, The Living God Inside You 58, The Decision Has Been Made 98, The Ganges River 111, Neither Violent Nor Victim 120, Jail Break 127, Excuse Me! 170, Fixing the Dog 173, I Can't Believe I Heard You Right 175, Opening Presents 196, Lilly 200, He's The Asshole 207, The Mosque of Ali 209, He Just Sat Back Down 222, I Just Stopped Walking 229, Welcoming the Enemy 266)*.

While at first it may seem that spontaneity is something inherently beyond practice, something simply gifted to extraordinarily creative people, this is actually not true. I learned this when I joined an improvisational comedy troupe in college. When I first visited my college and saw the troupe perform, I remember thinking, "I can't believe those people go up on stage with nothing planned, get a few simple suggestions from the audience, and are able to create a theatrical experience that is consistently enjoyable and very funny to watch." Two years later I joined the group and discovered that there is a whole structure to improvisation—a skill set that I've found extremely useful not only in puting on a good show, but in responding flexibly and resourcefully to the conflicts that arose constantly during the two years that I worked as a wilderness trip leader for "troubled teens." The skills of improvisation helped me find all kinds of ways to *connect* with the youth I worked with, and through that connection, the ability to guide and lead them. Since there's no single way of connecting with another human being, the benefits of learning how to flexibly improvise— repeatedly when necessary—is *huge.* Flexibility supports connection, and connection in turn supports flexibility and spontaneity: when we maintain connection both with ourselves and others, we can access the most (apparently) amazing spontaneous solutions because we are completely and fully acting out of the information of the moment—an exciting place to live from.

Training and *practice* provide a strong foundation from which spontaneity can happen in a useful way, just as musical training provides the foundation for creative musical improvisation. Some of the people in these stories had significant life experience or training that informed and provided a basis for what they were able to do. Other people underwent certain specific *preparations* because they knew they were likely to face a difficult situation *(A Little Preparation 195, Size Matters: part two 43, Flex Cop 76, The Dork Police 85).* Whether through life experience, communication courses, conflict resolution seminars, meditation, reading, or practice (nothing beats plain old practice), training and preparing ourselves with the skills to respond resourcefully in likely conflict situations can provide the invaluable groundwork from which to be spontaneous.

I hope you've found it useful to think about some of the broader generalizations that can be drawn from these stories. No doubt you will have insights of your own. As you go about your life, I hope you'll find that these stories have collected in your memory like water in a deep well, from which, at any time, you can draw up just the story that you need.

Mark Andreas

About Mark Andreas

Mark received his undergraduate degree in Peace and Global Studies at Earlham College, after which he got two years of hands-on experience in conflict mediation and leadership as a counselor/trip-leader for the Monarch Center for Family Healing. He was in charge of facilitating groups of "troubled" youth on a round-the-clock basis both in individual therapy and group process during three-week-long backpacking expeditions throughout the western United States.

Mark currently offers individual sessions assisting people in achieving life-goals and resolving limitations using NLP and other methods for personal transformation and development: www.markandreas.com. He also continues to explore the realms of conflict and community through his Science Fiction and Fantasy writing; his first novel, *Storysong*, is due to be published early in 2012: www.storysongandreas.com. Mark lives in Boulder CO.

Index